HANSARD SOCIETY SER
POLITICS AND GOVERN

Edited by
F. F. Ridley

HANSARD SOCIETY SERIES IN POLITICS AND GOVERNMENT

Edited by
F. F. Ridley

The Hansard Society Series in Politics and Government brings to the wider public the debates and analyses of important issues first discussed in the pages of its journal, *Parliamentary Affairs*

British Government and Politics Since 1945: Changes in Perspective

Edited by
F. F. Ridley and Michael Rush

OXFORD UNIVERSITY PRESS
in association with
THE HANSARD SOCIETY FOR
PARLIAMENTARY GOVERNMENT

Oxford University Press, Walton Street, Oxford OX2 6DP
Oxford New York
Athens Auckland Bangkok Bombay
Calcutta Cape Town Dar es Salaam Delhi
Florence Hong Kong Istanbul Karachi
Kuala Lumpur Madras Madrid Melbourne
Mexico City Nairobi Paris Singapore
Taipei Tokyo Toronto
and associated companies in
Berlin Ibadan

Oxford is a trade mark of Oxford University Press

Published in the United States
by Oxford University Press Inc., New York

© Oxford University Press, 1995

First published in Parliamentary Affairs, 1994
New as paperback, 1995

A catalogue for this book is available from the British Library

Library of Congress Cataloging in Publication Data
(Data available)

ISBN 0-19-922239-8

Printed in Great Britain
by Headley Brothers Limited, The Invicta Press,
Ashford, Kent and London

CONTENTS

CONTRIBUTORS TO THIS VOLUME

Gavin Drewry is Professor of Social Administration, Royal Holloway and New Bedford College, University of London

Philip Giddings is Lecturer in Politics, University of Reading

Derek Hearl is Lecturer in European Studies, University of Exeter

Sir Bernard Ingham was Chief Press Secretary to the Prime Minister, Margaret Thatcher

Simon James is the author of *British Cabinet Government*

Dennis Kavanagh is Professor of Politics, University of Nottingham

Austin Mitchell is Labour Member of Parliament for Great Grimsby

Philip Norton is Professor of Government, University of Hull

Dawn Oliver is Professor of Law and Dean of Faculty. University College, London

F. F. Ridley is Senior Fellow at the Institute of Public Administration and Management, University of Liverpool

Michael Rush is Professor of Politics, University of Exeter

Michael Ryle was Clerk of Committees, House of Commons

Anthony Seldon is Founding Director of the Institute of Contemporary British History, London

Colin Seymour-Ure is Professor of Government, University of Kent

Donald Shell is a Senior Lecturer in Politics, University of Bristol

Cover photograph by Ben Curtis

Preface

Fifty years is a nice round figure, and there are now many books looking back to 1945 or surveying the period since. This volume, however, tries to look forward as well as back, taking stock of central features of the British system of government. There is a clear thread of continuity. The central institutions of government are still there, Crown, House of Commons, Lords, Prime Minister and Cabinet, civil service, Conservative and Labour parties and first-past-the-post elections. They have changed, of course, but continuous change in an established framework is itself a form of continuity: 'new wine in old bottles' as generations of students of the British constitution have been told.

Criticism and reform proposals are also part of the tradition. The 'what's wrong with . . . ?' debate has gone on since 1945. That said, there has been a change in recent years as more and more writers ask for a new constitutional settlement; what's more, some politicians are edging that way. New wine may need new bottles after all and catalogues are available. In retrospect, perhaps the last fifty years of our not just unwritten but unentrenched constitution were not as glorious as originally hoped. 'Scope for improvement' is the least one would put in the report. The focus here, however, is not advocacy but stock-taking—though some advocacy there is, and it would be a dull book without.

The present book is designed to help students of British government and politics at whatever level. There are plenty of textbooks that try to cover the subject as a whole, but all need supplementing by further discussion of particular topics. Each chapter is written by a specialist. Readers will recognise names. They represent different viewpoints and a variety of approaches. That is deliberate. Uniform style textbooks are useful, but variety adds interest and reminds readers that government and politics can not be studied through one interpreter. This volume can therefore be read straight through as a set menu: chapters by different hands, a full meal but less monotonous than might otherwise be the case; or it can be taken à la carte, chapters read as the topics concerned came up for study.

Of course, no books on British government and politics should be written solely for students. Written that way, they mislead about the nature of the subjects which, in the end, should foster what is often called political literacy—not just an understanding of the political systems but judgement on its merits or faults and some real interest in participation. We are back to the reform debate. And in this debate students are citizens like others. All of what appears here, moreover is written for those others, the politically interested citizen, as well as for students, in style as well as substance. It is customary to bow to the general reader in introductions. Sometimes that seems a formality but here it is genuine: the chapters are written for all with a live interest in British politics by writers with a live interest themselves.

The appeal this book should have reflects its origins in a special issue of *Parliamentary Affairs: Journal of Comparative Politics* to mark the fiftieth anniversary of the Hansard Society for Parliamentary Government, as does its appearance in the OUP's new Hansard Society series on contemporary issues in government and politics. The Hansard Society's purpose is to promote understanding and encourage debate about parliamentary democracy in general, and British democracy in particular, among all sorts of people: observers (students, journalists, voters) and practitioners (parliamentarians, political activists, interest representatives). The perspective is broad and even if next year's situation is a little different from this year's, the issues addressed will remain relevant for some time to come.

F. F. Ridley

Consensus: A Debate Too Long?

BY ANTHONY SELDON

1995 marks the fiftieth anniversary of the end of the second world war. It also reminds us that there has been a longer period of twentieth century British history to study since 1945 than during the period 1900–45. Yet historical writing, and still more university study, remain disproportionately concerned with the earlier period. To help rectify the imbalance, Peter Hennessy and I established the Institute of Contemporary British History in 1986. The years since have seen an increased willingness to take postwar history seriously, and two new academic journals (*Contemporary Record* and *Twentieth Century British History*) have been established. But one can not deny that the study of British history since 1945 is still in its infancy.

This special anniversary edition of *Parliamentary Affairs* provides, then, an appropriate moment to consider the principal debate that has emerged on postwar British history, and one that has interested both political scientists and historians, the existence or otherwise of a postwar consensus. Has British politics, in short, been determined more by agreement and continuity between both parties in government, or have discontinuity and adversarial politics been the norm?

This article will examine the origins of this debate and go on to consider whether the postwar consensus in fact ever existed, what supporters of consensus believed it to be, when it might have existed, and what this author believes it to entail. It will continue with consideration of why consensual policies are in fact likely in a two-party political system with a simple-majority first-past-the-post electoral system as in Britain, and will conclude with consideration of the future of consensus beyond the mid 1990s.

The origins of the debate

The term 'consensus' was first popularised with the publication of Paul Addison's seminal 1975 study, *The Road to 1945*. Addison argued that the unique conditions and experience of the second world war gave birth to a consensus (elite) about postwar domestic policy. 'When Labour swept to victory in 1945, the new consensus fell like a branch of ripe plums into the lap of Mr Attlee.'[1] But as he readily admits, the term predated his own usage of it. He traces it back to the writing of J. P. Nettl in 1965, and to the work of Samuel Beer, who discussed 'policy convergence' between the Labour and Conservative Parties in his *Modern British Politics* of the same year (though Beer also saw deep value differences remaining between both parties).[2] The first time the word consensus was used academically in this modern context may have been by Angus Calder in his *The People's War* (1969), in which he argues that the final phases of the war led to the forging 'by all three major parties of a consensus which became the basis of the postwar welfare state.'[3] The consensus theme was given added piquancy in the late 1960s and early 1970s when it came under attack from two quarters. Enoch Powell articulated a series of policies, on the economy, social policy and race, directed square on against the existing policies of both parties. The Marxist left at the same time castigated Labour for adopting consensual policies which strengthened capitalism and the existing social order rather than seeking anti-consensual policies to destroy capitalism.

Andrew Gamble took up the consensus theme in his *The Conservative Nation* (1974). He had been very struck by the shift in Conservative attitudes during the war and how a group of Tories who had been marginal prior to 1939, especially Macmillan and Butler, had now become among the chief shapers of the direction of policy. To Gamble, the Macmillan-Butler nexus was pivotal, 'both going back to Peel and the Tamworth Manifesto, and to Disraeli, to help them think through what the 1945 general election result meant. That is why I thought it was legitimate to talk about a domestic political consensus'.[4] Both Addison and Gamble twenty years on have revised their initial positions, especially the former. Both now would want to extend their original notions of consensus beyond domestic policy to include a significant policy overlap in elements of foreign policy.[5]

The consensus debate was little visited in the academic literature for some years after the mid-1970s. The arrival of Mrs Thatcher as Prime Minister, and her seeming attack on many of the aspects of the postwar consensus, altered that. Dennis Kavanagh was the first to give the debate its new and high profile airing.[6] He noted how in 1979 Mrs Thatcher made mockery of consensus: for her, conviction and principle in politics were paramount. He cited Mrs Thatcher in 1981 responding to an attack by her predecessor, Edward Heath, for her doctrinaire, non-consensual policies: 'For me,' she said, 'consensus seems to be the process of abandoning all beliefs, principles, values and policies.'[7] Kavanagh set about itemising those areas, or 'planks', of the postwar consensus which were being wholly or partly dismantled by Mrs Thatcher, and so helped give birth to a whole new literature, not to say a host of examination questions in political science courses.

The last five years have seen a more critical academic spotlight pointed on the consensus. Ben Pimlott has denied that it ever existed. Meanwhile, an army of mostly younger historians, including Kevin Jefferys, Harriet Jones, Neil Rollings and Nick Tiratsoo, using documents at the Public Record Office and in party archives, have sought to cast doubt on the existence of consensus in key areas of policy. Consensus might appear to have existed, they would argue, when looked at from a very broad perspective. But when viewed from close to the ground, or the documents, the reality was very different. To an extent, the difference typifies the different approach of historians, who tend to see the trees, and political scientists, who prefer to see the whole wood. By the mid-1990s, the term consensus had fallen into some academic disrepute. Much of this is because of confusion about what exactly is meant by it.

Did consensus ever exist?

A number of commentators have argued that discontinuity has been prevalent in postwar Britain. Among them have been S. E. Finer, writing in 1975, and Beer in a volume published in 1982. But Ben Pimlott is the leading figure for the prosecuting counsel. In a powerful piece of polemic, 'The Myth of Consensus', Pimlott argues that 'consensus is a mirage, an illusion that rapidly fades the closer one gets to it'.[8] He believes that there is little evidence that the main political actors regarded themselves as part of a national consensus in the 1940s to 1970s. The key date of 1945, he says, saw the most ferocious election campaign in postwar history, and the Attlee government that followed saw deep battles between the parties over a wide range of policies, and these disputes between political leaders continued after Labour lost power in 1951. If consensus then can not be found among the party elites at Westminster, Pimlott argues, still less can it be found among party followers, who he believes were more divided in the 1950s and 1960s than in the 1980s, after consensus is alleged to have finished. As he puts it, 'Sandbagged in their electoral trenches, early postwar voters can be seen as the anonymous infantry of two implacably opposed armies in an era of adversial politics, with the middle-way Liberals floundering in no man's land'. Not to be found, then, among either party leaders or voters, Pimlott does at last locate consensus somewhere: 'The British postwar consensus could be defined', he says, 'as the product of a consensus among historians about those political ideas that should be regarded as important'.

This high calibre pounding from the artillery of one of Britain's most senior contemporary historians in fact makes as little impression as the seven-day British barrage before the battle of the Somme opened on 1 July 1916. Not because the exponents of consensus are taking cover as were the Germans in deep dugouts and cellars, but because Pimlott's guns were given the wrong grid references. His shells fell in areas in which his protagonists were not fighting. Nevertheless, all commentators and students of postwar Britain have reason to be grateful to him. Just as the Somme barrage could be heard in Britain over one hundred miles away, and the light seen along the Western Front, so too has his rhetoric served to illuminate the whole consensus debate and bring its contours into relief. So where can the consensus proponents be found to be resting their case?

The content of consensus

Consensus is a Latin word meaning agreement. As Pimlott helpfully reminds us, its first English usage was scientific, denoting harmony in body organs. Not until the middle of the nineteenth century did the word begin to be applied to the body politic, and thereafter it retained an organic connotation.[9]

In one sense, British politics since the 1680s has been dominated by consensus. Both the two main parties, whether Whigs and Tories in the eighteenth and nineteenth centuries, then Liberals and Conservatives, and since the 1920s Labour and Conservatives, have been in broad agreement on many issues, above all the acceptance of parliamentary democracy and constitutionalism. The only party to question it this century has been not Labour but the Conservatives, who under Andrew Bonar Law came close to inciting the Ulster Unionists to disobedience against the will of Parliament in the years immediately before 1914. Compared to the politics of Germany, Spain, Italy or even France this century, political parties have been close. Extremes of left and right, violent changes of policy direction, and refusal after 1914 to accept the legitimacy of the elected government of the day have not been features of British politics. Among liberal democracies with regularly alternating governments, perhaps only Republican and Democrat administrations in the United States have seen as much continuity as in Britain. Both countries have electoral systems, which might ceteris paribus have been expected to deliver adversarial politics. But things in politics seldom are equal.

In the nineteenth century little policy difference separated both main parties in Britain: both extended the franchise, both introduced factory reforms, both introduced permissive trade union reform, both led Britain into foreign wars. This century, the last Liberal governments of 1906–14 were interventionist in social policy, but the Conservatives introduced comparable reforms in Baldwin's second government of 1924–29. The Liberals took Britain into the first world war, the Conservative-led National government into the second world war. The Liberals had worked for Home Rule for Ireland prior to 1914; the Conservative-dominated Coalition government of 1918–22 granted self-government to most of Ireland in 1921. Labour's first two governments of 1924 and 1929–31 were remarkable not for introducing socialist domestic or pro-Soviet foreign policies but for their pragmatism and moderation, never seen more forcefully than under their highly orthodox Chancellor, Philip Snowden. It was the Conservatives, not Labour, who did more to introduce public ownership of industry prior to 1939, despite Labour's Clause 4 in its 1918 Constitution committing the party to just that. Were it not for the prevalence of Coalition governments (1915–22) and National governments (1931–40), both of which tended to obscure the clarity of alternating party competition, consensus might indeed have been widely discussed in relation to governments before 1945.

Many different meanings have been given to consensus in the literature, and indeed have been implicit so far in this article.[10] Three main groupings have been considered as putative parts of a consensus.

Consensus among party supporters. This 'popular consensus' is the easiest to contest, as a quick examination of party literature suggests major differences in preferences between Labour and Conservative voters, still more among activists. Yet as Rodney Lowe has argued, 'public opinion, particularly as perceived at elections, demanded social security and "full employment"'.[11] The evidence indeed suggests a sizeable common ground embracing most voters for the three main parties for most of the postwar period, favouring the welfare state, full employment and strong defence. Political parties, anxious to maximise votes, offer policies that attract this middle ground. The close identity of policy on offer between Labour and Conservative Parties could indeed provide an explanation of the low Liberal vote in the 1950s and 1960s. When the parties offered more ideological policies in the 1970s, then a gulf between them opened up, helping explain the rise of the Liberals in the 1970s and the birth of the Social Democratic Party in 1981. But much more empirical research needs to be carried out before one can pronounce definitively on the existence of a popular consensus throughout postwar Britain.

Consensus among Whitehall officials. Here it is suggested that the permanent feature of British life, the civil servants, provided an administrative consensus. Public choice theory, which stresses civil service independence in the face of political direction, and traditional socialist-Marxist critiques of the civil service, which highlight the upper middle class backgrounds and outlooks of senior civil servants, both in their very different ways support the notion of administrative consensus. In contrast to the US political system, where the top echelons of the Washington departments are appointed afresh with each new administration, is the British experience, where incoming governments do not appoint new officials (merely political advisers in Whitehall departments and certain key positions at the Prime Minister's Office). There is indeed much evidence to suggest, as does Nicholas Deakin, the existence of a Whitehall consensus.[12] Not just did top civil servants remain through changes of government, but departments themselves, and sub-groups within them, had their own favoured policies. The Treasury thus, once converted to Keynesianism in the 1940s, remained sceptical about monetarism until the 1970s, rejecting out of hand the ideas of bodies like the Institute of Economic Affairs which since the 1950s had been challenging Keynesian orthodoxy.[13] Above all, the civil service disliked adopting radical policies, and as a body the bureaucrats within it favoured the continuation of consensus-type policies.

Consensus among the party elites when in office. This is the brand of consensus stressed by Kavanagh and by his co-author of *Consensus Politics*, Peter Morris. As they write, 'the *governmentalists* in both political parties were overwhelmingly drawn from the centre of the political spectrum and, for all the differences of nuance and rhetoric, it is the continuity of policy which stands out'.[14] This governmental-elite interpretation of consensus allows for:

Differences in *rhetoric* between the parties, with Conservatives stressing the virtues of freedom, and Labour equality. Differences in rhetoric have indeed been far more marked in the postwar period than differences in policies.

Differences in *ideology*, which in fact rarely overlapped between Labour and Conservative Parties, except in the sense that Marxist commentators like Ralph Miliband see both Labour and Conservatives as supporting Parliament's democracy and gradualism.[15] Party ideologies remained widely divergent in the postwar period, but when it came to giving these ideologies voice when in office, the differences dried up.

Differences in what party followers say when their party is *out of office*. When Labour and Conservatives were in opposition, they both articulated anti-consensual policies. But once office was regained, they largely abandoned their radicalism, as did the Conservatives in 1970–72.

Differences in what radical MPs say when their party is *in office*. This reading of consensus can happily accommodate the presence of the Bevanite left in 1951 and their heirs in 1968–70 or the Suez group in the Conservative Party in 1954–56. It is what the leaders do in office, not what their backbenchers say, that is important.

Kavanagh and Morris argue that there were significant continuities in five principal areas of British policy from the Attlee government until the mid-1970s. Their five planks of the postwar consensus are the mixed economy, full employment, trade unions, welfare, foreign policy. The extent to which there was indeed a broad continuity between governmental policy in these five areas will be discussed below.

Not just do different commentators refer to three different groupings to include in the consensus, as described above, but they also argue for different *intensities* of consensual expression. Here, again, a degree of ignorance about exactly what is being argued seems to have made the debate more fraught than it needed to be. Three different levels of intensities stand out.

Positive or cheerful agreement. This is the sense in which Pimlott sees the term being used: 'Consensus is said to exist not when people merely agree, but when they are happy agreeing, are not constrained to agree, and leave few of their number outside the broad parameters of their agreement.'[16] But one has to say that no writer on the consensus subscribes to this cheerful school.

Agreement on specific policies. This again is a less than wholly plausible interpretation of consensus, as the precise policies often differed in substance, and certainly in the methods by which they were sold or justified, as governments changed.

Agreement on the broad framework, or on the parameters in which party disagreement would take place. This is by far the most satisfactory measure of the intensity, as it denies both happy acquiescence and inflexibility. Policies did alternate between the 1940s and the mid-1970s, but usually within a defined band, or snake.

The timing of consensus

Three points are at issue here: when did consensus begin, how long did it last, and when did it end? All are the subjects of lively debates.

Addison in his 1975 first edition of *The Road to 1945* stressed the achievement of the Coalition government of 1940–45 as the begetter of the postwar consensus. Kevin Jefferys has since argued persuasively, if over-dogmatically, that it was the Attlee government that deserves the credit for the postwar settlement.[17] Little consensus on postwar social policy existed in the Coalition government, Jefferys argues, and apart from the Education Act and family allowances, no major social legislation was enacted until after the 1945 general election. Addison himself subsequently conceded part of the case: 'I certainly exaggerated the extent to which "middle opinion" already prevailed on the front benches in 1945', he wrote in 1993.[18] One may conclude that the postwar consensus or settlement originated cumulatively between 1940–48, and leave the historians to continue to debate the fine print.[19]

How long consensus lasted arouses even wider dispute. Deakin has argued that 'real' consensus existed only from 1943–48, with an 'afterglow' between 1951–56 and a new convergence (on planning) from 1961–65.[20] Philip Williams argued that there were dangers in putting too much weight on Butskellism, a term (derived from the *Economist* in 1954) coined to show the continuity of economic policy between the Labour Chancellor, Hugh Gaitskell (1950–51), and the Conservative Chancellor, R. A. Butler (1951–55). Williams argues that Gaitskell was much more socialist in his thinking, and hence the election defeat for Labour in 1951 marked a decisive turning point in economic policy.[21] The case for discontinuity in economic policy has been put forward even more trenchantly by Neil Rollings in an essay entitled 'Poor Mr Butskell'.[22]

Consensus in social policy has meanwhile been attacked by Harriet Jones, who has stressed the radicalism of important elements in the Conservative Party. Even in the 1940s and 1950s these elements, she argues, did not accept the universality of the welfare state. Resistance to welfare was not confined to a radical fringe, like the arch-rightwing

MP, Waldron Smithers, but neo-liberal influence extended to the very core of the party before 1951, including Churchill, Butler and Woolton. After the 1951 election, the improvement in the world economy meant that cuts in welfare did not occur in the 1950s. But she argues also that the Conservatives in the 1950s instead held down expenditure on capital programme on education and the NHS below levels one might have expected had Labour been in power.[23]

All of this work is an important addition to knowledge, but it does not of itself undermine the reality of a broad consensus between the policies pursued by both main parties when in office. The fact that Conservative leaders discussed cutting back universal welfare provision is in fact irrelevant to the argument that when the Conservatives were in power after 1951 they retained, and indeed in some areas extended, the welfare state. In economic policy, the Conservatives may have had a greater willingness to use monetary policy than Labour, but economic policy was directed at the same end, maintenance of full employment in a balanced economy.

A number of termination dates have been put forward for the consensus ending. Some have favoured 1970, when Heath began to pursue 'Selsdon type' neo-liberal policies (although to read too much liberalism into Heath's 1970 policies is to mistake substance for rhetoric), others prefer 1975, when Mrs Thatcher was elected Conservative leader, or 1979, when she became Prime Minister, or the 1980s, when the consensual policies began to be reversed in earnest. Martin Holmes meanwhile sees the postwar consensus not ending, but reaching its highpoint, in the 1970s, most particularly from 1972–76, between Heath's U-turn and enactment of the 'highly socialist' Industry Act of 1972, and the IMF loan of 1976 which forced Labour into abandoning any plans of radicalism.

Trying to put a precise date on the end of the postwar consensus is as futile as trying to pinpoint its origin in the 1940s. It was above all a cumulative process, of both accretion and dismemberment.

The reality of consensus

At this point the author comes clean. I believe that it is meaningful to talk about a postwar consensus from the 1940s to the late 1970s (and beyond) in many spheres of policy. By consensus is meant a broad parameter of agreement on many key areas of policy between the leaderships of both main parties when they are in office. Total agreement on all aspects of policy, ideological agreement, rhetorical agreement, agreement on detail, agreement between government and opposition front-benches, agreement between party activists or ideologies, and all the other straw men erected by the anti-consensualists, are all ruled out by this definition.

The main areas of agreement are as itemised below:

Constitution. Both parties in government have accepted the constitution, parliamentary sovereignty, and have not introduced wholesale or fundamental reform.

The union. Both have supported the union, avoided devolution to Scotland or Wales, and worked to keep Northern Ireland within the union.

Interest groups. Both governed in consultation with the principal interest groups in the country, including trade unions and business interests.

Public ownership. Both supported the status quo on public ownership realised by 1951, with the principal exception of steel (privatised in 1953, renationalised in 1967).

Economic policy. Both put the maintenance of a high and stable level of employment as their primary aim of economic policy, in marked contrast to the position before 1939.

Social policy. Both parties supported free and universal provision of welfare benefits.

Labour relations. Both parties subscribed to voluntarism into the late 1960s, when both turned to legislation.

Criminal justice. Both parties subscribed to similar beliefs of rehabilitation and reform.

Europe. Both parties in office were Atlanticists in the 1950s and pro-European in the 1960s and 1970s.

Immigration. Labour opposed the 1962 Act, but when in office after 1964 legislated similarly.

Decolonisation. Both parties shed Britain's empire, Labour enthusiastically, the Conservatives more reluctantly.

Defence. Both supported the nuclear deterrent and the appropriate modernisations.

The attack of consensus came after 1979, when the Thatcher government enacted the following:

Inflation control was put above employment as the prime aim of economic policy.

Interest groups, above all the trade unions, were marginalised.

The balance of public/private ownership was tipped decisively in favour of private ownership in the economy (industry, housing).

Why did it exist?

A variety of factors were responsible for the policy convergence that did exist.

Civil servants. Governments came and went. So do ministers, even more quickly. Individual civil servants provided continuity, and civil service culture, traditions and favoured policies endure long after individual civil servants move on. If one considers who have been the individuals who have most shaped British policy since 1940, the names of Sir Edward Bridges, Sir Norman Brook, Sir Frank Lee, Sir Robert Hall, Sir Burke Trend and Sir William Armstrong bear comparison with the weight carried by most departmental ministers. The civil service dislikes change. It favours continuinty of policy, advises against and tries to block radicalism, whether from left or right. The civil service was content to enact the Keynes-Beveridge inspired policies in the 1940s and cheerfully supported their continuation until the 1970s.

The electorate. The Labour and Conservative Parties wanted to win general elections. The mass of British voters favoured moderate policies, which included full employment, the welfare state and a strong defence. Policies favoured by the far left, such as unilateral disarmament and wholesale nationalisation, or by the right, including dismantling the welfare state, would have resulted in removal to the margins of British politics. This explains why the leadership of both parties remained so adamant to marginalise their radical MPs, hence Attlee's and Gaitskell's onslaught on the Bevanite and post-Bevanite left. Attachment by the electorate to the welfare state also explains its survival largely untouched until the late 1980s, long after other aspects of consensual policies had fallen to Thatcherite policies.

Constraints of time and electoral majority. Radical departures in policy would have required a set of circumstances which did not exist. The first two Labour governments, of 1924 and 1929–31, were discouraged from embarking on radical courses in part due to their absence of a parliamentary majority and their brevity in office. Similar handicaps were experienced after 1945. The Labour government of 1950–51 was discouraged from radicalism by its wafer-thin majority of six, the governments of 1964–66 and 1974–79 laboured under similar handicaps, with no overall majority at all during 1974 and from 1977–79 (hence the 'Lib-Lab Pact'). The governments which did enact the radical shifts all had abundant time (Coalition and Labour governments, 1940–50, and the Thatcher governments, 1979–90) and also secure majorities.

Constraints of money. Financial stringency acted to prevent the adoption of some radical policies, such as the abolition of private education for the 5–7% of children in independent schools. However much the right wing of the Conservative Party may have wanted to keep hold of the empire, lack of funds made decolonisation a virtual inevitability. The appeal to the IMF for funds to bail out Britain in 1976 effectively ended socialism under Callaghan as Tony Crosland declared 'the party is over'. Britain's relative lack of wealth did at least yield some dividends for Labour and Conservative leaderships as they sought to outflank their more ideological partisans.

Absence of external shocks. Shifts in policy agenda often follow dramatic events, war, revolution, depression. The 1914–18 war changed the position of many groups in British society, women, trade unions and the organisation and ambitions of British government. It produced new demands from the British electorate. The second world war and the depression that preceded it gave birth to the postwar settlement, a far more dramatic shift than anything that had followed 1918. Following 1945 came two and more decades of relative social harmony and economic growth. Not until the late 1960s did cracks appear, rising unemployment, inflation out of control, violence breaking out in Northern Ireland, union and student militancy in mainland Britain, government apparently suffering from overload, unable to meet all the demands being expected of it. These factors helped change the public mood and demands of government as the 1970s, 'the decade of disillusion', petered out into the 'winter of discontent' of 1978–79.

Climate of ideas. In the 1940s the intellectual and indeed popular mood favoured the innovations of the postwar settlement. The press also, including its right-wing variants, was largely benign. Intellectual opinion tended to remain supportive of consensus policies until the 1960s, when a Marxist critique took hold of many intellectuals and advisers to the Labour Party. This thinking was implacably opposed to British government support for the USA in the Vietnam war, and at home it attacked Labour for adopting policies that supported rather than undermined capitalism. These ideas attracted little support in Wilson's government of 1966–70 but made much more headway among ministers and Labour MPs from 1974–79. That they did not find their way into policy can be explained by a variety of other factors (IMF loan, anxiety about loss of electoral support, lack of will from senior ministers, above all Callaghan and Denis Healey).

In the 1970s another ideological shift occurred, this time on the right of British politics. The neo-liberal, laissez-faire ideas of F. A. von Hayek, Milton Friedman and others had been in circulation since the 1940s, and the Institute of Economic Affairs, which did so much to popularise these ideas, had been founded in 1957. But it was not until the Centre for Policy Studies was established in 1974, and Mrs Thatcher elected leader of the Conservative Party in 1975, that the ideas began to take root in British politics. This critique was then incrementally introduced after 1979. Unlike the flirtation with a much milder form of these 'new right' ideas in 1970–72 under Heath, this time there was to be no turning back.

Interest group endorsement. Interest groups rapidly coalesce around a status quo and resist any attempts to change it that should result in a dimunition of their influence. The BMA resisted the creation of the NHS in the 1940s, but it also attacked the attempt to change it in the late 1980s and 1990s. Trade unions have lobbied throughout for a maintenance of full employment. Both unions and employers sought to retain the voluntarist tradition in industrial relations. Pressure groups are thus a great force for conservatism, which meant that once the postwar settlement was in place, they battled to keep it.

To sum up, there are a variety of factors which result in policy change. From 1940 to 1950, they favoured a radical shift in the agenda of politics. From 1950 until the mid-1970s, they favoured retention of the status quo. These factors, many of which interact, are shown diagramatically below.

INDIVIDUALS
Ministers
Officials
Intellectuals
Political activists

CONTINGENCY   GROUPS
War   Government departments
Depression   POLICY   Interest groups
Financial Crisis   CHANGE   Think tanks
Breakdown of order   The electorate
                                       Political parties

IDEAS
Collectivist ideas
Laissez-faire ideas

The future of consensus

What will be the future of the political consensus? In the 1980s one can see that in several areas (full employment, conciliation of trade unions) it was abandoned by the Thatcher governments. At the same time, under Neil Kinnock's leadership (1983–92) the Labour Party moved significantly to the right (defence, acceptance of much of the privatisation).

In the 1990s there has been a further policy convergence, with the front-benches of Labour and Conservative Parties closer on many issues than at any point since the 1970s. The reasons for this convergence have much to do with the parties' leaders. John Major is to the left of Mrs Thatcher on most issues, and his own brand of Conservatism has far more in common with the One Nation Toryism of Butler, Macmillan and Heath than the neo-liberalism of Mrs Thatcher. Major's Cabinet is also signficantly to the left of the parliamentary party. John Smith chose to continue the centrist policies of Neil Kinnock and to distance himself from his more ideological MPs. So has Tony Blair. In the 1990s also, the free market think tanks that so fired the Conservative Party after 1975 have been largely marginalised (with the exception of the Adam Smith Institute, which retains some influence in part because Major finds its colourful head, Dr Madsen Pirie, compatible). Think tanks on the centre-left, incuding Labour's own Research Department, the Institute for Public Policy Research and Demos, are not tapping out neo-Marxist but rather neo-market policy prescriptions. Both Labour and Conservative Parties are also driven by concern for the electorate, which strongly supports centrist policies, accounting for the large following for the Liberal Democrats.

As to policies, Labour admits it is a pipedream to imagine one can return to full employment. It has accepted that it will not renationalise the two-thirds of Britain's state-owned industry and services privatised since 1979, but would subject the privatised concerns to greater regulation. It will not reclaim council houses sold to private buyers, and it has accepted the logic of more cost-effective ways of targeting social policy. Unilateralism and abandonment of NATO and the European Community/Union are now forgotten policies: indeed, Labour has become more pro-European than the Conservatives.

Had Labour won the 1992 general election, a Neil Kinnock government (and this is obviously speculative) would have signed up to the Social Chapter, would have raised taxes on higher income groups rather than VAT, and might have devalued rather than left the ERM. It would also have produced policies attractive to its core supporters in the public sector, in the regions and Scotland.

The rhetoric of party competition in the mid-1990s suggests the parties are as far apart as ever. The reality is that Labour and Conservative front-benches share a great deal in common: only relatively narrow ground divides them. One can be confident that consensus, the dominant feature of British politics since the eighteenth century, will thus continue into the twenty-first.

Conclusions

This article has suggested that consensus rather than discontinuity is the norm. Such a consensus existed until the early years of the second world war. The Conservative Party had to accept a leftward move of the policy agenda in the 1940s. A new consensus then endured from the 1940s until the mid-1970s. In the 1970s and 1980s, Labour had to accommodate itself to a rightward shift in the governmental agenda. By the early 1990s it had accomplished the shift. As consensus is defined as a broad area of agreement between the leaderships of both main parties when they are in office, one can not say for certain that a new consensus has emerged. A Labour government after the next election, might after all feel constrained to return to the radicalism of Michael Foot's remit as leader (1980–83). But that is at best unlikely, and one can say with some confidence that consensus politics will continue to be the norm of British political life.

1   P. Addison, *The Road to 1945* (Jonathan Cape, 1975), p. 14.
2   Correspondence with author.
3   A. Calder, *The People's War* (Jonathan Cape, 1969).
4   A. Gamble, *The Conservative Nation* (Routledge and Kegan Paul, 1974). Conversation.
5   Conversation. Addison has written an Epilogue to the second edition of *The Road to 1945* (Pimlico, 1994).
6   D. Kavanagh, 'Whatever Happened to Consensual Politics', *Political Studies*, 1985; *Thatcherism and the End of British Politics* (Oxford University Press, 1987); D. Kavanagh and P. Morris, *Consensus Politics From Attlee To Thatcher* (Blackwell, 1989).

7   D. Kavanagh, 'Whatever Happened to Consensus Politics'.
8   B. Pimlott, 'The Myth of Consensus', in L. M. Smith (ed), *The Making of Britain: Echoes of Greatness* (Macmillan, 1988). See also S. E. Finer, *Adversary Politics and Electoral Reform* (Wigram, 1975); S. Beer, *Britain Against Itself* (Faber, 1982).
9   B. Pimlott, ibid, p. 12. H. Young, *One of Us* (Macmillan, 1989), p. 408.
10 Discussed in R. Lowe, 'The Second World War, Consensus and the Foundation of the Welfare State', *Twentieth Century British History*, 1990.
11 Ibid, p. 181.
12 N. Deakin, 'In Search of the Postwar Consensus', Suntory-Toyota International Centre for Economics, London School of Economics, 1988.
13 Lord Croham (former Permanent Secretary to the Treasury, 1974–77) at Institute of Contemporary British History, 1994.
14 Kavanagh and Morris, op. cit. p. 15.
15 See R. Miliband, *The State in Capitalist Society* (Weidenfeld and Nicolson, 1969).
16 Pimlott, op. cit., p. 12.
17 K. Jefferys, *The Churchill Coalition and Wartime Politics 1940–45* (Manchester University Press, 1991).
18 P. Addison, 'Consensus Revisited', *Twentieth Century British History*, 1993, p. 93.
19 Lowe concludes that 'consensus was not a mirage in the 1940s', but concurs that its constantly evolving nature in the decade creates problems in trying to pin down its origin. Op. cit.
20 Deakin, op. cit., pp. 29–30.
21 P. Williams, *Hugh Gaitskell*, pp. 312ff.
22 N. Rollings, 'Poor Mr Butskell', *Twentieth Century British History*, forthcoming.
23 H. Jones, *The Conservative Party and the Welfare State 1942–55* (Oxford University Press, forthcoming).

Britain and Europe Since 1945

BY DEREK HEARL

ONE relatively mundane but nonetheless still perhaps insightful interpretation of the last fifty-odd years of British history is that it has been a period during which the entire polity has had to come to terms with a new post-war, and especially post-imperial, role. Little by little, by fits and starts, with many hesitations and even some reversals, yet in the long run seemingly inexorably, the United Kingdom has been forced to come to terms with the reality of a new political and economic environment. From having been a world power with global interests and responsibilities, Britain has steadily and unquestionably become less and less significant an actor on the world stage. At the same time, of course, as its *world* power status has waned over the half century, Britain's importance as a *European* power has grown steadily to the point that it is now one of the most important and influential member states of the European Union. The corollary of this has been that European politics and political structures have begun to play an increasingly important role in purely domestic affairs. Not surprisingly, the management of this transition from global to European power has been a very difficult one for élites, institutions and public opinion alike. This article, then, consists of a more or less chronological, and necessarily selective, overview of some of the main features of this transition and of Britain's post-war involvement in Europe, followed, by contrast, by an assessment of some aspects of that involvement in institutional and political terms.

Historical overview

THE AFTERMATH OF WAR

It is still sometimes forgotten or overlooked, at least in Britain, that the original impetus towards post-1945 unification in Europe was much more the *political* goal of the creation of a lasting peace among the countries of the recently ravaged continent than it was one of economic advantage. Furthermore, this was a goal of which many British politicians and observers thoroughly approved. Churchill's famous speech at Zürich in September 1946 when he called for 'a sort of United States of Europe' in which both France and Germany would take part, is a case in point. Not that the idea was in any way new. The dream of a united and peaceful Europe can be traced back many centuries, most notably perhaps to William Penn who in 1693 called for a body that uncannily resembles today's Consultative Assembly of the Council of Europe. But it was in the twentieth century that it really achieved academic, intellectual, and above all political, respectability. Such personalities as the Austrian Count Richard Coudenhove-Kalergi and the French and German statesmen Aristide Briand and Gustav Stresemann argued during the inter-war years for '*Pan Europe*' as Coudenhove-Kalergi called it. However, such utopian solutions were rejected in favour of various forms of national independence and/or rival alliances in economic and military fields. But in 1945 things seemed very different and such attitudes could no longer be sustained. In the aftermath of war, a 'window of opportunity' finally opened up for the Pan-Europeans.

These were the years when national political systems were being re-established, political parties rebuilt (and in some cases created) and elections held, while a new breed of politicians and administrators was moving in to take over from their tired, disillusioned and frequently discredited predecessors. At this time there was an important, indeed crucial, coincidence of both psychological (or perhaps 'psychopolitical') and practical factors. The first was a massive disappointment with the pre-war political and international system. The second, more 'practical', factor was simply the sheer scale of destruction wrought by the war and the almost impossible task of reconstruction. Wholly new, and more cooperative, ways of thinking and organising seemed called for.

However, this essentially continental experience contrasted very strongly with the post-war situation in Britain, as well as among the Free French Forces led by Charles de Gaulle. Understandably both saw themselves as victorious rather than as liberated. The British political elite's faith in their own national way of doing things had not been shattered by the humiliation of defeat in war, as it had in so many countries on the European mainland where there was widespread disillusion with the mistakes of the inter-war period. 'It is perhaps the sheer political and economic chaos of world war II that accounts for the general attraction of the European option in the years just after 1945. If the competition among nation-states had led to "total war" twice within the first half of the twentieth century then European cooperation suggested itself as an appropriate theme for the future.'[1]

It is hard nowadays to imagine the sheer scale and horror of the destruction of much of the continent's industrial and physical infrastructure in the immediate aftermath of the war. Throughout Europe, canals, bridges, roads and railways were at best severely damaged and often altogether unusable. Factories and harbours, city centres and industrial complexes lay in ruins. It is estimated that in Germany a quarter of all housing stock had been destroyed, while a further quarter was utterly uninhabitable. Agricultural and industrial production was down to a third of pre-war levels and there were very severe refugee problems, widespread disease, malnutrition and even starvation. In short, in country after country the very notion of nation-state itself was widely believed to have failed and politicians and public alike were searching for a new, more cooperative and more integrated approach to the problems not only of reconstruction, although that was naturally the immediate concern, but also more generally.

During the war, Resistance members, many young, idealistic and still in their formative years, had become accustomed to the twin notions of working closely with—indeed often trusting their very lives to—fellow citizens of all political persuasions from conservative to communist as well as working with allies in other countries in pursuit of the over-riding common goals of political freedom and national liberation. 'The Resistance itself had had a kind of supra-national dimension; none of the national resistance movements could have survived without outside support; the nations whose honor they had saved had been liberated rather than victorious.'[2] The importance of this factor is not to be underestimated since, in the years following the war, many members of the Resistance went into politics, some eventually going on to high office. The attitudes such people had learned in adversity tended to be taken with them into post-war politics.

The more idealistic and non-adversarial approach to democratic politics extended to the European arena as well. This was particularly the case in the Benelux countries, in Italy and, of course, in Germany, if not so much in France which, because of de Gaulle's influence, had not seen its national pride damaged to the same degree. In Great Britain, by contrast the perception was very different and this is certainly one of the most important underlying reasons why Britain was largely to stay aloof from various schemes for European integration in the early post-war years. The issue was viewed very differently in a country which not only had not been defeated in war but which still had important world-wide economic and political interests outside Europe. Indeed, Churchill clearly saw Britain's role in such an enterprise as that of a close and supportive ally, not that of a full partner. Speaking in Zürich in September 1946: 'In all this urgent work France and Germany must take the lead together. Great Britain, the British Commonwealth of Nations, mighty America, and I trust Soviet Russia, must be the friends and sponsors of the new Europe and must champion its right to live and shine.'

In the meantime, the newly elected Labour government in Britain had more urgent priorities. The dangerous new bipolar world of superpower dominance by the United States and the Soviet Union made it imperative for Britain to consolidate the Atlantic connection. At the same time, the government was soon to be embroiled in the complexities of decoloni-sation, first in Burma and India and then more widely. Economic considerations too, above all the need for secure food supplies which continental Europe could not in any case have met at that time, pointed away from Europe and toward the Commonwealth.

This was not the American view. Washington felt that some form of

European Union, particularly but not only in the military field, was a highly desirable goal and that Britain would be a valuable element in such a project. The extremely important and generous post-war American economic aid package to Western Europe, the Marshall Plan, provided a powerful vehicle for political pressure in this direction. The United States made it a condition of the aid that the recipient states should establish a common organisation to administer it among themselves, leading to the Organisation for European Economic Cooperation (OEEC) of which Britain, as a recipient country, was of course a member. At the same time, Britain moved closer to Europe in military terms. Early fears of a resurgent Germany and subsequently much more realistic ones engendered by an increasingly strident and aggressive Soviet Union, again at American urging, led Britain to become a founder member first of the Brussels Treaty Organisation (now the Western European Union) and then, soon after, of NATO itself.

Economically and politically, however, Britain's face remained resolutely turned away from Europe throughout the 1950s. Even the establishment of the European Coal and Steel Community in 1952 by France, Germany, Italy and the three Benelux countries left the United Kingdom cold, declining even to take the proposal seriously, let alone participate. The elaborate system of Commonwealth preferences provided complementary trading links for Britain, while its domestic cheap food policy was very important to the government, allowing foreign imports into the country at low world prices and paying direct subsidies to the relatively small number of British farmers in order to prevent them being driven out of business at home.

During the following decade the entire situation began to change. The Commonwealth links were beginning to weaken and the 1956 Suez debâcle underlined the decline in the UK's world power status. And finally, and most importantly of all, the new EC was increasingly outperforming the UK economically. Between 1958 and 1971 UK output rose by 43%; in the EC countries it rose by 98%.

Britain first applied for full membership of the European Economic Community in June 1961 after a lengthy and somewhat tortuous reassessment of the political and economic benefits of doing so. According to an important study of this episode, the principal grounds for the application were predominantly political and very largely concerned with the role of the United States which was hostile to the EC's high tariff policies. Neverthless, the fact that the Community was growing so fast economically meant that there was growing support from the Treasury and increasingly, of course, also in business circles. A major concern was that, if it became too successful, it might replace Britain as the USA's major partner. Meanwhile, Charles de Gaulle, who had become President of France in 1958, had begun to make noises about foreign and defence policy cooperation between the EC states (and obviously under French leadership). This worried the British very greatly who feared the consequences of the French President's openly anti-American policies.

For all these reasons, it seemed to Britain's Prime Minister, Harold Macmillan, that the only way to preserve 'Atlanticism' in general, not to mention the so-called 'special relationship', always a very sensitive issue to the British, was for the UK to join the Community. Nevertheless, the application when it came was hesitant, due partly to divisions between and especially within both major political parties, but particularly among the governing Conservatives themselves, many of whom were deeply attached to the idea of British sovereignty and to the Commonwealth connection.

The negotiations were long and tortuous and became bogged down in detail perhaps because, it has been alleged, the French were making things difficult in the hope that they might break down irretrievably. Finally, in January 1963, following several sessions of talks in which good progress was made, they finally began to look like succeeding. It was then that President de Gaulle dropped his bombshell. At a press conference in January 1963 he announced a *de facto* veto of the British application on the grounds of Britain's essential 'un-Europeanness' and too close links with the United States. 'He did not consider that Britain had accepted a European vocation; ironically, he quoted the same doubts as had been expressed in conservative quarters in Britain. "England in fact is insular, maritime, bound by her trade, her markets, her suppliers, to countries that are very diverse and often very far away ... how can England, as she lives, as she produces, as she trades, be incorporated into the Common Market?"'[3] Some observers at the time believed that another reason for the French veto was the Nassau Agreement between Macmillan and Kennedy in December 1962 under which the Americans agreed to supply Polaris missiles to the United Kingdom, an offer which was not made to France.

Towards the end of that year, Macmillan resigned as Prime Minister on health grounds, to be replaced by Sir Alec Douglas-Home. The Conservatives lost the general election the following year and Labour returned to power under Harold Wilson as Prime Minister. Although at first the new government was not in favour of UK membership of the Community, there were powerful forces in the Labour Party that were, most notably the right-wing Deputy Leader of the Party and Secretary of State for Economic Affairs, George Brown, and it is suggested that in order to secure Brown's support, Wilson made some commitment to him on membership of the EC. The realities of office may also have contributed to convincing Wilson that membership was necessary, in the same way as they had convinced Macmillan before him, though, as with Macmillan, his conversion was hardly marked by enthusiasm. A second Application was made in 1966 as part of a deal between different factions in the Labour Party. Again, however, within four months there was a second de Gaulle veto on much the same grounds as the earlier one, that is that Britain was not ready for EC membership. This time the British insisted that the application lie on the table and did not formally withdraw it. Nevertheless, the veto remained in force until after de Gaulle's resignation from the presidency in 1969. It was lifted shortly afterwards by his successor, Georges Pompidou, and full scale negotiations began a few weeks later.

Labour lost the 1970 election and it fell to the new Conservative government under Edward Heath to complete the negotiations. Although Heath was, of course, (and still is) a fully committed European, he had to contend with considerable public hostility which the Labour opposition was quick to exploit. Since, however, the application had been submitted when it was in office, the Labour Party was forced to concentrate upon the 'terms of entry' which rapidly came to dominate the discussion. The result was that the arguments became confined to technicalities and bread and butter issues rather than ones of principle. Indeed, it may well be that the marked lack of idealism and popular enthusiasm for the European adventure that has been manifested in the United Kingdom ever since stems directly from this episode. The principal problems for the negotiators were what were to be done about the sterling balances (essentially a hang-over from British Empire days), the Common Agricultural Policy, the Community Budget and Commonwealth Preferences. The British were unable to gain any major concessions on any of these issues, thereby giving the Labour opposition plenty of material to beat the government with. Nevertheless, the deal was done and the United Kingdom joined the Community on 1 January 1973 together with Denmark and Ireland (but without Norway, where the government had lost an advisory referendum on the issue).

Virtually from day one, British politicians and civil servants appear to have treated their new Community partners in a tactless, even arrogant manner, immediately raising such sensitive questions as the locations of the various Community Institutions and criticising them for being inefficient. They did not appear willing to abide by accepted procedures and pushed their own national interests too stridently, especially that of a substantial budget for the new European Regional Development Fund. British ministers showed little patience with the Community's slow and tortuous consensus-building methods, preferring to indulge in the more confrontational style of politics with which they were familiar at home. Unsurprisingly, the principal effect of all this was very considerably to annoy other member states as well as EC officials and almost certainly made them less willing to accede to British demands. In short, there seems from the very beginning to have been a serious clash of political cultures at work, British adversarialism versus Continental consensualism, and this has not always worked to British advantage.

In March 1974 Labour returned to power and again defeated the Conservatives in October in an election fought partly on the terms of entry in general and the agriculture, fishing and budget issues in particular, with the Labour Party committed to renegotiation. Again, this was very largely an attempt by Wilson to keep his divided party together—everyone could at least agree that the Tory terms were bad. Further, and again in attempt to get the party off the hook, he promised to put the results of the renegotiation directly to the people in a referendum. 'For the government, membership of the EC was an issue that cut across class lines. It also allowed the Prime Minister to promote national unity in pursuing the national interest. There is no surer way of united a divided nation than for its leaders to wrap themselves in the national flag and conduct a campaign against an external foe. It was just unfortunate that the foe in this case consisted of Britain's partners in the Community, and the battle damaged relationships that were already strained.'[4]

The renegotiation concentrated on the same hoary old issues (apart from sterling which was ceasing to be a reserve currency anyway and therefore no longer a problem), that is, Commonwealth preferences (especially New Zealand butter), the Common Agricultural Policy and the Budget. The last was certainly the most difficult and deadlocked negotiations had to be resolved by a summit conference in Dublin. In the end agreement was reached and represented a marginal improvement over the existing terms which the government promptly presented as a major victory. Neverthless, the Labour Party at large refused to endorse the revised terms and the Party Conference voted against them.

The Referendum took place on 12 June 1975, with both major parties, but especially Labour, very divided. It was a unique event in British constitutional history (unlike Scottish and Welsh devolution, the only one held across the UK as a whole). Although merely advisory in theory, Parliament having the final word, there was never any chance that MPs and Peers would have been able to do anything other than endorse the decision of the electorate. It is distinctly odd, therefore, that the potentially very serious damage to the near sacred doctrine of parliamentary (as opposed to popular) sovereignty which the referendum represented, compounded as it was by the suspension of collective Cabinet responsibility to allow ministers to campaign on opposite sides, appears to have been little discussed, or even recognised, either at the time or subsequently. Be that as it may, on a turnout of 64.6%, 13,378,581 people (67.2%) voted yes and only 8,470,073 (32.8%) no, a decisive victory by any standards and one which, it might have been imagined, would have put paid to the issue once and for all.

In the event, however, the rows between Britain and its partners continued over such varied things as environmental and pollution standards, lorry drivers' hours and the compulsory use of tachographs, the Regional Development Fund and the problem of 'additionality' (the principle that EC aid must not be a substitute for national government aid).

James Callaghan replaced Wilson as Prime Minister in March 1976 and promptly raised the issue of the British contribution yet again. Once more British ministers and officials were mostly confrontational and undiplomatic, not only on this issue but also concerning the development of a Common Fisheries Policy and in negotiations for the establishment of the European Monetary System. Callaghan had an overall majority of two which was soon eroded by by-election losses, forcing him to turn to the Liberal MPs to keep him in office. Part of the price the latter demanded for entering the subsequent Lib-Lab Pact was proportional representaton for the forthcoming European elections. This, however, was anathema to much of the Labour Party and consequently the government stalled on the issue. Even when the arrangements for holding the elections were agreed and a target date of May/June 1978 set, the government failed to keep up with the necessary timetable and eventually the entire election had to be postponed for a year. When it finally did take place, the parliamentary debate was long and hard, in many ways foreshadowing the Maastricht ratification process fifteen years later. Needless to say, in spite of the Prime Minister's personal support, no majority could be found in the Commons for proportional representation and so far all European elections in Great Britain have taken place under the traditional first-past-the-post electoral system (in Northern Ireland, however, the STV system of proportional representation is used).

In 1979 after a successful motion of no confidence following the outcome of the Scottish and Welsh devolution referendums, Callaghan called a general election which was won by the Conservative Party and Margaret Thatcher became Prime Minister. By the time the first European election was held the following month, the Labour Party had adopted an extremely negative position in regard to British membership of the EC. Its manifesto not only called for fundamental reforms but threatened that if they were not obtained Britain should withdraw from the Community altogether. Four years later, at the 1983 general election, Labour, led now by Michael Foot, had hardened its position to one of unconditional withdrawal. In the interim, in 1981, the Labour Party had suffered an extremely damaging split, one which for a time seemed to threaten a major realignment of British politics with the formation of the Social Democratic Party. Although the ostensible reason for the breakaway, as the leading 'Gang of Four' saw it, was the undemocratic constitutional changes in the Labour Party, it was quite clear that Labour's official policy on the European question was also a major cause.

However, following Foot's replacement as leader by Neil Kinnock after the massive electoral defeat of 1983, the Labour Party gradually shifted to a more pragmatic stance. In an obvious attempt to try to heal the very deep cracks in the party, Kinnock argued that even if Labour were to take office at the next election, the UK would by then have been a member of the Community for approaching twenty years. The detailed arrangements for a subsequent withdrawal would then have to be negotiated, a process which might itself take a considerable time, and would in any event be very gradual, lasting perhaps several years as commitments were slowly unravelled. In short, immediate withdrawal was simply not on the cards and in the interim Labour's duty was to act positively to get the best deal it could for Britain for as long as it remained a member. In this way, Kinnock was able first to put the entire issue on the back burner and then to defuse it altogether. The sea change came when, following his speech to the 1988 Trade Union Congress, Jacques Delors, the new—and socialist—President of the European Commission, managed to convince the TUC that 'Social Europe' could guarantee better conditions for workers than could the individual member states. After that, it was only a matter of time before the Labour Party itself came around to the same view.

Over the years that official Labour Policy was shifting from an overtly hostile position towards membership of the European Community to a more positive one, the Conservative Party under Mrs Thatcher seemed to be moving in the opposite direction. 'After 1979 British policy had seen a continuation of the predominantly suspicious British attitude to European integration, although it was now accepted that the question of membership was closed. The pervasive concern became, therefore, the attempt to remodel the Community in the British image, that image reflecting certain features common to both major parties and to traditional British post-war policy, although there were also distinctive Thatcherite elements.'[5]

The first problem to raise its head following the Conservative victory in 1979 was yet again that of the budgetary contribution. The latter, the net difference payments to and receipts from the Community, had long been considered by the British to be unfair and a number of temporary corrective measures had been negotiated previously. Mrs Thatcher, however, sought a permanent solution to the problem, about which she felt particularly strongly. It was one on which she was prepared to make few if any concessions, and the vigour with which she pursued the issue for several years before it was finally settled at the Fontainebleu Summit in 1984 shocked her fellow heads of government. Nor was the Prime Minister prepared for Britain to join the newly established Exchange Rate Mechanism, which she considered both dangerous and impractical, although, apparently against her better judgement, her government did so later. She also refused for a long time to contemplate any reform of the Community institutions, a process which several other governments set considerable store by. On the other hand, from the beginning the government strongly supported the principle of completing the Single Market, which Jacques Delors was proposing, and consequently the United Kingdom did put its signature to the Single European Act at the end of 1985.

Throughout the whole of her period in office, Mrs Thatcher's abrasive style and her constant refusal to compromise became as much a byword in European circles as it was at home. She took particular exception to any pretensions on the part of the EC institutions, and particularly the President of the Commission, to assert their authority and was reportedly furious at Delors' speech. She almost immediately counter-attacked with her own Bruges speech in September 1988 which was widely interpreted both as an offensive against Delors' vision of a Social Europe and as a hymn to nationalism. In retrospect, the Bruges speech does seem to have been a turning point since the Prime Minister's ever more strident tone on European questions increasingly began to affect the Conservative Party itself. It became easier for long-standing, but latterly rather quiescent, anti-marketeers to raise their heads again, and the latent division in the party began to open up once more. On the other hand, many Conservatives, including perhaps a majority of the parliamentary party, continued to be staunch Europeans, with many openly appalled at this new turn of events. Matters eventually came to head in Sir Geoffrey Howe's devastating resignation speech in November 1990 in which he made it clear that there were deep and unbridgeable divisions within the government on the European issue. Mrs Thatcher was forced from office some days later.

John Major became Prime Minister in November 1990 at the head of a government divided on the European issue as never before. He promptly declared his intention of seeing Britain at the heart of Europe and set about building good personal relationships with his fellow heads of government, notably the German Chancellor. However, it soon became apparent that the new Prime Minister's very different and much more conciliatory personal style did not herald any weakening of British opposition either to continental notions of a 'federal vocation' for the Community, as early drafts of what was to become the Maastricht Treaty on European Union put it, or to the detested Social Charter, which the government firmly believed would have harmful effects on employment. In the event, John Major did succeed in having the first removed from the Treaty text altogether and obtained an 'opt out' for Britain from the second, as well as from the next stages of Economic and Monetary Union for which the Treaty provides. Since then, of course, there have been considerable problems, not only in Britain but also in a number of other countries, notably Denmark, in ratifying the Maastricht Treaty. These problems have only served to exacerbate the continuing division inside the Conservative Party where the ranks of the 'Eurosceptics' seem still to be undiminished.

The 'Europeanisation' of British politics?

The first part of this chapter has largely concentrated upon the *politics* of the UK's involvement in and with Europe since the 1940s. This second part will highlight a few aspects of the impact that European Union membership has had upon a number of British political *institutions*, that is upon the government itself, Parliament, local authorities and the political parties.

Government. Easily the most powerful EU institution is the Council of Ministers, each full meeting of which consists of departmental ministers from the Member States and their advisors. It is here that all the main decisions are taken and European legislation finally enacted. The enormous growth in the Council's activities over recent years, not to mention the enhanced position of the presidency which each member state including Britain holds in rotation, has meant that ministers and civil servants now have to devote an ever increasing proportion of their time and effort to this function.

This has been compounded over the past twenty years as increasing interpenetration of EU and national policy-making and implementation has led to new ways of working in the Council. Governments, reluctant to abandon control to the more supranational Commission and Parliament, have devised ever more elaborate ways of working involving a welter of committees and specialist working parties concerned with negotiating and elaborating proposals for Community legislation or other action, but increasingly concerned also with their detailed implementation. Already by the end of the 1980s, hundreds of days were being spent on meetings at ministerial and ambassadorial level and more than 2,000 on committees and working parties staffed by civil servants and other experts. Even this number was to increase substantially over the following years when the detailed legislative arrangements for the 1992 Single Market Programme were being worked out. Now, however, that that programme has successfully been implemented, the frequency of such meetings can be expected to diminish, at least to some extent.

At the same time there has been a significant increase in direct contacts between the ministries of member states, which often by-pass the offical EU institutions altogether. The inevitable consequence of all this has been that direct involvement in European affairs by ministers and civil servants has increased dramatically. Nearly every day dozens of such people travel to Brussels and other Community capitals, sometimes for only a few hours, to attend the many committees which the above 'comitology' system has spawned. Hardly a ministry is exempt, while it is said that the Foreign Secretary, in particular, now meets his opposite numbers more frequently, and for much longer periods of time, than he does his Cabinet colleagues.

Parliament. Parliament, too, has seen its position significantly affected, albeit for different reasons, as a result of EU membership. The European Communities Act of 1972 is itself cast in almost frighteningly wide terms; 'All . . . rights, powers, liabilities, obligations and restrictions . . . created or arising by or under the Treaties . . . are without further enactment to be given legal effect or used in the United Kingdom . . .

and be enforced, allowed and followed accordingly.' This is clearly a massive erosion of at least the formal *legislative* powers of the UK Parliament and constitutes a major, indeed fundamental, change in the British constitution, notably in the doctrine of parliamentary sovereignty which insists that any state power in the United Kingdom must derive from Parliament in Westminster. This has serious implications for all forms of power sharing, not just European integration but judicial review and regional devolution in Britain.

It is obvious that the Act constitutes a major breach of this principle and this perhaps explains why loss of 'sovereignty' has been such a sensitive issue in Britain. In other member states national parliaments, subordinate as they are to written constitutional provisions or Bills of Rights, are not directly identified with national sovereignty in this way. By contrast, in Britain where traditionally there have been no other constitutional safeguards against abuse of power or loss of citizens' rights than Parliament, virtually *any* restriction on parliamentary power is seen as highly dangerous.

In more practical terms, too, Parliament is now faced with a vast number of EC reports, draft directives, regulations and other provisions, many embodied in highly detailed Ministerial Orders which are not subject to normal legislative procedure. Indeed, such Orders, although still having to be laid before Parliament, are typically considered untouchable, at least to the extent that they merely implement Community provisions. This has led to the suspicion that governments may be making use of the procedure to impose additional regulations of their own devising, smuggling them, as it were, past Parliament under the guise of European law. For example, it has recently been claimed that out of some 80 new, allegedly European, regulations affecting the catering industry less than 20 were actually required by Community law, the remainder having originated entirely from within the British government itself.

Another important area in which Parliament has seen its position weakened as a consequence of European Union membership is that of ministerial accountability. It is now virtually impossible to question British ministers about the discussions they have, or even the legislative decisions they make, in the Council whose deliberations have hitherto almost always been considered confidential, subject to the traditional secrecies of diplomatic intercourse. This is certainly an area which arouses considerable disquiet, especially when, as frequently happens, national ministers who have been at the same meeting in Brussels seem on return to their own capitals to have completely different recollections of what took place. The situation may marginally improve as a result of the limited experiments that have taken place in televising selected Council meetings and, more especially, if current plans to publish the results of votes in the legislative sessions of the Council are implemented in due course.

On a more positive note, both Houses of Parliament have set up specialist select committees to deal with European Union business and the ability of these committees to investigate and report on matters of their choosing has certainly been a very valuable one. The House of Lords Committee in particular has acquired a considerable reputation for the excellence of its reports.

Local Authorities. Local authorities in the UK began to feel the effects of Community membership almost immediately following British accession. EC regulations in the fields of employment law, VAT, and especially the award of public service contracts, had to be observed virtually from the start, and the impact of these and other provisions has grown steadily over the years, particularly following the passing of the Single European Act and the completion of the Single Market at the end of 1992. A wide range of new Health and Safety rules covering such disparate things as bathing beaches, consumer protection, environmental standards and the planning of new roads, has also affected local authorities significantly.

Perhaps most important of all, grant aid under the various 'structural' (Regional, Social, etc.) funds aimed at, for example, job creation and/or infrastructure development is now available to many local authority-supported schemes. As a result, a large number of councils, either alone or in cooperation with others, now employ specialist staff to deal directly with the European Union and some have even opened liaison offices of their own in Brussels. Finally, of course, the recent establishment of the Committee of the Regions under the Maastricht Treaty has for the first time given local authority representatives from the UK an institutional input of their own into EU decision-making. There are 24 members of the committee from the UK, with 24 alternates, appointed by the government from local councillors and acting in a personal capacity.

Political parties. Following UK accession in 1973, each of the three main parliamentary parties was allocated seats in the then still nominated European Parliament. The Conservatives and Liberals took up their seats from the beginning but Labour at first declined to do so, leaving its seats vacant. The two Liberal MEPs, one from each House, joined the Liberal and Allies Group in which they remained until the party lost all its seats following the 1979 move to a directly-elected Parliament. Similarly, the Labour MEPs, when they did eventually take their seats, have always sat in the Socialist Group. The Conservatives, by contrast, did not have sufficient affinity with the then Christian Democratic Group for them to sit together and eventually, together with two or three Danish colleagues, they formed a European Democratic Group of their own.

In the meantime, in 1978, in preparation for the forthcoming direct elections, three EC-level party federations, one Christian Democrat under the name of European People's Party, one Liberal and one

Socialist were formed as extra-parliamentary organisations to draw up common election manifestos and coordinate their campaign efforts. Again, although the Labour and Liberal Parties joined their respective federations, not without some difficulties in the latter case, the Conservatives continued to be independent and unaligned. This remained the position until the beginning of 1993 when the European Democratic Group finally dissolved and the UK Conservative MEPs joined the European People's Party Group on an individual basis, i.e. without committing the party at home which has so far not joined the EPP proper.

The Maastricht Treaty now recognises a new role for European-level parties and party federations. The former rather loose Confederation of Socialist Parties, for example, has now reorganised much more tightly as the Party of European Socialists. In due course, the enhanced importance given to such organisations may give the British Conservatives a problem in deciding whether or not to affiliate fully to the overtly federalist (and Social Chapter supporting) EPP. On the other hand, the problems the British Liberal Democrats have long had with some of *their* allies may now have been eased by the recent departure of the (essentially Conservative) French Republican Party from the European Liberals, Democrats and Reformers which many party activists may now find more to their taste than was previously the case.

Conclusion

One thing that the preceding sections have shown is that, over the last thirty years or so, a new cleavage has opened up in British politics cutting straight across its traditional left-right structure. Setting pro-Europeans against anti-Europeans (although many of the latter would not accept this designation), this has obviously varied in intensity over time. Sometimes it has been relatively quiescent, at other times it has been sufficiently important to threaten the party system itself. The 1981 split in the Labour Party, when the SDP was formed, is only the most dramatic example; there have been plenty of others. Indeed, the reported divisions in the current Conservative Cabinet, not to mention the embarrassments it suffered during the long drawn out Maastricht Treaty ratification process, bear eloquent witness to this. Nor does this new cleavage show any signs of disappearing as the reaction in the Conservative Party both within and outside Parliament to the recent row over the qualified majority needed in the Council of Ministers clearly demonstrates.

Indeed, there are likely to be plenty of opportunities for further controversial issues to come to the fore over the next few years, any of which can be expected to put further strains upon this new fault line in British politics. It is entirely possible, for example, that attempts will be made in some quarters to try to use the powers contained within the 1986 Single European Act to implement some of the provisions of the

Social Chapter, thereby by-passing the UK's Maastricht Treaty 'opt out'. If this were to happen, and the chances of it doing so will presumably be enhanced with the EU's enlargement to include Austria and the three Scandinavian states, the reaction of a British Conservative government can only be imagined. On the other hand, the doctrine of subsidiarity (under which the European Union is supposed in future to act only when the aims of any legislation can be most effectively achieved at that level) has now become justiciable and therefore potentially enforceable in the courts. There is clearly a rich field here for conflict between the member states, or some of them, and the European Union institutions themselves.

Nor should it be forgotten that plans for Economic and Monetary Union are already going ahead and may yet be achieved by the target date of 1999. The European Monetary Institute, designed to be the forerunner of the European Central Bank enshrined in the Maastricht Treaty, is already in place and, notwithstanding British assumptions to the contrary, the Exchange Rate Mechanism is once again functioning more or less normally, albeit among a restricted inner core of countries.

Fnally, within a couple of years, a new intergovernmental conference will take place to review progress and to consider further institutional reforms. One likely outcome of this will be concrete proposals for a fully-fledged Constitution for the European Union along the lines of the little-noticed Herman Report recently adopted by the European Parliament. This will be certain to raise all the old issues of sovereignty, federalism and subsidiarity in a new and stark form. Controversies over the design and operation of the European Union look like remaining at the heart of British politics for a long time to come.

1   L. Lindberg and S. Scheingold, *Europe's Would-be Polity* (Prentice-Hall, 1970), p. 2.
2   S. Hoffman, 'The Fate of the Nation', *Daedelus*, Summer 1962.
3   S. George, *An Awkward Partner: Britain and the European Community* (Oxford University Press, 1991), p. 34. The following section draws on this book.
4   George, op. cit., p. 76.
5   W. Nicoll and T. Salmon, *Understanding the New European Community* (Harvester Wheatsheaf, 1994), p. 255.

The Media in Postwar British Politics

THE half-century since 1945 has produced no remark about the press
and politics with quite the resonance of Baldwin's jibe against Beaverbrook and Rothermere—that they were seeking 'power without responsibility—the prerogative of the harlot through the ages'. Roy Thomson's
unguarded claim in 1957 that the award of an ITV franchise was 'a
licence to print money' perhaps comes closest; appropriately so, since
the insinuation of television into political life is the dominant feature of
the period. Little in the nest, including tardily the Chamber of the
House of Commons, was undisturbed by this cuckoo.

However, TV did not displace the press. Editors discovered in the
1920s that radio was a complementary medium, not a head-on rival,
and the same proved true of TV. Radio largely eschewed politics, so in
1945 the press and the public meeting remained the dominant media of
political discourse. The tradition was typified in Mr Attlee's election
campaign of 1950, when he trundled round the country in the family
car, with Mrs Attlee (somewhat alarmingly) at the wheel, in a classic
hustings tour. Forty years later the situation had been transformed.
Political activity has always been conditioned to a great extent by the
nature of the dominant means of communication available for carrying
it on. By 1992 this meant campaign strategies that put TV coverage at
their very heart. Claims that 'TV is the campaign', heretical until the
early 1970s, were long since truisms. It may not be true that politics
and media, politicians and journalists, are entangled with each other
more than ever before (the sniggering sense included), but the expansion
of media within our lives—25 hours a week watching TV, on average,
in the 1990s, and a thick doormat of daily newspapers—has altered
the terms of the relationship. Compared with the first half of the
twentieth century, to put it emotively, politicians have become the
clients of the media, where formerly media were the clients of the
politicians.

The more complex the entanglement, the more difficult is the question
about the political effects of media. Almost any question about political
life since 1945 could turn out to have an answer in which media are a
factor. Is the questioner interested in the short term or the long term?
In unintended effects, or intended? In effects upon knowledge, upon
attitudes, or upon behaviour? Upon process, or upon outcome? Precise
answers are difficult too, for media cannot often be isolated as a
variable. Party strategists would have paid generously at every election

© Oxford University Press

since 1945 for solid information about how to manipulate votes through media. But that question remained obstinately unanswerable, whether about the wisdom of Churchill's anti-Labour 'Gestapo' smear in 1945, or about Heath's failure to impose his interpretation of the February 1974 mining dispute ('Who Governs?'), or about the truth of the claim that 'IT'S THE SUN WOT WON IT' in 1992.

Upon less structured things than election results the influence of media is even less clear, though often more intriguing: the rise and fall of careers and reputations (Enoch Powell, Jeremy Thorpe); of whole parties and movements (CND, Militant, the SDP); or of shifts in ideology. This article, necessarily selective then, speculates simply about some prominent themes in the relation of politics and media since 1945 and about their impact on political institutions and behaviour. The first is the tension of power and accountability between politicians and media; second, the mutual adjustment of politics and television; and thirdly, the continuing issue of press partisanship.

Media and politics: power and accountability

The veteran *Sunday Times* political correspondent James Margach subtitled his memoirs, published in 1978, *The War Between Fleet Street and Downing Street*. Although the main title was *The Abuse of Power*, Margach saw the war as neither surprising nor exceptionable. Media and politicians have methods and objectives which often coincide (a common interest in words as a tool of persuasion, for instance), but which also conflict. Part of the enduring conflict is for power over the public understanding of the meaning of events, as politicians and journalists struggle to impose rival versions of the truth.

In addition to this, however, politicians' attitudes to the media (certainly politicians at Westminster) are overlain with beliefs about the kind of media desirable in a parliamentary democracy. These separate views can themselves come into conflict. Press freedom has predominantly been seen in the twentieth century as freedom from government interference. Yet managing the news to present an unpopular policy in the best light may involve threats or cajolery, such as Eden used against the BBC in the Suez crisis and Mrs Thatcher used in the Falklands war. Labour governments have thus had to confront the temptation to intervene in order to try and get a more sympathetic press. Conservatives have had to deal similarly with the desire to temper the principles of public service broadcasting, so as to reduce what they perceived as an anti-Conservative bias in the BBC. Suez was just the first (or most public) in a line which, from the early 1970s onwards, included a litany of complaints about broadcast coverage of Northern Ireland.

Tensions since 1945 have thus taken two forms. Some have featured media as Goliath, with politicians in the role of David, seeking to hold overmighty media barons accountable to their publics. Others have reversed the roles, with media playing tribune of the people and seeking to hold politicians accountable to the public. Both forms run through the process of mutual adjustment by politics and television and through politicians' dealings with the press. But they are clear also in those areas in which media have been subject to specific government policy.

For the press, politicians' concern until the Thatcher administration was with the fear of contraction in the number of newspaper titles and of excessive concentration of ownership. The period was punctuated by three Royal Commissions, in 1947–49, 1961–62 and 1974–77. The focus in the first was upon newspapers' performance—accuracy, bias, diversity—in addition to ownership and monopolistic tendencies. The second was set up as a direct result of the closure of the *News Chronicle* and the London evening *Star*. The *News Chronicle* was the last remaining mass circulation daily supporting the Liberal Party. The Liberals won only 6% of the votes cast in the 1959 general election (distributed among 216 constituencies) and the *News Chronicle*'s circulation of 1.2 million comprised about 8% of the Fleet Street total— meagre beside the 4.2 million of the *Daily Express* and 4.5 million of the *Daily Mirror*. The Macmillan government's willingness to set up a second Royal Commission, under the former Labour Attorney General, Lord Shawcross, thus reflected a 'democratic' impulse—though this required little generosity of spirit, as the Conservatives were in no danger of losing their dominance in the party press. The third Commission was set up by the Wilson government, concerned again by editorial standards and concentration, but with particular awareness of the increasingly bad labour relations of Fleet Street.

Not one of these inquiries, however, led to strong government action. Each time, mid-Victorian fourth estate rhetoric rationalised inactivity and accompanied an invisible shrug of the shoulders about party bias and contraction of numbers. Ministerial discretion to refer takeovers to the monopolies commission was considered enough to take care of concentration. It was not surprising if a Labour government, by 1977, was reluctant to tackle the print unions; while subsidy schemes for weak papers might have turned out to damage Labour's own chief supporters, the Mirror group papers.

Policy about broadcasting was marked equally by official inquiries, in 1949–51, 1960–62 and 1974–77. These were about the management of expansion, chiefly as new TV channels and longer broadcasting hours became practical. A fourth inquiry, in 1985–86, was supposedly about how to finance the BBC, which Mrs Thatcher thought needed shaking up, preferably by the abolition of its guaranteed licence fee income. But that issue inevitably broadened into scrutiny of the structure of broadcasting in general. Independent or 'commercial' TV, as it was sniffily called after its inauguration in 1955, was seen at first as an alternative to the public service system of the BBC. Public Service was a phrase that did not come into common use until the late 1970s, but the principles went right back to the incorporation of the BBC in 1926.

Their essence lay in giving audiences what they needed (which included, but went beyond, what they already knew they wanted); assured finance, not dependent upon audience ratings; the provision of an equal service regardless of audiences' location (an important engineering consideration in the earlier days); special attention to minorities; and political independence. Such were the regulations laid upon the commercial broadcasters, however, that gradually the entire broadcasting system came to be regarded as one of public service. This was especially true after the Macmillan government accepted the caustic criticisms of ITV in the Pilkington Committee report (1962) and awarded the third TV channel to the BBC (BBC2).

By the later 1980s the technical limits on the number of possible TV and radio channels were rapidly disappearing. With them went the historic justification for a publicly controlled broadcasting monopoly. The Thatcher government's preference for deregulation was therefore applied to the 1990 Broadcasting Bill, which set up an auction system for future ITV franchises. Applicants were simply to bid what they guessed they could afford to pay the Treasury out of earnings from advertising revenue. The system was drastically modified by the introduction of a quality threshold, so that the eventual Act produced companies with less money available for programming but with many of the old public service requirements intact. These included high quality news and current affairs, of precisely the kind which governments from time to time found so frustrating.

What the 1990 Act did not fully address was the issue of cross-ownership and conglomeration. All the postwar public inquiries listed above proceeded on parallel tracks with barely a wobble of convergence. In retrospect, it is extraordinary that the Wilson government still thought in the mid-1970s that policy about press and broadcasting could sensibly be made in isolation from one another. The reason, perhaps, is that politicians persisted in seeing them from the vantage point of ownership not consumption. After all, it was owners, editors and executives with whom they mainly had to deal. For the citizen/elector, on the other hand, newspapers, magazines, radio, TV, and the new products that simply did not exist in the 1950s, such as VCRs, cassette tapes, CDs and videogames, were all to some degree substitutable or overlapping products. Politicians, right up to the mid-1990s, were treating different products differently, for purposes of regulating trade, competition, taxation, technical development and public morals (no video-nasties permitted, but some pretty nasty novels and films).

It took the expansion of the Murdoch empire to bring into focus the implications of cross-ownership and conglomeration — but not until the mid-1980s. By 1994 the most distinctive aspect of his empire was neither its size nor its international scope but its unique position in the satellite TV market. Murdoch's Sky channel was classed as non-domestic for regulatory purposes, and this exempted it from the 1990

Broadcasting Act's limitation on cross-ownership between satellite TV and newspapers. How far and how quickly Sky's share of the viewing audience would grow remained an open question. But, added to the roughly 30% of national daily circulation made up by his papers (*The Times*, *Sun*, and *Today*), plus comparable figures on Sundays (*Sunday Times*, *News of the World*) and control of libraries of film and TV programmes in the USA, Sky made Murdoch's a formidable empire. Of him more than anyone with whom politicians had to do business since 1945 it could be asked: which is the greater danger to democratic politics—a giant international media mogul or a government that intervenes to curb him? When the Major government did announce a review of cross-ownership rules in 1994, however, the example of Murdoch was less a motive than the fear that continuing strict limits, including about multiple ownership of TV stations, would harm British companies' competitive chances in an increasingly global market.

Politics and television come to terms

For most of the postwar period, TV posed problems less of policy than of coping day to day with an unexpected guest who, when invited as a courtesy to make himself at home, proceeds irritatingly to do just that. Indeed, it is tempting to see the entire period since 1945 in these terms, since newspapers, too, had to adjust to TV. (The national press clung on to its share of the total advertising cake, for instance, while ITV's grew from zero to one third, only at the expense of magazine, cinema and provincial press advertising). The simplest reminders of TV's growth are that in 1950 there were about 350 thousand TV licences and in 1990 about twenty million; and that in 1961 people spent about 13.5 hours a week watching TV, while in 1990 they spent nearly twice as long. On the other hand, politics, in so far as it can be separated from 'news' and 'international' stories, has never become popular viewing. The official Party Political Broadcasts have generally been amongst the most unpopular of all programmes. Post-election surveys in 1992 found two-thirds of viewers saying there had been 'too much' election coverage—by no means an unprecedented finding.[1] An ITV survey in 1992 ranked programmes about politics 28th in popularity out of 36 subjects, with only 9% of viewers claiming to be very interested.

The adjustment, one might say, was done by the politicians and the broadcasters, then, more than by the viewers. The process can be summarised as a shift from broadcasters being, first, observers of politics, to being, next, discreet participants, and finally to becoming more recently so essential as to be part of the structure. Where TV was at first an instrument applied to politics, it had become by the Thatcher era part of the environment within which politics was carried on. Put another way, the terms of exchange shifted. TV increasingly operated on its own terms, with the politicians making the adjustments.

The public service background has already been indicated. For reporting politics, this meant extreme caution, to avoid audiences being unwittingly exposed to biased or partisan programmes, or even to unbalanced controversy. Least of all could the broadcasters editorialise. These principles naturally constricted political coverage to the verge of strangulation. All that listeners could hear in 1945, apart from the news, was the daily fifteen-minute report on 'Yesterday In Parliament', a weekly round-up called *The Week In Westminster* and the occasional scripted talk. Worse still, the BBC's '14-days rule', invented as a protection against pressure from politicians, excluded reference to any matter likely to be the subject of discussion in either House of Parliament within the coming fourteen days. The rule survived until 1956, when it was quietly abandoned during the Suez crisis for the embarrassment it had steadily become. But its existence—and the fact that the BBC itself invented it—epitomised the extent to which broadcasters began by deferring to the political institutions they had to report.

During the 1945 election, similarly, the BBC avoided the risks of controversy simply by ignoring the campaign's existence until the results were announced, and by leaving the parties to produce their own election broadcasts. These took the form of alternating nightly talks, varying in length up to half an hour. Not until 1959, after testing the water at by-elections the previous year, did the broadcasters dare to report an election campaign. The initiative was Granada's, and it was typical of the fresh approach brought by ITV. The BBC had been overly worried about infringing the fairness requirements in election law; ITV was prepared to take a chance. Equally, ITV took a less deferential approach to interviewing politicians. Archive film shows interviewers such as Chris Chataway and Robin Day less inclined to call politicians 'sir' and more inclined to press them for clear answers.

The 1959 election is the single most important symbolic date, arguably, in the history of political broadcasting. Ministers had already begun to appear on discussion programmes from the early 1950s (though they still needed Downing Street permission). Eden had won plaudits for his televised election broadcasts in 1955 and was the first Prime Minister to address the nation face to camera (twice) during the Suez crisis. Macmillan used TV imaginatively in a fireside chat with the visiting American President, Dwight Eisenhower, in 1958; and he cultivated what broadcasting professionals regarded as a fine television manner. But election TV signalled the beginning of an adjustment to the new medium by political institutions in general and not just by the top party leaders. This was perfectly logical, since election campaigns are the most concentrated, intense form of competition for political power, with the highest stakes, and they turn entirely on successful communication to the voting public.

An immediate example of politicians adjusting to suit TV was the invention by Labour's General Secretary, Morgan Phillips, of the daily campaign press conference at party headquarters during the 1959 election: thus was born one of the key rituals of modern campaign communications (often influential, for example, in setting the day's news agenda). With each successive election, parties sought more ingenious methods of improving their coverage. These ranged from small detail to grand strategy. Harold Wilson discovered that to squash a heckler on camera he needed to repeat the heckler's comment for the microphones before demolishing it. His opponent in 1964, Alec Douglas-Home, did not learn that trick, nor realise that even if he was drowned in a hall, his microphone would enable the TV audiences to hear what he was saying. Wilson was the first, too, to go walkabout for the TV cameras, providing them with movement and visual interest. Mrs Thatcher brought the technique to its apotheosis in 1979 by cradling a calf. Such devices, applied equally by politicians when in office, became the commonplaces of political news coverage. It seemed not the least odd, for instance, that workmen scattered litter in a London park so that Mrs Thatcher could come and be filmed picking it up again in the cause of a tidier Britain.

As to 'grand strategy', election campaigns were increasingly masterminded from 1979 on the advice of advertising and marketing specialists. The Party Election Broadcast reached new heights of sophistication in Hugh Hudson's film about the Kinnocks in 1987. Hudson had made the successful nostalgia movie, *Chariots of Fire*. His PEB was popularly known as 'Kinnock—the movie'. The typical PEB, so to speak, was now biked round to the BBC by courier and handed over as a cassette. Mrs Thatcher included the former Saatchi and Saatchi senior executive, Tim Bell, among her strategists. Christopher Lawson, a former Mars executive, was a marketing adviser in 1979. Harvey Thomas, who had staged rallies for the American evangelist Billy Graham, 'produced' the Conservative annual conference. The playwright Ronald Millar crafted her speeches (including 'The lady's not for turning'). Gordon Reece, a television director, coached her in interview technique, getting her to lower her voice and eliminate the occasional note of shrillness. Comparable developments in the Labour Party were typified in the central role of Peter Mandelson, appointed communications director by Neil Kinnock as part of his reorganisation after succeeding Michael Foot as Leader in 1983.

By the 1990s, it could be taken for granted that candidates for office, from constituency level upwards, would be chosen partly on the basis of their skill as TV performers, that they would dress for TV, do their hair for TV, speak in soundbites for TV. TV had effectively enveloped politics. The changes that led to this position can be summarised in two ways. The first focuses on places in which politics is carried on. The broadcasters' first move was into existing locations. They were welcomed into Parliament well before world war two, even though they were prevented from broadcasting it live. As early as 1954 the Conservative party annual conference was televised (including Sir Winston

Churchill—who never agreed to take part in a studio broadcast). From 1959 election campaigns embraced broadcasting. From 1975 the Commons permitted direct radio broadcasting. From 1985 the Lords, less fearful of the impact upon their character and procedures, let in the TV cameras.

In 1989, finally, the House of Commons also agreed to be televised on an experimental basis. This decision followed twenty-five years of intermittent debate, in which the doubters had dominated, sometimes narrowly (for example under Richard Crossman's Leadership of the House in 1966). The House's overwhelming desire was to minimise the extent to which the cameras would affect what they were observing. In the spirit of the old 14-days rule, the Commons persisted in seeing TV as a threat, not an opportunity, a medium which should be bent to its needs, rather than providing scope for innovation. When organising the experiment, therefore, the House kept firm control over the use of the film, although it was happy to contract out the actual business of filming. It imposed strict rules, too, about camera angles and permissible shots. In the event of disturbances, for instance, the camera was to shift immediately to the Speaker. Close-ups, reaction shots—the crudities of nose-blowing and forty winks—were all banned. There was little doubt the experiment would be judged a success by MPs and the public alike, and in 1990 it was put onto a permanent basis.

The next development in TV's progress was the discovery of new locations in which politicians could be observed or interviewed. The election press conferences are an example. Membership of the European Community brought an increase in summitry, with summit press conferences as one of the rituals. These were all the more noticeable because of British Prime Ministers' continuing reluctance to give press conferences at home. Ted Heath gave three rather grand conferences in the plush surroundings of Lancaster House during the early years of his administration. But journalists found them lacking in hard news, and they disliked seeing their questions used as fodder for the cameras. Informal conferences, on the other hand, became quite common, in the form of quick question-and-answer sessions on the move as a minister emerged onto the pavement or greeted journalists at an airport. Jim Callaghan's unguarded remarks during the 1978 'winter of discontent' (which prompted the *Sun*'s headline, 'Crisis? What crisis?') were made in precisely such circumstances as he came down the aircraft steps on arrival from the sunny Caribbean.

One step on from these occasions was the creation by broadcasters of their own studio locations in which politicians could perform. Forgotten programmes, with similar self-explanatory names, dot the years, from In the News (1950), through Press Conference (1952) to more recent examples such as This Week, World In Action and Newsnight. A few have lasted years, such as Panorama, founded in 1955, and radio's Any Questions?, recycled for television as Question Time. The formats vary, with more or less emphasis on a high profile presenter/interviewer, a documentary or outside broadcast approach, and the studio interview or discussion. But in every case the programme provides an opportunity for politicians to reach the public by a means that has no other purpose and would not exist but for the existence of TV and radio. This is the difference from the broadcasts discussed in the previous paragraphs. The Commons worried about TV precisely because they do have another purpose, and Members did not want it distorted by the intrusion of a mass medium. In TV's own locations, there was no such problem. Moreover, as such locations expanded in the 1970s, they became increasingly attractive to politicians. The House of Commons was ultimately more at risk from being bypassed, as political debate shifted to the studio, than if it had let the cameras observe its own proceedings.

The second way in which the progress of political broadcasting can be measured is by the changing attitudes of broadcasters and of rules about access to the medium. The attitude epitomised in the 14-days rule was elaborated in an aide-memoire of 1947, agreed between the BBC and the politicians. This provided for 'ministerial broadcasts' to be made on matters of national importance at government request, with a possible right of reply for the Opposition if the BBC judged the broadcast to have been partisan or controversial. Anthony Eden discovered to his fury in 1956, during the Suez crisis, that he had no automatic right to broadcast at will. The BBC allowed Hugh Gaitskell to give a powerful riposte the night after one of Eden's addresses to the nation. Eden then explored the possibility of commandeering the BBC.

Gradually, however, as the range of channels and programmes increased, documents such as the aide-memoire became unpractical. The requirement of a balance of opinions within any given programme gave way to balance over a period of time or between programmes. Party managers' control over broadcast appearances by ministers and backbenchers declined. Ministers were capable of putting great pressure on broadcasters, often informally; but even the most public rows— about documentaries on Irish issues, such as Real Lives (1985) and Death on the Rock (1988)—often found the government complaining after a programme had been broadcast. Moreover, there developed a curious distinction, from 1963 onwards, between the political carbolic of 'balanced' current affairs programmes and the germ-laden mayhem of satire and comedy. This began with That Was the Week That Was (which made David Frost famous) and continued through to the scatology of Spitting Image and contemporary improvised comedy and stand-up routines.

Politicians broadly came to tolerate such programmes. 'Serious' programmes, however, were another matter. The difference was exemplified in the broadcasting ban on Irish extremists, imposed by the Thatcher government in 1988. This, ingeniously, banned the voices of

Republican and Protestant extremists—but not their words. The government could argue that broadcasters were simply on the same footing now as newspapers, for there was no restriction on reported speech: the voices only were banned. Broadcasters, who saw the ban as a blow to their professionalism, retaliated by dubbing different voices onto film of such leaders as Sinn Fein's Gerry Adams, thereby both largely obviating the ban and implicitly mocking it.

Mrs Thatcher wanted to deny terrorists 'the oxygen of publicity'. Her action was an unusually drastic acknowledgement of (or statement of belief in) the power of television. In its own way, possibly Canute-like, it was a fitting recognition, after nearly half a century, of television's pre-eminent place in political life.

Press partisanship

By comparison, the relationship of politics and the press went through no such fundamental changes in the postwar period. The dominant feature, from a politician's point of view, was the continuing practice of newspaper partisanship. This was a tradition going back far beyond the beginning of the twentieth century. If there was a change after 1945, it was that newspapers became less predictable and manageable by the parties. In the 1945 election campaign, Clement Attlee knew that the mass circulation *Daily Herald* would play the party tune: Labour, through the TUC, owned nearly half the shares and controlled the paper's editorial policy. Indeed, the editor had to account for his stewardship each year at the party conference. In the 1945 campaign the paper organised a big election rally at the Albert Hall. Harold Wilson or John Smith, in contrast, had to persuade the *Daily Mirror*—Labour's surviving mass-circulation supporter after 1964—to back the party. The Conservatives, paradoxically, did not own any papers by 1945. Proprietors were more likely to be Conservative anyway, but both parties found themselves securing party loyalty by the lavish distribution of peerages and knighthoods. If you could afford it, one of the surest pathways to the Lords after 1945 must have been by purchasing a newspaper. During Wilson's premiership in the 1960s there were at one time at least four peerages within the Mirror group.

A second and entirely different kind of change accompanied the shift by newspapers to a tabloid format. In the 1959 election 5.7 million readers read two tabloids (*Daily Mirror* and *Daily Sketch*), while 10.4 million readers read seven broadsheets. The *Daily Mail* (1971) and *Daily Express* (1977) subsequently went broadsheet. The *Daily Herald* and *News Chronicle* disappeared. Most new papers—*Daily Star* (1978), *Today* (1986) and above all the *Sun*, relaunched when Murdoch bought it in 1969—were tabloid. So in the 1992 election campaign 11 million readers read six tabloids, while only 2.5 million read the five broadsheets.

Behind these figures lay important changes in the style of reporting politics. The old *Daily Herald* and its readers had taken politics seriously, as a matter of substantial argument and analysis. The tabloid papers of the 1970s had neither the same inclination nor the same style. The change of mood is caught by the comments in the Nuffield election study of 1979: 'The written text merely served to reinforce the "images" the headline writers wished to suggest to the readers, so much so that the medium of the headline was often more useful in propaganda terms than the accompanying article.'[2] That is to say, words were now in the service of pictures, not pictures in the service of words. By 1992 the familiar tabloid characteristics of sensationalism, personalisation, over-simplification, exaggeration, had gone so far that the *Daily Mirror* went through the campaign with only half a dozen very brief mentions of Liberal Leader, Paddy Ashdown, while the *Sun* dwelt in a world of fantasy and fun. Whole pages were spent on picture spreads about how to build yourself a soapbox like John Major's; on travelogues about 'Kinnockfree zones', such as the North Pole and the Moon, to which appalled voters could flee in the event of a Labour victory; and on reporting a clairvoyant's views about how Queen Victoria, Genghis Khan and Karl Marx would be voting if alive today. None of this was sinister. Much was clever and funny. Compared with the *Daily Mirror*'s electoral coverage of the 1950s, say, it was degenerate. Above all, as party propaganda, how could it possibly be countered, if not in its own terms?

Labour's problems also became worse, as the years went by, because the imbalance in the distribution of party papers increased. Of committed national dailies, four supported the Conservatives in 1945, two Labour and two the Liberals. The death of the *News Chronicle* in 1960 left the Liberals at best with the ambivalences of the *Guardian*. The death of the *Daily Herald* in 1964 and of its successor, the pre-Murdoch *Sun*, in 1969, left Labour with the *Daily Mirror*. The 1983 election saw seven papers supporting the Conservatives, one Labour and none the Liberal/SDP Alliance, and in the two elections since then the pattern has been much the same.

The large differences between circulation figures make the skew look worse still. The Conservative share of the vote in every election since 1945 has been smaller than its share of total circulation, and Labour's has almost always been larger. Up to and including 1959, the Conservative 'excess' varied around 5%. From 1974 it was never less than 10% and in the Thatcher era it was well over 30%. Only in 1950 did Labour manage half the circulation and not quite half the votes (46%). From Labour's point of view, what this boiled down to was that too many Labour voters were reading Conservative papers. Indeed, from 1979 onwards more Labour voters were reading the 'wrong' paper than were reading a Labour paper. Labour leaders could justly argue that they were unable to communicate with a large number of voters in their natural working-class constituency on their own terms. As for the

Liberals, they scored between 14 and 25% of the vote in all the elections from February 1974 onwards but never with anything more than heavily qualified editorial support in just one or two papers.

Taken together, these trends amount to a resurgence of press partisanship from 1979 onwards. In the consensus politics of the 1950s and early 1960s, the numbers might be skewed but the tone of partisanship was relatively muted. Papers seemed to have abandoned smears and scares, such as the *Daily Mirror*'s warmongering campaign against Churchill in 1951 (WHOSE FINGER ON THE TRIGGER?). In 1966 the *Daily Mirror*'s virtuous theme was 'First the Inquest—Then the Verdict', even though its eventual declaration of support for Labour was predictable. The growth of opinion polls—one in four election headlines in 1970 was about a poll—put a damper on partisanship too.

With the polarisation and stronger rhetoric of the Thatcher years, the tone altered. The change is well illustrated by a new fashion for knocking copy. A content analysis of election coverage between 1966 and October 1974 was able to conclude that papers consistently gave more space to the party they supported editorially.[3] From the 1980s, in contrast, papers gave more space to their opponents—to bash them. Thus in 1983 'The *Sun*'s leader columns displayed a talent for political invective but not for sustained argument',[4] and in 1987 the most distinctive feature of election coverage was 'well-prepared smears against individual politicians'.[5]

The implications of press partisanship are highly complex; they range from short run minutiae, such as shifts in ministerial reputations, to systemic changes, such as the fortunes of the Social Democratic Party or other fledgling parties. Partisanship is most conveniently studied in an electoral context, yet it grinds on year in year out. As Conservative Prime Ministers in particular know, a Conservative press is no guarantee of support for any given policy—or Prime Minister for that matter. Who needs enemies, John Major might well have thought, almost as soon as he won the 1992 election, with friends like the Conservative tabloids? The implications of partisanship are thus best dealt with in the speculative conclusions that follow.

Media impact: past and future

Individuals. Institutions comprise individuals, and the basic impact of media is upon people. It is worth considering politicians, first, in isolation from the institutions to which they give life. What would Churchill and Bevan, spellbinders both, have made of television, for example? Churchill was a meticulous rehearser of speeches and might not have liked the formats, albeit of practised informality, to which Eden and Macmillan readily began to adapt. Bevan, who complained that opinion polls took the poetry out of politics, might have viewed with distaste the more intimate forms that TV programmes were beginning to take at about the time he died in 1960. He might have been devastating in studio discussion; on the other hand he might have failed to adapt to the different rhythms, in the same way as his disciple Michael Foot. Foot, indeed, is a cautionary reminder that a superlative communicator in one medium may fail badly in another. Foot, in hall, hustings or House of Commons, was another spellbinder. But as a maker of soundbites in the 1983 election he was little short of disastrous.

What makes a good media performer is thus notoriously difficult to predict. On TV it is also difficult to measure, compared with the vulgar measurement of tomatoes and hecklers in a public meeting. Nonetheless, as party leaders had more and more to perform on TV in the 1960s,. their party colleagues necessarily made judgements about their effectiveness. These, of course, could be wrong. Alec Douglas-Home may have fared badly despite his media performances, not because of them. But Conservatives at Westminster, in Fleet street and beyond decided that he was 'bad on television'; and his own awareness of this belief was a factor in his willingness to stand down after the 1964 election defeat. Much later, a belief that Neil Kinnock would be an asset on television was a factor in his choice as Leader to succeed Michael Foot.

Media have affected politicians not only through their own performances but through their capacity to attract media attention. In this way, media can 'make' a politician. When isolated within the Conservative Party in 1968 for his outspoken, apocalyptic-sounding views on immigration, Enoch Powell attracted enormous spontaneous public support, including 110,000 letters in just a few weeks. Media virtually became his constituency, and in the 1970 general election he was treated both as an issue and almost as a one-man party. Such an example has been highly unusual. It is easier now to think of comparatively recent, less contentious cases, such as Ken Livingstone or Edwina Currie. But it is misleading to single out individuals more or less at random, and the point is better generalised. That is, in the television age people have a new forum in which to gain the kind of celebrity — and gain it quickly — that may be turned to political advantage. Preceding reputation, too, can help. Chris Chataway was an Olympic athlete and newsreader before becoming an MP in 1959. Colonel Colin ('Mad Mitch') Mitchell of the Argyll and Sutherland Highlanders became a TV celebrity in 1967 through his leadership of British troops in the final stages of decolonisation in Aden. He quickly found a parliamentary seat (but turned out not to like the parliamentary life). Ken Livingstone was fastened on by broadcasters initially because of his radical leadership of the Greater London Council.

More clearly, perhaps, media can be seen to break politicians. This can happen through the drip of poor publicity. But it is clearest when resulting from sheer exposure. In the later 1970s the Liberal Leader Jeremy Thorpe was destroyed by newspaper exposure of contortions in his private life, including allegations that resulted in criminal charges. Earlier, in 1963, Macmillan's War minister, John Profumo, was driven from public life after admitting he lied to the House of Commons in denying an affair with Christine Keeler, a model who also had relations with a Soviet military attaché. In Mrs Thatcher's time, the exposure in 1983 of Cecil Parkinson's affair with his secretary, and fathering of her child, was a major setback to his political career. John Major's administration seemed positively plagued by such episodes, the first and most notable being the resignation in 1992 of his friend the Heritage Secretary, David Mellor, victim of electronic bugging and of what Mellor dubbed the media's alternative criminal justice system. Media will continue to make and break politicians. It is a product of the entanglement of politics and journalism. But we must now turn finally to consider politics in its institutional forms.

Elections, parties and pressure groups. The shape of election campaigns has always depended considerably upon the media through which they are conducted. As already pointed out, the invasive growth of TV in the postwar era has had an enormous impact. When we think of 'the national campaign', we think primarily of activities organised for TV or taking place in TV studios. Newspapers and TV have a symbiotic relationship. The press report election programmes as part of the campaign. Broadcasters analyse newspaper partisanship. Each medium takes up stories from the other in a rolling news agenda. Newspapers trumpet polls; broadcasters use them to back up questions that politicians would rather not be asked. As the broadcasters became less bound by the politicians' rules, they became more free to decide for themselves what where the important issues, rather than merely following the parties' priorities.

Personalities more than issues, however, were increasingly believed to be an inevitable focus of televised campaigns. With this claim came the argument, too (from the persuasive pen of Richard Crossman in the late 1960s, for instance) that TV trivialised politics. Certainly, it gave exceptionally large coverage to party Leaders at the expense of their front-bench colleagues. In 1992, for instance, Paddy Ashdown had twice as much news coverage as all the other quoted Liberal Democrats together; Neil Kinnock had the same amount as all the other Labour politicians; and John Major had more than 80% of the Conservatives.[6] In this way, along with their discretion in the choice of coverage, TV might have partisan consequences, even though it was not permitted partisan intentions. Some parties, such as the Liberals under Jo Grimond, probably benefited from concentration on personality. At other times, a party will want to emphasise its team. Government parties quite often want a quiet campaign; parties in opposition tend to want to stir things up. (In either case, of course, they may be wrong from the point of view of electoral effects.)

While the impact of the media on the nature of election campaigns has been fairly clear, the intended or unintended impact on election outcomes has been much more obscure. A variety of factors is involved and media cannot be reliably isolated. As media continue to diversify, with a plethora of TV and radio stations, not all of which may even be controlled from Britain, the situation is likely to become more uncertain. Furthermore, the argument that TV has partisan consequences goes beyond questions of electoral success and includes the nature of parties themselves. An increasingly strong case can be made that British parties are becoming predominantly election-fighting bodies. Between campaigns, core organisations remain in some strength (and very likely in overdraft), but traditional concepts of membership, in relation alike to funding and to activities such as canvassing and propaganda, are in decline. Policy research and development has shifted away to interest groups and think-tanks. Only as a pool of talent and a springboard to public office does party remain pre-eminent.

This may be to overstate the case. But the trend is surely in that direction, and media have been among the influences making it so. It is no accident that parties have been historically linked to newspapers: there are obvious affinities of purpose between the two (news, argument, shared interests and experience, etc.). The same link does not exist with broadcast media. Yet broadcast media now dominate—not least as most people's main source of political information. The tabloid press, at the same time, gives less space to politics. Except during election campaigns, therefore, parties are losing one of the chief means through which daily reality was given to the concept of party membership and loyalty.

While TV has helped to eliminate party as an intermediary between leaders and voters, it has also played up the importance of leaders themselves. This is true in terms of talk-show appearances, House of Commons Question Time, tabloid news values—even the annual party conferences. In these last, the Conservative Leader used only to take part on the final morning, until Heath came for the full programme, to maximise his TV coverage. Within the leadership group, in turn, TV has played up the importance of the Leader himself or herself. Beyond that, the focus on leaders helps the very emergence of leader-based parties from nowhere. As with media's ability to catapult an individual to celebrity, so the 'Gang of Four' were helped greatly in their launch of the SDP in 1981 by a tide of prime-time national TV exposure. You could indeed join SDP—but most conveniently by telephone call and credit card payment, to a number taken off the TV screen. Equally, a party built on slim foundations could dissolve like spring snow when its moment had passed and merger with the long established Liberals was expedient.

Similar media tendencies have increased the importance of pressure groups relative to parties, both in generating and promoting policy and in the political process at large. Policy-oriented groups, in fields like health and social services, depend heavily on publicity as a form of leverage on Whitehall and Westminster. They seize on such opportunities as inquiries by the Commons departmental select committees. Again, membership of these groups may be extremely small. On the other hand, a movement such as CND used its numerical strength to maximise publicity. Even here, however, the great marches from (originally to) Aldermaston in the later 1950s gave way in the 1980s to the rather different symbolism of protest camps at Greenham Common airbase. These could be just as newsworthy but depended less on mass participation.

CND never officially put up parliamentary candidates. Changes in the nature of parties, however, make it more likely that pressure groups will do so in the future. The Greens perhaps provide an example. The environmental movement started in the form of various pressure groups, with a policy range too narrow to be suited to the British parliamentary electoral system. In the media climate of the 1980s, however, it became plausible for a Green party to emerge, albeit with scant success. In sum, many of the simple divisions between parties and pressure groups are becoming blurred, and media have been one of the causes.

Parliament and Opposition. The centrality of Parliament to British government and politics is habitually a matter of contention. As a representative and deliberative assembly, it is necessarily dependent to some degree on the news media of the day. There can be no doubt that at the start of the postwar period it was privileged by comparison, say, with parties or trade unions in the treatment accorded to it by a public service broadcasting system such as the BBC. Parliament took precedence in political news; there were the special programmes such as Yesterday in Parliament. The establishment of ITV did little to change this. Other developments described earlier did reduce the privilege — but more by making room for broader constituencies, as channel time grew, than by diminishing Parliament. The threat that TV might bypass Parliament was more from MPs preferring the studio to the Chamber than from MPs being shut out of TV altogether. Even so, the televising of the Commons came not a moment too soon for the institution's reputation.

It seems likely that in the long run TV will change the shape of Parliament. But throughout its history Parliament has been changing in response to changes in communications technology, and its fundamental purposes need not from this cause alone be disturbed. In the shorter run, one can see Prime Minister's Question Time, for instance, developing into a kind of press conference, with MPs taking the role played elsewhere by journalists. Mundane debates, attracting less coverage, would presumably be less affected. Already, too, one can observe the boost given by TV reporting to the select committees, especially when examining ministers and high-profile outsiders such as Robert Maxwell's sons. In the Chamber, TV may highlight the party leaderships (amplifying failure and success alike). In focusing on the committee, it will favour the backbenchers.

Those trends assume larger significance as the mass circulation press reduces its detailed coverage of parliamentary affairs—especially of debates. When a dedicated parliamentary channel becomes widely available, the historic role of print media will have been largely usurped. The broadsheet papers too, despite increases in pagination from the 1960s onwards, have cut their reports and increased the element of sketch and commentary. Considered the other way round, however, the press remains extremely important in helping to set the parliamentary agenda. The point was made in a quintessential English way by a letter to *The Times* in 1973 from Harold Wilson when Leader of the Opposition. 'The raw material of parliamentary debate', he claimed, 'is in fact what members read in the press.'

This section can conclude by noting that the media have become particularly important to the parliamentary Opposition. Compared with ministers, the Opposition has nothing actually to do. The floor of the House is its main regular forum of publicity and of credibility. Opposition members are well aware that their coverage decreases in the recess. With the entry of TV to Westminster, Neil Kinnock stopped bothering to meet the political correspondents for a weekly session. He spent even more time than before, in coordination with backbenchers, working to make the twice-weekly Prime Minister's Question Time the critical occasion for projecting Labour effectively.

Such opportunities were all the more important with the decline of the Labour press. The broadcasters' principles of balance and impartiality were an increasing boon for the Opposition, routinely ensuring them representation, proportionate to their electoral strength, in more or less every political programme. For the Liberals and other minor parties, the importance was correspondingly greater.

Prime Minister and Cabinet. The Prime Minister's job description is informal and flexible. The conventional view that he is 'first among equals' suggests an inherent instability. It is logically impossible to be both first and equal: in practice, Prime Ministers must sometimes tend more in one direction, sometimes in the other. Given the secretiveness of Cabinet proceedings, media have a crucial role in suggesting what the relationship is at a given moment and whether 'equality' should be seen as disunity and weakness or as consensus and strength. John Major, for instance, might not have been perceived so frequently as weak if he had not followed a famously dominant predecessor.

Media management has thus been an important task for Prime Ministers throughout the postwar period, and its importance has surged with the expansion of TV and of a more maverick style of press partisanship. Clement Attlee could leave most of it to his Press Secretary, Francis Williams. His successors from Eden onwards, as we have seen, had to spend more and more time on it themselves, not only as managers but also as performers. In addition, they have developed the Downing Street press office into an influential part of the Prime Minister's entourage.

TV has also increasingly drawn Prime Ministers and the Cabinet away from their natural parliamentary base. This is a grander version of the bypassing effect. Measured by the comparatively small amount of time she spent in the Chamber, Mrs Thatcher was the least parliamentary of modern Prime Ministers[7], and TV probably had something to do with it. The televising of the Commons is unlikely to make much difference, for the pull of the TV studio is too strong.

This development is one of several which support the claim that TV has been presidentialising the office of Prime Minister. TV, so the argument might run, helps a Prime Minister to dominate his colleagues; provides a basis of popular authority and approval independent of reputation and performance in the legislature; gives high priority to mobilising public opinion as a leadership role; and can effectively portray a Prime Minister as a quasi-Head of State. The argument can not be taken too far. So long as Prime Ministers depend upon parliamentary and party arithmetic for their continuation in office, the central importance of the House of Commons will remain entrenched. However much Prime Ministers hog campaign coverage, their election remains indirect, not a plebiscite. The Downing Street press office, raised to new efficiency under Mrs Thatcher's Press Secretary Bernard Ingham, gives the Prime Minister the advantage over his colleagues in managing the news; but media are always alert to signs of Cabinet tension. Despite Mrs Thatcher's occasional queenly trappings ('We are a grandmother now') and the novel unpopularity of the royal family in the 1990s, John Major was certainly very far from becoming a symbolic focus of the nation.

If there is doubt about the extent of presidential roles and powers in the premiership of the 1990s, however, there can be less about the aspects of presidential style; and it is these with which media are most clearly associated. The most intriguing issue about which to speculate is their impact upon the pathway to the premiership. Long parliamentary apprenticeship is not a prerequisite of party leadership in other countries, such as Australia or Canada. With changes in the nature of party and with the proliferation of political arenas within TV, what are the chances, as the Hansard Society marks its 50th anniversary, of a major party Leader emerging, possibly even a Prime Minister, whose power base and appeal lie primarily in media and only secondarily in party and legislature? This would be confirmation indeed of the entanglement of politics and media, and of the claim that media, of the two, are the primary force.

1   J. M. Wober, *Televising the Election*, ITC Research paper, 1992.
2   D. Butler and D. Kavanagh, *The British General Election of 1979* (Macmillan, 1980), p. 238.

3   C. Seymour-Ure, 'National Dailies and the Party System' in O. Boyd-Barrett, C. Seymour-Ure and J. Tunstall (eds), *Studies in the Press* (HMSO, 1977), pp. 159–202.
4   D. Butler and D. Kavanagh, *The British General Election of 1983* (Macmillan, 1984), p. 188.
5   M. Harrop in D. Butler and D. Kavanagh, *The British General Election of 1987* (Macmillan, 1988), p. 180.
6   D. Butler and D. Kavanagh, *The British General Election of 1992* (Macmillan, 1992), p. 169.
7   P. Dunleavy, G. W. Jones and B. O'Leary, 'Prime Ministers and the Commons: Patterns of Behaviour 1968–1987', *Public Administration*, 1990.

The Lobby System: Lubricant or Spanner?

BY SIR BERNARD INGHAM

THIS Spring the Parliamentary Lobby Journalists—otherwise known as the Lobby—came under the most grievous threat in their 110-year history. First, the House of Commons' Catering and Administration Committees banned snoopy, intrusive and possibly occasionally noisy journalists from the Commons' Terrace overlooking the Thames. Then others threatened to make the Members' Lobby, just outside the Chamber, a scribe-free zone.

The latter move would have emasculated the Lobby—the journalists, that is, if not entirely the Members' concourse. It would have destroyed at a stroke their distinctive privilege as a particular group of more than two hundred journalists who work in the Palace of Westminster. They exist as a Lobby only because they are licensed to reach parts of the Palace of Westminster—and, most notably, the Members' Lobby—denied to other British and foreign journalists working in the Press Gallery.

'Lobby rules and practice', the group's guidebook, points out that 'there is no formal "association" of Lobby journalists'. The Lobby is merely the means by which Madame Speaker, through the Serjeant at Arms, regulates access. The list is, in short, a mere administrative convenience, though the Lobby elects its own officers and holds occasional social functions. Their only other 'privileges' are to receive twice-daily briefings from the Prime Minister's Chief Press Secretary, occasional briefings from ministers and access to advance copies of government documents.

It is as well to establish at the outset the unglamorous basis of this celebrated outpost of the Fourth Estate for I have little doubt that it will survive the MPs' threat to continue its unique role in informing and entertaining us for many years to come. Denial of access to the Members' Lobby would not spell its end as such. There are many watering holes and quiet corners in the Palace where Lobby business could be transacted with MPs. But it would be highly inconvenient to both daily journalist with deadlines to catch and politician alike. After all, they need each other. Journalists need stories and politicians need to be written about. As Auberon Waugh put it: 'Politicians can forgive almost anything in the way of abuse; they can forgive subversion, revolution, being contradicted, exposed as liars, even ridiculed, but they can never forgive being ignored.' Politicians and journalists have a symbiotic relationship. They literally feed off each other.

This was immediately demonstrated by protests from more enlightened—or perhaps just thirsty—MPs when the committees banished writers from the Terrace. Who, they complained, was now going to buy their summer drinks? This was an entirely reasonable question. Among their many burdens in life, newspaper proprietors, through their readers and advertisers, and holders of broadcasting licences fill the expensive role of victuallers once-removed to our parliamentary representatives. Some might say they also have much to answer for, especially during rowdy winding-up speeches after 9pm. One thing is certain: politicians and journalists are interdependent.

Unfortunately, they can not depend on each other. Of course, journalists have never found politicians entirely reliable. They are brought up to distrust them as a race. So much so, that they even tend to think the first Baron Acton was a wet for suggesting that power merely tends to corrupt. They are convinced that it most certainly does and they therefore subject politicians to close scrutiny. Politicians bear this with a more or less patient shrug. They have no option. Like journalists, they are conspiracy theorists, too. But the cause of the recent Commons' sanctions-laden atmosphere clearly owes more to journalistic excess than to over-sensitive MPs. The storm clouds have been gathering for years.

How the skies came to darken over the Members' Lobby is a relatively recent story which gathered pace during the 1980s. It is a consequence of Watergate, the death of the age of respect and restraint, the development of television, the media's growing self-importance and MPs' collective failure to insist on a certain modicum of media behaviour.

The Lobby was born in more decorous times a century earlier out of the formal recognition in 1850, after years of strife over the public disclosure of Parliament's affairs, of parliamentary reporting through the construction of a Gallery for reporters. In fact, it took MPs another 34 years to stomach the idea of allowing a single 'gentleman to enter and remain in the Members' Lobby'. Speaker Peel sanctioned him to take up his lonely station round about the time that General Gordon was dispatched to Khartoum and Greenwich was adopted by the Prime Meridian Conference as Universal Time in the face of strong protests from the French. Plus ça change.

The identity of this pioneer remains lost along with the Lobby's records. They were incinerated by a world war two bomb and surprisingly no one survived—or survived and bothered—to recall the origins of today's controversial institution. Some think the first of the many was Sir Henry Lucy who wrote a distinguished column for *Punch* as 'Toby MP'. At all events, he had few privileges other than being there.

'The Press Gallery at Westminster', published by the *Blackburn Times*, records that for a long time they 'went no further than the right to talk to any Member who was so good as to stop and pass the time of day with the phenomenon'. Those who followed—and a very select crowd of 'seven or eight sitting round the table talking to the Prime Minister' were soon noticed—had to content themselves 'with writing their carefully phrased pieces and with being as inconspicuous as possible'. Like children, they were expected to be seen not heard, though increasingly they were noticed. They pontificated at length in the third person on the political situation rather than the news of the day and attached their initials such as APN (A. P. Nicholson) and EJ (Edward James) to their articles.

For virtually sixty years—wars apart—they wore tall silk hats on duty, even above mustard-coloured tweeds. And they became such a part of the Palace establishment that they formed, with members of the Gallery, a special press platoon of the Parliamentary Home Guard during world war two. This brought with it such privileged duties as sharing in the 'Guy Fawkes' search of the vaults before royal openings of Parliament.

War, like mud, is a great leveller. But to this day the Lobby is regarded as a journalistic elite even though the distinction between comment and the reportage, which is the normal currency of members of the Press Gallery, has been almost unrecognisably blurred. Some would say that it has been entirely fused with the virtual abandonment, to the disgust of some MPs, of parliamentary reporting for the record. Nonetheless, full-time political commentators, as distinct from parliamentary sketchwriters, are more likely to be found within the Lobby's ranks than outside it. They are supposed to be the diagnosticians rather than mere mechanics.

Their role from pontification to interpretation evolved slowly after world war one with the development of popular journalism. Only twenty years ago 'The Press Gallery at Westminster' wrote:

'Not so very many years ago, it was the custom for newspapers to print whole tracts from Government reports and White Papers, Bills and other official documents, with little or no attempt to explain them except, perhaps, in the leader columns. But as the interest taken by the man and woman in the street in public affairs grew, it became necessary to explain and expound official policies in popular terms as they arose. So another task was added to those borne by Lobby journalists. They had to find out and then explain what all these documents meant, what would be their effect on the ordinary person, what was likely to happen when they came before Parliament and generally to build them up into a news story easily understood by the casual reader.

Gradually, the importance of this new development became apparent to all. 'Politics' ceased to be a somewhat obscure and puzzling game, played by a few relatively leisured people largely for their own amusement, and became the concern of all. The fact trebled and quadrupled the work of and responsibilities of the Lobby Journalists.'

Hence the post-war growth of the Lobby, slowly extending through provincial evening newspapers and political weeklies such as *The Economist* to radio and television.

David Rosser, the *Western Mail*'s former lobby editor, gave us a personal glimpse of life in the Lobby 50 years ago in his 1987 memoir *A Dragon in the House*: 'It was ... in a sense a much more casual life, especially on the output side. It was quality much more than quantity which mattered in those early days. By that, I mean one was not expected to file two, three, four or more "inside" political stories a day. Today a Lobby Correspondent is not thought to be on top of the job unless he or she ... turns in numerous pieces every day and regularly makes the front page.'

These 'numerous pieces' are now often as much, if not more, about the personalities of our politicians as the 'ishoos' which Tony Benn MP used to regard as paramount. Indeed, for a period earlier in 1994 politics was solely about personalities as the various personal problems of an assortment of Tory ministers and MPs—Tim Yeo, David Ashby, Alan Duncan, the Earl of Caithness, the late Stephen Milligan and Hartley Booth—were paraded before us. In fact, the capacity of the Prime Minister's personality to cope with this rush of personalia became a political issue.

Thus the Lobby is not merely about fact and its interpretation but also about gossip—the very lifeblood of politics and its media coverage—perception and entertainment. To survive, newspapers have to sell copies and attract advertising, and radio and television programmes need to secure audiences—ratings.

I arrived on the periphery of this changing world in 1965 when I came down from Yorkshire as a *Guardian* reporter to join the Labour and Industrial Correspondents Group. I mention this in order further to demystify the Lobby. Labour and Industrial Correspondents, along with many other groups of specialist correspondents such as defence, diplomatic or agricultural, operated under similar rules to those of the Lobby. Such was—and is—their generally close relationship with their informants, whether ministers, MPs or officials, that they followed the cardinal rule of the Lobby never to identify their informant without specific permission. This is an entirely sensible rule because the closer the journalist and his informants become, the more confidences are exchanged and the more necessary it is for both informant and writer to know where they stand if the relationship is to survive.

It may well be that the assumption that informants are speaking unattributably—that is, not for identification—was, and remains, stronger in the Lobby than among other groups. But my point substantially holds. There are only two sensible ways of communicating with journalists: on the record, meaning that the informant can be identified and quoted; or unattributably, meaning that the journalist can use the information gleaned only on his own respnsibility and can not identify his source. A third method—off the record—has substantially fallen into disuse since it is madness, in these treacherous times, to tell a journalist something the informant does not wish to see in print or broadcast.

In 1967, when I became Press and Public Relations Adviser to the National Board for Prices and Incomes, the Lobby was losing one of its privileges. With the increasing specialisation among journalists, advance or 'proof' copies of White Papers and other government documents, which Lobby members uniquely received before MPs so that they could prepare their reports in a more considered way under embargo, were beginning to reach other correspondents more familiar with the particular issue. Technically, as I discovered at the NBPI, I had to seek the permission of the Prime Minister's Chief Press Secretary before I could supply journalists outside the Lobby with 'Confidential Final Revise' or 'proof' copies of its reports. Generally speaking, such documents now also go to specialist correspondents, where they exist, as a matter of course. The Lobby correspondent sweeps up the rest. He is more a jack of all trades, albeit armed with with political 'spin', than he was in the 1960s when Labour correspondents used to disparage Lobby members as 'mere general reporters'.

It also became clear in the early 1980s that some, though not many, included public relations among their portfolio of interests. I came across evidence that briefs on the Queen's Speech, prepared in No. 10 for the specific assistance of Lobby correspondents and issued under embargo a few hours ahead of the sovereign's reading the contents in the House of Lords, were finding their way into the City. This led to a change of rule which stated: 'The Lobby decided by ballot held in April 1982 that: It is an abuse of Lobby membership and incompatible with that membership if members pass information gained through Lobby facilities, and not available elsewhere, to interests outside journalism. In no circumstances should advance copies of documents, or information in them, be provided to such outside interests. Any breach may be followed by a recommendation to the Serjeant-at-Arms that Lobby facilities be withdrawn from the members concerned.'

In 1986 the House of Commons itself decided to set up a register of journalists' interests. This applies to members of the Press Gallery as well as the Lobby. I first heard the concept of such a register canvassed by Barbara Castle when she was First Secretary and Secretary of State for Employment of Productivity in 1968–70. She argued that, with the wide currency given to their reports and commentaries, it was perhaps just as important to know where journalists and commentators came from as MPs.

Notwithstanding these tribulations, Lobby correspondents have retained an aura to this day. This is perhaps inevitable for an organisation which twice daily receives a briefing from the Prime Minister's Chief Press Secretary and meets the Leader of the House of Commons (primarily to discuss government business) once a week. It also used to see the Leader of the Opposition and the Leader of the Liberal Democrats once a week but latterly these have petered out. No doubt they will be revived as another general election approaches.

The aura arises not only because Lobby journalists hourly rub shoulders with those at the centre of political power but also because of the secrecy which has traditionally, though decreasingly, surrounded its activities. The Lobby's rules have given rise to much amusement and ridicule. Margaret Thatcher had much fun with them when she addressed the Lobby's centenary lunch at the beginning, evocatively, of 1984 — an irony which was not lost on her.

It was, she said, 'the first time that the Fourth Estate has avowed its Secret Service. Today the organisation that never was is ... Today in the Savoy the Lobby is made Flesh. I for one rejoice in your fleeting identity — in your being let out, as it were — for it simplifies my ... task of proposing the health of an organisation which otherwise would not exist and would never meet.'

This was reference in the rules, prior to their revision in the late 1980s, that 'Members are under an obligation to keep secret the fact that such meetings [with ministers and others] are held and to avoid revealing the sources of their information'. This was taken so literally in the early 1950s that some clarification had to be entered in the Lobby rules. Accordingly, it passed a resolution in 1955 'that it is consistent with Lobby practice that members of the Lobby may tell their Editors, or Acting Editors, the sources of their information at Lobby meetings on the rare occasion that this may be vital'. It added that Lobby members 'must, on every occasion that such information is passed on, explain to their Editors or Acting Editors, that the source is strictly confidential'. Rule 9 went on to issue warnings about careless talk: 'Don't talk about Lobby meetings before or after they are held, especially in the presence of those not entitled to attend them. If outsiders appear to know something of the arrangements made by the Lobby, do not confirm their conjecture or assume that, as they appear to know so much, they may safely be told the rest.'

Mrs Thatcher, as she then was, thus felt it necessary in her centenary lunch speech to make clear that 'Celestial Blue is on the record'. That, she said, was what she understood she would have been called in closer days gone by when old Lobby hands were speaking among themselves in code about a meeting with the Tory leader. The Labour leader was known as Red Mantle.

Just how seriously former members of the Lobby took their responsibilities is illustrated by David Rosser in *A Dragon in the House*. He records how he got a blow by blow account in the Library Corridor of one of those rare events — a secret session of the Commons. This was during the Suez crisis in 1956. His informant was the late Colonel Marcus Lipton, Labour MP for Battersea. Mr Rosser says that he broke another Lobby rule in taking Colonel Lipton's account down in his pocket book. He was just about to dictate his story down the phone to Cardiff when his early Lobby mentor, Guy Eden, of the *Daily Express*, poked his head around the door, asking 'What's happening?'

Mr Rosser explained that he had got a leak from the debate and would pass it on later. Mr Eden promptly cut him off. 'I realised I had put my foot in it', Mr Rosser added. 'What he [Mr Eden] had done, in fact, was to save me from the frightening experience of having to answer to the House of Commons for an unmitigated breach of privilege, and even more. He must have saved my career.'

Secret sessions of the House are not to be reported. I hope that the Commons will not be so unwise as to put this aspect of parliamentary privilege to the test in the current frontier-rolling media climate. My money would be on disclosure if, as Mr Rosser did, a Lobby correspondent came across a willing informant, steaming with indignation as Sir Marcus reportedly was. In my experience, many journalists are of the view that, if someone is daft enough to tell them something, they should report it.

Lobby rule changes over the 1980s show the extent to which the media, in concert with informants, have eroded Parliamentary privilege over recent years. In 1982 the Lobby's rules stated: '. . . any reference to the proceedings of a Select Committee held in private will almost certainly be raised on the floor of the House with the Speaker, with a view to obtaining his opinion as to whether or not it constitutes, prima facie, a breach of privilege.

References to the reports of Select Committees are covered by the following ruling given publicly by Mr Speaker King on 24 March 1969: 'Any publication of a draft report before the report has been agreed to by a Committee and presented to the House is treated as a breach of privilege; but when the report has been presented to the House, though not yet available to hon Members in printed form, it is not an offence against the House to publish the findings of the Select Committee. It is certainly inconvenient, however, and discourteous to the House when this is done. I cannot go further than that . . . No question of privilege is involved.'

You can see the way the wind was blowing by the resolution, recorded in Lobby rules, passed by the Lobby the following month: 'That the chairman and secretary of the Lobby inform the Speaker that, in the absence of any positive and public ruling, members of the Lobby are free to use any information reaching them concerning reports of Select Committees of the House of Commons once they have been technically laid before the House.'

In recent years leaks from select committees have become commonplace, whether of matters under discussion or of tentative conclusions, and the Commons has shown no determinations to uphold rules. This is presumably because MPs, for their own political reasons, feed journalists with what they want them to write. Consequently, the Lobby's latest rules make no mention of questions of privilege. MPs have only themselves to blame.

Thus we see progressively reflected in the Lobby's own rules the increasing flexibility with which the relationship between media and parliamentarians has been conducted. It was only a matter of time before relations with the Chief Press Secretary came under scrutiny or attack. I approached the task when Mrs Thatcher recruited me as the fifteenth Chief Press Secretary in 1979 with some trepidation. As I recorded in my book *Kill the Messenger* in 1991, 'If there was anything that caused me concern it was the Lobby'.

My fears arose not simply because I had had relatively little contact with it in my role as Director of Information since 1968 in two rather specialist Departments — Employment and Energy. I knew from those who had done the No. 10 job before me, in more restrained times, how bruising it could be. Joe Haines, Harold Wilson's Chief Press Secretary, had, for example, been provoked into pulling up the drawbridge towards the end of his two bites at the job in 1975 and communicating with the media, including the Lobby, only by written press notice. Trevor Lloyd-Hughes, an earlier Wilson Chief Press Secretary, and Donald Maitland and Robin Haydon, both diplomats who did the job for Ted Heath, had also regaled me with tales of almost daily derring-do with the Lobby.

I was under no illusion that life would be easy. I knew that its rule No. 10 — now no more, another casualty of the new journalism — was more honoured in its breach than in its observance. It read: 'The Lobby correspondent should bear in mind that the purpose of a meeting is to elicit information not to score political or debating points.' This rule was positively flouted, with malice aforethought, in my earliest years when members of the Lobby were heard to be planning a "baiting" session of my deputy, Neville Gaffin. Deputy press secretaries have a thankless job. But Chief Press Secretaries soon recognise that provocation is an essential part of a Lobby correspondent's weaponry. It is important not to respond as I did when first I described Francis Pym, after ITMA's Mona Lott, as 'being so cheerful as keeps 'im going' and John Biffen as 'that well-known semi-detached member of the Cabinet'.

I was, in fact, trying to defend each Cabinet minister from remarks which the Lobby not unreasonably felt disqualified them from office. Mr Pym, the minister responsible for the coordination of government presentation, had made a speech of inspissated gloom about the economy in the same week that Chancellor Sir Geoffrey Howe had been exceptionally upbeat about it. Mr Biffen had gone on television in 1986 — a year before Mrs Thatcher won her third general election with a 100-plus majority — to suggest she was a liability to her party and should be replaced by a collective leadership. My forthright — and insightful — attempts to excuse their behaviour in the face of insistent

Lobby objections to their remaining in the Cabinet earned me a lasting reputation for rubbishing Her Majesty's ministers. But at least we are no longer led to believe that the Lobby's purpose is not to score political or debating points but 'to elicit information'.

My twice-daily encounters with what Jonathan Aitken MP fancifully described as 'Ingham's Hallelujah Chorus'—if only they had sung Handel Ingham's score!—followed a familiar post-war pattern. I described it in *Kill the Messenger* as follows:

'At 11am members of the Lobby saunter over to No. 10 from their offices in the Palace of Westminster for the first briefing of the day in the Chief Press Secretary's room. My deputy and I sat in extremely comfortable arm chairs on either side of the grand fireplace with a set of tongues on the hearth. My press officers sat with their backs to the windows looking out into Downing Street. The Lobby used the settee and the black plastic chairs stacked against the wall for their convenience. I would tell them what the Prime Minister was doing that day and what Government news events, announcements or publications to expect and then I would place myself at their disposal. They could ask anything they liked and I would answer as I wished. We would each form our own conclusions.

The questions could range from what the Prime Minister had had for breakfast—which would have been relevant, had she made a habit of having breakfast, during a salmonella, listeria or BSE scare—to the intricacies of Anglo-Soviet relations. Sometimes it became lively; on others the briefing died of boredom. The entire process was repeated at 4pm when two of my staff and I went over to the Lobby room in the roof of the Palace looking steeply down on to Westminster Bridge and the Thames and across to St Thomas's Hospital. This time, if there were no alarums or running news stories, the Lobby would begin to fish for stories, testing me out against other informants. For me, it was a fascinating commentary on who, outside the Lobby room, might of been saying what, to whom and why.'

There were no greater fishers for stories than the so-called Sunday Lobby—a group within a group made up of the political correspondents of Sunday newspapers. They were, in fact, called 'The Fishing Fleet' for that is all there was left to do after the bulk of the Lobby had trawled the political waters with a wall net for the other six days. Their desperation on Friday afternoons, when I saw them, made them particularly dangerous. Among their celebrated coups was hounding me into accurately affirming that 'the government will not throw good money after bad defending the pound. You can't buck the markets'. As the pound sank to near 1:1 parity with the dollar, interest rates were raised decisively, as they should have been earlier. A press secretary is always at the mercy of events, his tongue and the Lobby, especially the Sunday Lobby.

My role in this brief sterling crisis, like my remarks about Messrs Pym and Biffen, should never have become known. Even the present Lobby rules, revised after 'the Great Lobby Revolt', as I described it, in

1986, sold out to members the threat of 'exclusion from attendance' for breaching the agreed basis on which briefings are held 'until he or she has indicated to the Lobby officers and committee that they accept the rules'. And the basis under which I gave all 5,000 formal Lobby briefings in my eleven years at No. 10 were the same: I attended at the invitation of the Lobby, even when for convenience they came to No. 10, and spoke unattributably, or on 'Lobby terms'. The furthest those journalists under pressure to 'source' a story could go was to describe me as 'sources close to the Prime Minister' or 'government sources'.

That was the basis on which all previous Chief Press Secretaries had conducted their operations except when Mr Haines took to issuing press notices and when, for a time, the now Sir Donald Maitland experimented unsuccessfully by briefing on the record. Ironically, bearing in mind the attitude I came to encounter, Sir Donald found the Lobby preferred him unattributably.

The unattributable relationship may seem curious when the Chief Press Secretary is the Prime Minister's spokesman and when, for example, the United States' presidential spokesman is on the record and even seen speaking on behalf of his leader and government on televison. But our systems differ. The US head of state is an executive president who seldom goes near Capitol Hill. He takes decisions and announces them either on television or through a televised press conference held by his spokesman. The British Prime Minister, who is merely primus inter pares in a devolved Cabinet system of goverment, is expected to report directly to Parliament and hold himself or herself fully accountable to the Commons. Ministers are very firmly the front men and civil servants, to define the precise position even of politically-appointed press secretaries such as Mr Haines, are backroom boys. The Lobby system is thus a prime example of homo sapiens adapting to his constitutional environment. 'Sources close to a Prime Minister' may kid no one in the know, but it observes constitutional niceties.

The Lobby system is, of course, open to abuse by both minister (or his press officer) and journalist. As I pointed out in *Kill the Messenger*:

'It can encourage journalistic licence because there is no requirment to quote an informant. Equally, it can promote recklessness in Government because (theoretically, at least) unattributable remarks can be denied. In practice, there are many checks and balances against abuse by Government. Not the least of these are the breakdown in respect among journalsits ... and, I am sorry to say, a pervasive malice in journalism ... There are not, however, many sanctions against journalists who abuse the system other than for No. 10 to cut them off for a time when No. 10's guidance is most needed.'

I never had much faith in the Lobby's right, under its own constitution, to recommend the Serjeant-at-Arms to withdraw accreditation from members. Just imagine the fuss an editor would kick up over his interference in his prerogative to decide who reports what for him—not to mention the opportunity it would have presented those Lobby members who were increasingly gunning for the system during the 1980s.

The attack began early in my No. 10 career. One of the leading 'reformers' was Peter Hennessy, now Professor of Contemporary History at Queen Mary and Westfield College, who in 1984 wrote *Sources Close to the Prime Minister* with BCC journalists Michael Cockerell and David Walker. On the strength of a brief spell in the Lobby in 1976 for the *Financial Times*, followed by six years as *The Times*' Whitehall correspondent, he said the Lobby was lazy, self-serving and easily manipulated.

This did not go down too well with the Lobby. One member, Adam Raphael, former political editor of the *Observer* who was by no means an unqualified admirer of me, wrote:

'At risk of sounding self-defensive, this is a ludicrous misunderstanding of how the system actually works . . . The idea that such a large, disparate body can be collectively gulled by being drip-fed information from No. 10 is inherently implausible. The White House press corps, in which I have also worked, is a far tamer and more deferential group than the Lobby, yet the authors frequently refer to Washington as a paradigm they would like to copy. The authors also fail to understand that formal Lobby briefings comprise only a small part of the information gathering process.'

The Chief Press Secretary does not have a monopoly of information, as *The Guardian*'s former political editor, Ian Aitken pointed out in a so-called BBC TV panorama exposé of the lobby system. He said that before he could move a yard from the Palace of Westminster to a No. 10 briefing, 650 MPs were eager to offer their ideas, points of view and arguments, not to mention gossip. All too often, the Chief Press Secretary is forced to react—as I was over the remarks of Messrs Pym and Biffen.

Nonetheless, the effort to Americanise the Lobby system with the Chief Press Secretary regularly on the record gathered sway. British journalists showed themselves to have been deeply affected by the Watergate affair into believing that they only had to turn a stone in Whitehall and something extremely nasty would crawl out and make them rich and famous. This influenced journalists in a variety of ways. But some were undoubtedly smitten by a zealotry for openness or transparency and inevitably saw the Lobby's rules, couched as they were in a language of freemasonry, as an inviting target. 'Ingham on the record', became their cry. Readers were entitled to know who was saying what. The time had come to end the 'fraud' in hiding sources of information from them. It would then be impossible for me to 'manipulate' the Lobby or systematically to 'rubbish' members of the Cabinet as I had Mr Pym—under persistent and indignant pressure from the

Lobby. In any case, some were heard to argue, Mrs Thatcher was too powerful and her spokesman must be curbed.

All this was reinforced by the entirely natural desire by news agency, radio and television reporters, though not all allowed themselves be driven by it, to have a name, a voice and a face to go with my briefing.

I gave the Lobby no encouragement. With Mrs Thatcher's support, once she accepted the case for the Lobby—she was neither the first nor will she be the last Prime Minister to wonder whether it was worth pandering to—I made it clear I had no intention of going on the record. And since I was offering the briefings, that was that.

And so it might have been but for Anthony Bevins who emerged from the Westland affair convinced, so he told me, that if he had been outside the Lobby he would have had a ball with his freedom. I took that with a pinch of salt as he informed me privately after a Lobby briefing in No. 10 that he was to become political editor of the embryonic *Independent* and had made it a condition of his employment that he would not attend Lobby briefings. He wanted, however, to be sure that—as a Lobby member with continuing access to the Members' Lobby—he would still be able to secure advance, embargoed copies of White Papers and other government documents. I saw no reason to be churlish. As a member of the Lobby, it was up to him whether he attended my briefings. I also permitted myself the thought that life in the Lobby might be less tedious shorn of Mr Bevins' conspiracy theory. Professor Hennessy described Mr Bevins as a 'possesed soul' as he prepared to boycott my briefings.

In *Kill the Messenger* I noted that superficially Mr Bevins 'had a lot going for him', adding: 'Observance of the Lobby's own rules had been honoured only in the breach for years and the situation was steadily deteriorating. By the time I arrived in Downing Street, a Chief Press Secretary could not count on their being observed. Indeed, he can be absolutely certain they won't be if it is to the advantage of some correspondents—which in turn puts pressure on the more responsible.' That partly explains the steady abbreviation of 'Lobby rules and practice' during the 1980s. There is no point in having conventions which are ignored and cannot be enforced.

In spite of considerable sympthy among Lobby members for his aims, Mr Bevins' determination to avoid my allegedly corrupting influence and the 'collective pressure' which, he claimed, I exerted on correspondents when they met me for group therapy might have been a mere footnote to Lobby history but for *The Guardian*. On 18 September 1986—just before the appearance of the *Independent* as a competitor— its editor, Peter Preston, wrote to me suggesting there was political, journalistic and reader dissatisfaction with the Lobby: 'Accordingly, I have this week instructed my political staff that, when Westminster business recommences, they shall attend—as normal—your daily briefings, but that instead of employing any of the customary and increasingly threadbare circumlocutions … they shall refer openly to "a Downing Street spokesman" or "Mrs Thatcher's spokesman" and, as relevant, quote what that spokesman says …'

Mr Preston had made a cardinal error. He had, in effect, tendered his resignation from the Lobby to me. But it was no more my Lobby than it was No. 10's, the government's or Parliament's. It was — and is — the Lobby's Lobby. Consequently, I wrote back: 'If you wish to change the system you will have to find a way of addressing the Lobby, since I assume from your letter you wish to act constitutionally. In the meantime, I should say I have no proposal to change existing practice.'

What I did not say but wrote in *Kill the Messenger* was that, if *The Guardian's* political staff turned up at a Lobby briefing under his new instructions, 'I was perfectly at liberty to tell them and the rest of the Lobby to take a running jump at themselves. I would say what I wanted to say, and unless I could say them on my terms I wouldn't say a word'. I left no one in any doubt about my intentions or my retribution by withdrawing help if anyone attended my Lobby briefings — which only I could give — and dishonoured the terms on which they were held. Only the *Scotsman* followed the *Independent* and *The Guardian* into what the saw as a principled wilderness and which I regarded as targeted assault on No. 10.

The evidence confirming this soon appeared. It emerged that the editors of these three newspapers had no objection to unattributable briefing per se. Their other specialists were systematically attending unattributable collective briefings in government departments, including the Foreign Office. To their chagrin, their staffs, not all of whom agreed with their editor's boycott, rapidly discovered that No. 10 would not be mucked about by their bosses but could make life very uncomfortable by refusing to make its guidance available to them at midnight and declining them access to the Prime Minister's plane on foreign visits. They had not thought it through.

'The Great Lobby Revolt' was instantly heralded as a success, especially when all the Opposition party leaders — Messrs Kinnock, Steel and Owen — meaninglessly pledged themselves to end unattributable briefings if they ever became Prime Minister. But Mr Preston failed to secure the support of the editors of *The Times* and the *Daily Telegraph*. The Lobby officers would have been dismayed had I capitulated to outside forces and eventually the Lobby also refused to be browbeaten, though it was a fairly close run thing.

The machinations and discussions which took place within the Lobby over the next six months illuminate the condition of 1980s' political journalism. First, the Lobby officers quickly established a majority of 21 against any change in the non-attribution rules (76–55) but a majority of 10 for a speedy inquiry into Lobby practice. The bedrock of the opposition to any change in the rules was — and remained — the older hands and the provincial press who, lacking the power of national media, saw a potentially valuable source of guidance being muzzled since an informant is always likely to say more unattributably than on the record.

The Lobby received eighteen submissions, including my own, to its inquiry. Three strands of opinion emerged. Among those who wished to see the Lobby system ended, David Owen said it had been unable to withstand the movement towards greater openness in public life 'and would be better abandoned'. Labour MP Tam Dalyell claimed that 'as interpreted by Mr Bernard Ingham, it is wholly unacceptable that the Prime Minister's press secretary should be a civil servant'. Joe Haines believed that the non-attribution rules had broken down anyway. Robert Southgate, head of news at Central TV, argued that through the Lobby system the government 'is able to set the political agenda and through non-attributable briefings manipulate or distort facts without the risk of subsequent culpability'. And Mr Preston asserted that 'a situation in which many powerful politicians wanted attribution whilst the journalists resisted it would be to set logic on its head'.

The middle-of-the-roaders, including David Nicholas, editor of ITN, and Mr Aitken, of *The Guardian*, essentially wanted more on the record and for No. 10 briefings to be sourced as coming from Downing Street. They seemed not to understand that this would end the unattributable system. To all intents and purposes, the source would be disclosed.

Among those in favour of retaining unattributable briefings, the Newspaper Society, representing the provincial press, saw it serving the best interests of regional newspapers while welcoming any move towards more attribution. Of three former Chief Press Secretaries who backed it (including Sir Trevor Lloyd Hughes and Henry James briefly Margaret Thatcher's press secretary and deputy press secretary to Harold Wilson and Ted Heath), Sir Tom McCaffrey (James Callaghan) said it was the 'least objectionable' way of keeping the public informed.

My evidence, setting out the government's position, said it had no plans for changing the relationship. The government believed that:

'i. the prime source of information from the Government will — and should — remain on the record statements by Ministers to Parliament and published material; the Lobby system supplements this flow of information.

ii. the lobby system accordingly gives due recognition to the primacy of Parliament as the channel for the communication of information by the Government to the nation.

iii. many journalists recognise that, within the constraints imposed by Parliament, the Lobby system facilitates the flow of information and guidance.

iv. as operated by this Government, the Lobby system serves without discrimination the interests of all Parliamentary Lobby journalists who wish to take advantage of briefings.'

My evidence added:

'The Government notes that journalists who seek to end unattributable briefings of the Lobby as a group by the Chief Press Secretary are in no way opposed to his (or others, including Ministers and MPs) briefing them individually on an unattributable basis, and seek such briefings as a matter of course. Indeed, journalists apparently, consider it would be entirely impractical — and undesirable — to end the well-tried system of unattributable briefing in favour of an exclusively on-the-record relationship between informant and correspondent.

The Government cannot accept that the Lobby should seek to treat differently collective briefings with the Chief Press Secretary.

In a free society, journalists using their own judgment are free to accept or reject information imparted to them. In the exercise of their judgment they will take account of the credibility — the track record — of their informant, whether he is on the record or briefing on Lobby terms. Their briefers are similarly guided by their perception of the integrity of the journalist or group of journalists with whom they are dealing.

The Government considers that, properly operated according to the conventions, the Lobby system can serve a useful purpse in our democracy and for that practical reason would wish to see it continue.'

Out of this, the Lobby committee sought to 're-establish a workable and sustainable system which does not provoke continuing debilitating conflict'. It deplored what became a regular practice by the *Independent* and *The Guardian* — the quotation of my remarks at unattributable briefings as supplied by those who attended them — and said it seemed reasonable to require a formal undertaking from members that they understood the rules and would abide by them. But it understandably wrung rung its hands, as neither an accrediting nor an enforcement agency, over the problem of enforcement.

The Lobby Committee did not get very far. It won an 80–5 majority for a simplification and clarification of its rules and a 76–8 majority for pressing for more on the record information 'wherever and whenever practicable — but not where it inhibits the flow of information from the Government to the public'. But the members refused to require written undertakings to observe its rules (54–31) or to exclude those who broke them: on this the vote was tied 42–42.

Returning to the drawing board, the Lobby Committee not unnaturally found the Lobby 'clearly divided and uncertain about its role'. It shortened and simplified the rules and got round the problem of discipline by suggesting a revised formula under which anyone breaching the agreed basis of briefings 'should be excluded from attendance [at Lobby briefings] until he or she has indicated to the Lobby officers and committee that they accept the rules'.

An increasingly weary Lobby accepted the revised rules 35–26, with five invalid votes. In the process, it rejected a last ditch attempt by James Naughtie and John Carvel, of *The Guardian*, to put the Chief Press

Secretary on the record. They would have had written into the rules: 'Normal practice in dealing collectively with representatives of the Prime Minister's office would be to attribute the information to Downing Street spokesmen.'

In practice, nothing changed. And the *Independent*, *The Guardian* and presumably the *Scotsman*, which I seldom saw, continued to boycott my briefings in London but to quote me second hand, not often accurately, on the basis of information supplied by other members of the Lobby in breach of rule. None of the boycotters had any difficulty attending my European Council briefings in Brussels and elsewhere. So much for media principles. I reached the conclusion that many journalists would not recognise a principle at five paces if it got in the way of their professional interest.

Certainly, for all their initial demands for on the record briefings, the boycotters had no difficulty in returning to the Lobby when John Major's Chief Press Secretary fell in with the Lobby's wish to be allowed to source his briefings as coming from Downing Street. This has, to all intents and purposes, ended the unattributable system. But with the best will in the world, I cannot see that this has brought a lasting improvement in either the flow of information or relations.

Instead, it underlines the problems of dealing with a media which seeks to exercise their imagined rights to the exclusion of their responsibilities as citizens of a country which provides them with a living and protection. This is what has brought the Lobby to its latest Terrace impasse with the Commons' Catering and Administration Committees.

Its rules used to prohibit the reporting, for example, of incidents within the Palace of Westminster such as the rows between MPs or, more spicily ministers and MPs. Margaret Thatcher reflected these in her speech to the Lobby's centenary lunch: 'After a century without a notebook—at worst, very discreedtly and unobstrusively using the back of an Order Paper; never running after a Minister, MP or Peer unless invited to do so; never in any circumstances making use of anything accidentally overheard in any part of the Palace of Westminster; after averting your collective gaze for 100 years from any incident, pleasant or otherwise, in those parts of the building to which you have acess, today you can confess—this is your life.'

Now such incidents almost routinely appear either in news or gossip columns even though the Lobby rules still remind members: 'There are mutual obligations resulting from this accreditation in other not to prejudice the special access granted at Westminster ... The work of a Lobby journalist involved close and sensitive relations with MPs and Ministers. These require common sense and tact in not compromising this position.'

Common sense and tact have long since been overtaken by conspiracy theory, an overweening sense of the media's self-importance, an abuse of power and a determination to publish and to hell with it. The only surprise is that the parliamentary worm has taken so long to turn. The Lobby, once a lubricant, is becoming a spanner in its own works. Our democracy deserves better.

Career Patterns in British Politics:
First Choose Your Party . . .

BY MICHAEL RUSH

CONSTITUTIONAL convention demands that ministers are drawn from Parliament. There are only two exceptions, one temporary, the other a special case. Temporary exceptions are those pending election to the House of Commons, as in the case of Sir Alec Douglas-Home when initially appointed Prime Minister in 1963, or elevation to the House of Lords, as in the case of Irwin Bellow awaiting his translation into Lord Bellwin on being appointed Parliamentary Under-Secretary for the Environment in 1979. The second exception is that of the Scottish Law Officers, the Lord Advocate and the Solicitor-General for Scotland, who must be members of the Scottish Bar, of whom there are not always suitable candidates for either post in Parliament.

Parliament is therefore an almost unavoidable part of the route to political office, providing not only the most important initial step but also the parliamentary and ministerial apprenticeships that normally precede membership of the Cabinet. This has long been so and has effectively discouraged the regular and widespread recruitment of ministers from outside Parliament. There have been notable exceptions, of course, but they have almost always been temporary in nature. In 1940, for example, Ernest Bevin was appointed Minister of Labour in Churchill's wartime coalition and a Labour MP resigned to create a by-election vacancy at which Bevin was duly elected unopposed. This practice can backfire, however, as Harold Wilson found in 1964 when he recommended peerages for two labour MPs to create by-election vacancies for two newly-appointed Cabinet ministers, Patrick Gordon Walker, who had been defeated in the 1964 general election, and Frank Cousins, the General Secretary of the Transport and General Workers Union (TGWU). Cousins was elected on a reduced majority, but Gordon Walker was defeated and had to resign as Foreign Secretary.

The House of Lords offers a guaranteed safe route into Parliament but is objected to by the Labour Party, especially for heads of government departments on the grounds that such ministers should be directly accountable to the Commons. For middle rank and junior posts this is less of a problem and Harold Wilson used life peerages to bring four such ministers into Parliament in 1964. Conservative Prime Ministers are less inhibited and peerages were used by Harold Macmillan to bring Sir Percy Mills, an industrialist, and by Margaret Thatcher to bring

David Young, a businessman, into their Cabinets in 1957 and 1984 respectively.

As a pool of ministerial recruits and as a route to ministerial office, however, the House of Lords is of limited importance. In 1900 no less than 45% of ministers were peers and it was still as high as 26% in 1940. Not surprisingly, the proportion of peers holding office varies according to the party in power, with more under Conservative and fewer under Labour (previously Liberal) governments. In the period since 1945, about one in five ministers in Conservative governments have been peers, compared with one in six or seven under Labour administrations. The Attlee government of 1945 included only ten peers, whereas in 1994 the Major government has as many as 23. But it is in the Cabinet itself that the decline in the number of peers has been most marked: more than half of Lord Salisbury's Cabinet in 1900 and eight out of twenty in Asquith's first Cabinet in 1908 were peers, but both the 1945 and 1994 Cabinets contained only two. This is the minimum number possible from the Lords under present arrangements, since the Lord Chancellor and the Leader of the House of Lords need to be members of the Cabinet. This highlights the most important change in the position of the upper house as a source of recruits for and route to ministerial office: at the beginning of the century any Cabinet post, with the notable exception of the Chancellor of the Exchequer, could be held by a peer, including the office of Prime Minister; by 1945 most senior ministers, especially those heading government departments, were normally MPs. Conservative Prime Ministers continue to be willing to depart from this norm — it has yet to achieve the status of a constitutional convention — but in practice the House of Lords places severe constraints on the ambitious politician, weighting the odds heavily against holding one of the great offices of state (the Lord Chancellorship excepted) and entirely precluding the office of Prime Minister.

The limitations of the Lords as a vehicle for political ambition is greatest for hereditary peers. They can at best hope to head a government department, but only under a Conservative Prime Minister; only middle-ranking and junior posts are likely to come their way. A number of life peers, on the other hand, find the Lords a reasonably pleasant and rewarding means of continuing their political careers after achieving high office as members of the Commons; yet others secure office for the first time or achieve a modest advancement in office as peers after long and faithful service as MPs. And many more, both hereditary and life peers, enjoy a career spent entirely on the backbenches in the Lords, assisting in the scrutiny of legislation and of government policy and administration, not unlike that of many backbenchers in the House of Commons.

In short, the substantial growth in the number of ministerial offices since 1900 (and since 1945) has been almost entirely to the benefit of

MPs and this, together with its long-standing constitutional and political dominance, has made the House of Commons the mainstream of political careers. Parliament in general and the Commons in particular, however, are dominated by party and it this dominance that ultimately is crucial to a career in British politics.

Two-party domination

British politics has long been dominated by party and since the middle of the nineteenth century it has been largely two-party politics, first Conservative and Liberal and then Conservative and Labour. This has been so electorally, as measured by the proportion of candidates standing and votes cast for the two major parties, and in parliamentary terms, as measured by the proportion of MPs elected for the two major parties. Thus in the period 1945–70 three-quarters of the candidates, over 90% of the votes cast and no less than 98% of the MPs elected to the House of Commons were either Conservative or Labour. It is true, of course, that since 1970 two-party domination has declined, so that between 1974 and 1992 little more than half the candidates and only three-quarters of the votes cast were Conservative or Labour, but the two-party domination of the Commons has fallen much less dramatically to 94%. Even when two-party hegemony was most under attack through the Liberal-Social Democratic Alliance in 1983 and 1987, the proportion remained as high as 93%, and it showed no change in 1992.

Moreover, any inroads into to Conservative-Labour domination between 1945 and 1992 have been made by other parties, principally the Liberals (later Liberal Democrats), the now defunct SDP, and the nationalist parties in Scotland and Wales. In 1945 eight independent candidates were elected, but five of these represented university seats which were abolished from 1950, and since then no candidate bearing an unadulterated 'independent' label has been elected. There have been a few candidates elected under labels such as 'Independent Conservative', 'Independent Labour' or 'Independent Liberal', but there was still a party connection for the electorate to see. As for third parties, the largest number of MPs elected at a general election from any party other than Conservative or Labour was the twenty Liberal Democrats in 1992, although the Liberal-SDP Alliance secured 23 seats in 1983. Even more discouraging for the would-be MP is that most Liberal and latterly Liberal Democrat MPs capture seats from their opponents, often at by-elections, and between 1945 and 1992 only four Liberals have 'inherited' Liberal-held seats—Emlyn Hooson at Montgomery in 1962 (lost in 1979 but regained by the Liberals in 1983), James Wallace at Orkney and Shetland in 1983, Matthew Taylor at Truro in 1987, and Liz Lynn at Rochdale in 1992. Small wonder that in 1959 Gerald Sparrow, a former prospective Labour candidate for Exeter, advised in a humorous book in 1959 entitled *How to Become an MP*, 'I beg of you consider very carefully which party you join'!

For those with ministerial ambitions, the facts of two-party domination are even more crucial. There has been no Liberal government since
the formation of the wartime coalition in 1915, although Liberals
subsequently served in that coalition, in the National government
formed in 1931 and in the coalition government during the Second
World War. No Liberal has held ministerial office since 1945. Only
Conservative and Labour MPs have held ministerial office since that
date and in the ensuing fifty years the Conservatives have been in power
for nearly twice as long as Labour. Indeed, Labour has suffered two
prolonged periods in opposition, the first between 1951 and 1964 and
the second from 1979, which remains unabated. Both these periods
have denied a number of Labour MPs office and frustrated the higher
ambitions of others who had managed to climb the lower rungs of the
ministerial ladder before those periods of opposition began.

Party is therefore crucial to political ambition and advancement,
acting not only as a gatekeeper to political careers but as a major factor
in the continuation and success of those who secure election to the
House of Commons.

Electoral opportunities

For the overwhelming majority of aspiring politicians the decisive hurdle
is therefore becoming a Member of Parliament. The opportunities for
doing so are governed by four factors: by the parties in choosing
candidates, by the frequency of elections, by the voting behaviour of the
electorate, all of which contribute to the fourth factor, the voluntary
and involuntary turnover of the membership of the House of Commons.
The selection of candidates is the most important of these and is dealt
with separately below. The Parliament Act 1911 stipulates that the
maximum period between general elections is five years, but politically
it is the Prime Minister who decides the date of a general election. Only
rarely, as in 1979, are elections forced on the government by defeat in
the House of Commons. On average general elections have been held
every three-and-a-half years since 1945, but in practice the period
between elections has varied from the seven months between the
February and October elections of 1974 to the full five-year terms of
1959–64 and 1987–92, with Parliaments of three-and-a-half to four
years the norm. In addition, casual vacancies between general elections
are filled through by-elections, but the number of these has declined
significantly since 1945. Until 1964 by-elections averaged about twelve
a year, dropping to between seven and nine between 1964 and 1979
and falling further to four or five a year thereafter. The main reason for
this fall is that fewer vacancies have been created by the appointment of
MPs to positions, such as judgeships or the head of a public corporation,
which are constitutionally incompatible with membership of the Commons; similarly, fewer MPs have been elevated to the Lords between
elections. Such vacancies have largely been avoided because they have

mostly involved MPs of the governing party and from the 1960s onwards governments have frequently suffered by-election defeats, many of which were avoidable by avoiding the appointment of sitting MPs. Death is now much the most common cause of by-elections, accounting for between three-fifth and four-fifths of vacancies in recent Parliaments, compared with between two-fifths and half before 1964.

The fate of candidates in all elections is, of course, ultimately determined by the electorate and much therefore depends on changes in party support between elections. However, a significant proportion of the seats in the House of Commons are safely held by one party or the other, regardless of the overall outcome of a general election, and substantially more than two-thirds of seats do not change hands from one election to the next. In these seats the crucial hurdle is largely predetermined by the earlier hurdle of selection as a candidate by the party. Only in marginal seats is the fate of the candidate really determined by the electorate, but that fate is largely decided by the fortunes of the party nationally. A favourable national swing will secure the election of candidates of the benefiting party at the expense of the hopefuls of other parties, whereas in safe seats only the size of the winning candidate's majority is affected by the national swing. The growth of regional disparities in electoral behaviour in the 1970s and since has not changed this state of affairs, merely the distribution of safe and marginal seats.

By-elections provide an alternative but more haphazard route into Parliament. They are a safe enough route for the main opposition party. Only ten times since 1945 has the main opposition party lost a by-election,[1] but for the governing party by-elections have come to be dreaded. Between 1945 and 1959 only four government seats were lost in by-elections and the normal impact was a significant reduction in the governing party's majority in the seat concerned. From the 1960s onwards, however, the governing party lost seats at by-elections with embarrassing regularity: governments suffered no fewer than 50 by-election defeats between 1962 and 1992. Large majorities often melted away and safe seats for the governing party became safe only at general elections, those lost in by-elections frequently reverting to their original allegiance at the next general election. By-elections do not provide a guarantee of election for governing party candidates, but they are no more a guarantee of re-election for the successful candidate at the subsequent general election. In the 1987–92 Parliament, for instance, the Conservatives lost seven seats in by-elections but regained every one at the 1992 general election.

The turnover of the membership of the House of Commons that general and by-elections produce inevitably varies, depending mainly on the swing of the electoral pendulum and on the number of MPs retiring at each general election. Britain's first-past-the post electoral system exaggerates the number of seats gained and lost by the parties relative to shifts in electoral support, so that as many as fifteen to twenty seats can change hands between the two major parties in response to a mere 1% swing. The number of MPs retiring at each general election is not constant, partly because short Parliaments, such as those of 1950–51, 1964–66 and February-October 1974, produce relatively few retirements. More importantly, there is cyclical process at work in which a large number of retirements (and therefore new entrants) at one election produces a similarly large number of retirements three or four general elections later. This is simply because, barring electoral defeat, most MPs, once elected, continue their parliamentary careers for at least fifteen to twenty years.

Much the largest turnover in the 1945–1992 period was in 1945 itself, resulting from not only the massive swing to Labour but also from a particularly large number of retirements—the last election having been ten years before in 1935. The average turnover between 1945 and 1992 was 26%, but it varied between the massive 74% of 1945 to the tiny 7% of October 1974; 1945 aside, the average was 23 per cent, with the four most recent Parliaments averaging 24%. The chance to exploit these electoral opportunities, however, is firmly in the hands of the parties, and to exploit them fully means being selected as a Conservative or Labour parliamentary candidate.

First steps

Candidate selection has long been largely in the hands of local parties rather than the national leadership or party organisations. The latter play a significant role in laying down the rules by which local parties choose candidates, in exercising a degree of 'quality control' by maintaining national lists of approved candidates, and retain a right of veto over candidates not to their liking. Although the national lists are too large to provide a means of imposing a candidate on a local party, they play a part, particularly in the Conservative Party, in determining the types of people who become candidates and MPs. The national veto can prevent the selection of a candidate the leadership does not want, without ensuring the selection of a preferred individual. There is a limited but important exception to this, in that the National Executive Committee of the Labour Party can impose a candidate of its choice at a by-election, as it did, for example in the cases of George Howarth at the Knowsley North in 1986 and Kate Hoey at Vauxhall in 1989. Both major parties have used their national vetoes sparingly and Labour's use of its power of imposition is infrequent, though not without significance.

Political recruitment can usefully be seen in terms of supply and demand. Demand factors—what sort of person the selectors are looking for—are more easily delineated than supply factors—who is available to be selected. For instance, the selectors may be looking for a candidate who is reasonably well-educated, neither too young nor too old, having a good knowledge of party policy (and possibly holding particular ideological views), with an understanding of local problems, and so on. Supply factors, however, are more difficult to pin down. Even a cursory examination of the socio-economic backgrounds of those who are selected as parliamentary candidates makes it self-evident that there are many more people with essentially the same socio-economic character-istic who were not chosen, the vast majority because they have no political ambitions. What distinguishes one group from the other remains a matter for further research, although some recent work has thrown significant light on the question.[2] The case of women candidates and MPs illustrates the supply side vividly: in 1945, 24 women were elected to the House of Commons and, although the number fell to 17 in 1951, in 1992 the number of women MPs was a record 60. Part of the explanation is a degree of prejudice on the part of some local parties, but much the most important factor is the relatively small number of women seeking a political career.

1: Socio-economic characteristics of MPs elected in 1945 and 1992

| | Cons. | | Lab. | | Lib.Dem. | Other |
| | 1945 | 1992 | 1945 | 1992 | 1992 | 1992 |
	%	%	%	%	n	n
Education						
Elementary	0.5	–	37.1	1.1	–	2
Secondary	15.9	14.0	15.8	17.3	2	1
Further ed	3.4	11.0	10.3	18.4	2	9
Private/self ed.	1.1	–	0.2	–	–	–
Graduate	74.9	75.0	34.3	63.1	16	12
Not known	4.3	–	2.3	–	–	–
Public school	79.2	59.8	22.3	13.2	9	2
Other	20.8	40.2	77.7	86.7	11	22
Oxford	29.0	25.0	9.3	11.8	4	–
Cambridge	20.8	19.6	5.3	5.5	2	–
Other UK	10.6	25.3	17.5	42.1	8	11
Polytechnics	na	1.8	na	2.9	1	–
Overseas	1.0	2.1	1.5	0.7	1	1
Service coll.	13.5	1.2	0.7	–	–	–
Non-grad. & NK	25.1	25.0	65.7	36.9	4	12
Occupation						
Professional	43.5	29.2	27.3	41.7	11	16
Business	46.9	52.4	11.8	4.4	4	7
Workers	–	1.2	43.4	24.3	1	1
Miscellaneous	4.8	17.2	16.3	29.5	4	–
Private means	4.3	–	0.5	–	–	–
Not known	0.5	–	0.7	–	–	–

The socio-economic characteristics of MPs undoubtedly reflect both supply and demand. For example, the widening of educational oppor-tunities in the 1960s clearly made more graduates available. In substan-tial part this may be seen as a supply factor, but it also reflects a significant move away from traditional working-class Labour MPs, as the marked decline in the proportion of workers shows. Similarly, the Conservative Party has become less elitist, drawing fewer MPs in 1992 than 1945 from a public school and Oxbridge background. A more detailed occupational background would also illustrate the fact that some occupations lend themselves more readily to embarking on a political career than others because of the expertise they impart and the contacts they provide. In many cases they allow would-be politicians the time to cultivate their political ambitions. In the not too distant past a secure financial base was a virtual necessity and largely remains so in the early stages of a political career, before election to Parliament. Law, teaching, journalism, many business occupations, and, more recently, political advisers and researchers all provide skills, money and the time which, though not vital, do much to facilitate a political career in its initial stages.

It is also apparent from Table 1 that there has been a degree of convergence in the socio-economic backgrounds of Conservative and Labour MPs between 1945 and 1992, but it should not be exaggerated and each party tends to draw its MPs from different sections of the population. As for the Liberals and other parties, their MPs tend to fall somewhere between the two major parties in socio-economic terms, but the same general observations apply.

The practice, common among the sons of peers in the eighteenth century, of seeking and securing election to the House of Commons as soon as they were of age has long been overtaken by the necessity of would-be MPs to establish themselves in another career first. Apart from particular occupations that facilitate embarking on a political career, there are a number of different routes or combinations of routes that can be followed. First and foremost is getting involved in local politics, not necessarily in the locality which the aspiring MPs eventually represents, but in establishing credentials as a loyal and useful member of the party. More particularly, an increasing proportion of would-be MPs involve themselves in local government, always more common in the Labour Party but of growing importance among Conservatives.

2: Local government experience of MPs, 1945 and 1992

	Cons.		Lab.		Lib.Dem.	Other
	1945	1992	1945	1992	1992	1992
	%	%	%	%	n	n
No experience	81.2	54.5	43.6	36.9	15	12
Local govt.	18.8	45.5	56.4	63.1	5	12

More recently, experience in elections to and membership of the European Parliament has provided another avenue for pre-Westminster experience. In 1992 eleven Labour MPs[3] and five Conservatives had been or were still Euro-MPs when first elected to the Commons, and a further six Labour and eight Conservative MPs had fought Euro-elections. However, movement between Europe and Westminster or vice-versa is not of a high order and largely separate career patterns have developed.

For MPs of both major parties the party organisations themselves have always provided a small number of parliamentary recruits, often individuals who have subsequently gone on to hold high office, such as Enoch Powell, Iain Macleod, David Howell and Tony Newton for the Conservatives and Denis Healey, Peter Shore, and, although he has yet to hold ministerial office, Peter Mandelson for Labour. This type of experience has always been more common among Conservatives, with the Conservatives Research Department and Central Office providing a significant number of MPs, but more recently the growth in the number of political advisers to ministers and research assistants to MPs has opened up yet another avenue for political advancement. This has benefited Labour MPs, such as Margaret Beckett, who was a political adviser in the Ministry of Defence, and Jack Straw, who was political adviser to Barbara Castle and Peter Shore, but the principal beneficiaries have been Conservative aspirants. In 1992, for instance, no fewer than fourteen newly-elected Conservatives has served as political advisers to ministers or research assistants to MPs.

The Labour Party has traditionally provided another route to Westminster in the form of sponsorship, mainly via trade unions but also through the Co-operative Party. Since 1959 sponsorship by the Co-operative Party has been subject to strict limits, particularly on the number of Labour-held seats that may be sponsored, largely because Co-operative nominees were winning selections at the expense of trade union nominees. There is, however, no limit on the number of trade union-sponsored candidates, other than the numbers individual unions are willing and able to support financially. For the most part, unions are more interested in sponsoring candidates in Labour-held seats. Although a number of unions have been willing to support candidates in marginal non-Labour seats and a few in safe Conservative seats, but their main concern is to secure union representation in Parliament. Thus from 1945 to 1992 between a fifth and a quarter of Labour candidates and between a third and three-fifths of Labour MPs have been sponsored by trade unions.[4] Apart from providing unions with a voice in Parliament and in the Parliamentary Labour Party, sponsorship gives Constituency Labour Parties (CLPs) financial help towards election expenses and, in some cases, provides additional support in running the local party. In 1945 the overwhelmingly majority of union-sponsored MPs had had direct industrial experience, although a significant number were trade union officials who had worked their way up from the shop-floor or coalface. From the 1960s onwards, however, an increasing number of union-sponsored candidates have lacked that industrial experience and are lawyers, teachers or journalists, or work for pressure groups, and have been adopted by unions as sponsored candidates before or after their initial election to Parliament. In addition, a growing number of trade union officials have entered union service as graduates rather than working their way up from shop-floor or coalface. More than a quarter of union-sponsored MPs in 1992 fell into this non-traditional category.

3: Constituency connections among MPs, 1945 and 1992

	Cons.		Lab.		Lib.Dem.	Other
	1945	1992	1945	1992	1992	1992
	%	%	%	%	n	n
None known	45.1	43.1	39.6	15.1	1	–
Regional conn.	13.0	28.4	14.4	18.2	8	7
Area conn.	16.7	13.8	15.3	17.2	8	1
Direct conn.	25.2	14.7	30.7	49.5	8	17

Although candidate selection is primarily a matter for local parties, this has not led to the selection of overwhelmingly local candidates: the 'carpet-bagger' is alive and well in British politics. Indeed, in the Conservative Party there has been a decline in the proportion of MPs with direct connections with the constituencies before selection. In the Labour Party, however, changes have been in the opposite direction. Not only has the proportion of Labour MPs with no known constituency connections declined sharply, but more significantly the proportion with direct connections has increased markedly. Furthermore, this is part of a growing trend, which showed only a small decline in 1992.

4: Labour MPs with direct local constituency connections

first elected	% direct connections
Pre-1979	29.4
1979–83	42.3
1983–87	50.0
1987–92	69.0
1992	61.4

In many instances these direct local connections take the form of membership of the local authority in which the constituency lies, but others have held office in their local CLP and, in two cases, involved wives succeeding their husbands as Members.

5: Previous electoral experience of MPs, 1945 and 1992

	Cons.		Lab.		Lib.Dem.	Other
	1945	1992	1945	1992	1992	1992
	%	%	%	%	n	n
None	83.1	32.4	68.7	58.7	7	14
One or more	16.9	67.6	31.3	41.3	13	10

There is also evidence that the competition for membership of the House of Commons has increased since 1945, especially in the Conservative Party where there has been a dramatic increase in the number of MPs who have fought one or more unsuccessful contests before being elected to the Commons. The 1992 figure is the culmination of a steady decline in the proportion of Conservative MPs being elected without having previously fought an election unsuccessfully. The Labour figures for 1945 and 1992 mask a similar trend since 1964, with an increasing prpportion of Labour MPs having previous electoral experience, until it was reversed in recent elections. Not surprisingly Liberal Democrat, though not other party candidates, are more likely to have fought unsuccessfully before being elected, often fighting the seat they eventually win.

Parliamentary careers

6: Age on first being elected, 1945 and 1992

	Cons.		Lab.		Lib.Dem.	Other
	1945	1992	1945	1992	1992	1992
	%	%	%	%	n	n
Under 30	14.5	5.9	2.8	3.3	5	1
30–39	35.7	52.4	27.6	42.1	8	8
40–49	30.4	38.7	38.3	42.1	6	10
50–59	12.6	3.0	21.3	11.8	1	5
60–69	5.3	–	6.5	0.7	–	–
70, or over	0.5	–	0.2	–	–	–
Not known	1.0	–	3.3	–	–	–

Only a small minority of MPs begin their parliamentary careers under the age of 30; most are first elected between the ages of 30 and 50, a substantial proportion between 35 and 45. Moreover, this concentration has become more marked since 1945: fewer MPs are elected under the age of 30 and notably fewer at the age of 50 or more. What this reflects is, first, the need for would-be MPs to establish themselves occupationally and financially; second, a decline in the number of MPs for whom a parliamentary career was a fairly late adjunct to their principal occupation; and third, the professionalisation of the role of the Member of Parliament. It is also evident that Conservatives tend to reach a point at which they can launch into a parliamentary career sooner than their Labour counterparts. This was noticeable in 1945, but had become considerably more marked by 1992.

7: Parliamentary service of MPs, 1945–74 and 1974–92

	Cons.		Lab.		(1974–92)		
	1945–74	1974–92	1945–74	1974–92	Lib. Dem.	SDP	Other
	%	%	%	%	n	n	n
Less than 5	9.0	6.5	10.4	3.2	1	1	2
5–9 years	23.2	21.2	28.4	19.4	2	2	15
10–14 years	18.0	9.3	16.1	16.6	4	7	1
15–19 years	19.5	13.9	16.5	21.9	3	9	3
20–24 years	13.8	17.8	12.2	15.9	2	3	–
25 or more	16.5	31.3	16.3	23.0	1	2	1

* Figures for 1945–74 relate to MPs whose membership of the House of Commons began in 1945 or earlier and ended in October 1974 or earlier; those for 1974–92 relate to those whose membership began in 1974 or earlier and ended betwen October 1974 and 1992, including the 1992 general election.

Parliamentary careers in Britain tend to be fairly long. The turnover of the House of Commons is not, on average, very large. Arguably the period 1945–74 saw the two-party system at its height, with seats in the House of Commons fairly evenly balanced between Conservative and Labour, but the period since 1974 was first one of largely minority government and then of Conservative domination. The figures in Table 7 largely conform with this conception and there is little difference between the parties. Those for the period 1974–92 present a more complex picture. This involved substantial Conservative gains in 1979 and 1983, subsequent losses in 1987 and 1992, offset by the prolongation of the service of a number of Conservative MPs in a period of Conservative domination. A similar lengthening of service benefited a number of Labour MPs as regional voting disparities enabled the party to tighten its grip in its industrial heartland in the northern half of England and in Scotland. Consequently, the median length of service rose from fourteen years for those leaving the Commons between 1945 and 1974 to eighteen years for those leaving between 1974 and 1992.

8: Causes of termination of membership of HoC, 1945–74

	Cons.		Lab.		(1974–92)		
	1945–74	1974–92	1945–74	1974–92	Lib. Dem.	SDP	Other
	%	%	%	%	n	n	n
Retirement	45.5	61.8	41.2	49.5	4	1	5
Defeat	24.4	23.2	27.3	33.2	8	23	14
Death	10.1	10.4	20.2	13.4	1	–	3
Resignation	8.8	2.7	7.4	3.5	–	–	–
Elevation to peerage	9.7	1.9	3.5	0.3	–	–	–
Succession to peerage	1.1	–	0.2	–	–	–	–
Disqual./expulsion	0.4	–	0.2	–	–	–	–

* See note to Table 7

Membership of the House of Commons is most commonly brought to a premature end by electoral defeat and this accounts for the end of between a quarter and a third of the parliamentary careers of MPs, but retirement at a general election has long been the most common means of ending membership of the Commons and in recent elections accounted for more than 50% of the turnover of the House. Although death has ended the parlimentary careers of more Labour than Conservative MPs, the gap has narrowed significantly since 1945, almost certainly as a result of the introduction of a parlimentary pension scheme from 1964.

Professionalisation of the MP

The length of parliamentary service, the growing tendency to retire from Parliament at or around normal retirement age, the recruitment of MPs from a fairly narrow age-band are part of a pattern of the increasing professionalisation of the role of the Member of Parliament. In 1945 MPs were paid £600, rising to £1,000 in 1946, from which they were expected to meet any expenses incurred in the performance of their parliamentary duties, other than telephone calls in the London area and the cost of travel between Westminster and their constituencies and their homes. Few MPs employed a secretary, let alone any research staff, and office accommodation for backbench MPs was virtually unknown. When the new chamber (which had been destroyed in 1941) was opened in 1950, the only desks available to backbench Members — apart from writing places in such locations as the Commons Library and writing rooms — were a few typists' desks in rooms in the Upper Committee Corridor of the Palace of Westminster. And the idea of telephoning a Member at Westminster was laughable. Only in 1946 did the House of Commons Library embark on creating a systematic research and information service for MPs.

Although the House of Commons does not meet notably more frequently in the 1990s than the 1940s (160 days compared with 170–180), the demands on the Member of Parliament have increased enormously. The volume of legislation, both primary and secondary, has grown massively, added to which is secondary legislation emanating from Brussels. Committee activity, both standing and select, has also increased greatly, the former in response to the House's legislative load, the latter in response to growing demands for the more effective scrutiny of policy and administration. And the demands made upon Members by their constituents has burgeoned almost beyond belief; the 'welfare officer' role, for example, takes up more MPs' time than any other single activity.

A quite separate development, largely associated with the type of individuals in both major parties being elected to Parliament, resulted in importance changes in Members' behaviour. The so-called 'Tory knights of the shire' and Labour's traditional trade union MPs declined in numbers and were replaced by Members who were not content to acquiesce unquestionably in party policy and troop through the division lobbies at the behest of the whips. They demanded a more active and critical role and backbench dissension has become much more common. Their demands led to major improvements in pay, services and facilities for MPs and eventually to the setting-up of the departmental select committees in 1979. In 1945 a substantial proportion of MPs, possibly a majority, were part-time Members; by the 1970s a majority were full-time in the sense that being a Member of Parliament was their main activity and in the 1990s few MPs regard their job as other than full-time, even though a substantial majority still have an extra-parliamentary income.[5]

Ministerial careers

In 1900 there were 60 ministerial posts; in 1945, 73; and in 1994, 111. This expansion was entirely to the benefit of MPs (as already noted, the number of peers in the government fell markedly). On the other hand, the proportion of MPs with ministerial ambitions has almost certainly grown since 1945. Although the evidence for this is largely anecdotal, there is little doubt that many of the Tory knights of the shire and Labour trade union MPs did not aspire to office. In contrast, a survey by the Study of Parliament Group of MPs first elected in 1992 found that 60% Conservatives and 43% of Labour Members hoped eventually to become ministers. The party difference is notable and probably reflects both the long perid of Conservative domination and a longer-lived aversion of some Labour MPs to the restrictions of office.

9: Ministerial experience of MPs, highest office held, 1945–92

	Cons.		Lab.	
	1945–74	1974–92	1945–74	1974–92
	%	%	%	%
None	58.9	37.1	62.2	52.9
Parl. Private Sec.	12.9	17.2	12.3	12.3
Junior whip	4.5	5.0	3.3	5.2
Parl. Sec./Under Sec.	11.1	15.1	9.2	9.4
Minister of State	0.8	9.3	1.8	5.8
Chief Whip/Dep. Ch.Whip	0.8	–	0.8	1.3
Law officer	1.4	1.1	0.3	–
Speaker/Deputy Speaker	1.1	0.8	1.3	1.0
Non-Cabinet minister	3.5	0.4	3.9	1.0
Cabinet minister	4.9	13.9	4.8	11.0
(excl. PPS) Total held office	28.2	45.6	25.5	34.7

* See note for Table 7: Cons. includes 2 MPs who subsequently represented other parties; Lab. includes 23 MPs who subsequently sat as SDP

Among MPs who left the Commons before 1974 approximately a quarter held ministerial office, but among those whose parliamentary careers ended between 1974 and 1992 the proportion rose to two-fifths — 46% of Conservative and 35% of Labour MPs. Most other MPs spent their entire careers in the Commons as backbenchers, although a minority served as opposition frontbenchers without ever achieving office.

Of course, much depends on party fortunes and this is reflected in the figures in the table. Indeed, as 1979 gets further and further away, the number of Labour MPs with ministerial experience will continue to decline, especially those with Cabinet experience. The fairly elaborate governmental hierarchy also means that only about one in ten MPs actually reach the Cabinet and most ministers do not rise above the rank of Parliamentary Secretary of Minister of State. However, the growth of the position or Minister of State, which usually involves a substantial degree of departmental responsibility, has resulted in a significant broadening of ministerial experience.

Apart from party fortunes, achieving (and losing) ministerial office also depends on periodic government reshuffles and these have tended to get more frequent since 1957. Attlee conducted only three major reshuffles between 1945 and 1951, Churchill (1951–55) only one and Eden (1955–57) only one (soon after the 1955 general election), but Macmillan (1957–63) had five in six years, including the notorious

'July massacre' of 1962, when he sacked a third of his Cabinet and made 24 ministerial changes altogether. Later Prime Ministers have varied in their frequency of reshuffles, with Heath (1970–74) and Callaghan (1976–79) each having only two, but Wilson and Thatcher reshuffled their governments almost annually and Major has followed their lead. Indeed, it almost seems that an annual reshuffle is widely expected, to the point of often appearing to be media-led. All this means, on the one hand, that although ministerial careers can last a decade or more (sometimes with the interruption of a period in opposition), changes of office are fairly frequent, both in moving up the hierarchy and once Cabinet office has been achieved. The average period in a major office is about two years, but the range is considerable and some ministers hold the same office for quite long periods of time — Lord Chancellors such as Lord Gardiner (1964–70), Lord Hailsham (1970–74 and 1979–87), and Lord Mackay (since 1988) are perhaps atypical in this respect, but others, such as Denis Healey (Defence Secretary 1964–70 and Chancellor of the Exchequer 1974–79), Sir Geoffrey Howe (Chancellor of the Exchequer 1979–83 and Foreign Secretary 1983–89), and Nigel Lawson (Chancellor of the Exchequer 1983–87) illustrate the point.

Given the extensive governmental hierarchy and the constitutional convention that ministers must be drawn from Parliament, it is not surprising that membership of the Cabinet is normally preceded by an extensive parliamentary apprenticeship and somewhat less extensive ministerial apprenticeship. The median length of parliamentary service for Cabinets formed between 1964 and 1992 ranged from 14.5 years (1992) to 23 years (1974) and normally only a small minority of ministers will not have had previous ministerial experience upon achieving Cabinet office. Even in 1964, when Labour had been out of power for thirteen years, well over half of Wilson's Cabinet had previously held office, although only four were former Cabinet ministers, including Wilson himself.

Continuity and change

Political career pattens between 1945 and 1994 are still marked more by continuity than change, although the changes that have occurred have been significant. National political ambitions in Britain remain fulfilled almost entirely through Parliament and overwhelmingly through the House of Commons, which is in turn the almost exclusive route to high political office. Britain has not moved towards the practice in some other countries, notably but not only the United States, of seeking to fill executive office from a much wider pool of recruits, either by abandoning or substantially modifying long-standing constitutional and political practice, or by finding quick, effective and acceptable ways of installing ministers in Parliament. Moreover, political advancement is not only through Parliament but through the party system, itself dominated by two major parties. None of this has changed.

Changes there have been, however. The demands made upon MPs have grown enormously both at Westminster and from constituents. The role of the Member of Parliament has become increasingly professionalised and the job is now essentially full-time. The change in the party system from a balanced two-party system to a system of 'ins' and 'outs' has had some effect and has the potential for a yet greater impact, should Conservative dominance be maintained. This is illustrated starkly by the fact that 66% of Conservative MPs in the 1992 Parliament have experience only as members of the governing party; conversely, 72% of Labour MPs have experience only of being in opposition. There were strong signs during the 1980s that Labour was becoming opposition-minded and the Conservatives government-minded. These attitudes of 'ins' and 'outs' will be substantially reinforced if Labour suffers a further electoral defeat. That in time may have a wider impact on the party system, the effects of which on Parliament could be profound. Alternatively, if the next election were to produce a hung Parliament, and it and subsequent elections led to minority government or coalition government becoming the norm, various possibilities emerge.

Much, of course, depends of the parliamentary arithmetic, especially whether the distribution of seats in the Commons is such that either a minority or a coalition government could be sustained with Liberal-Democratic support. Initially, a hung Parliament is likely to produce minority government (neither major party is used to or likes sharing power), which is potentially unstable, and political careers might become much more fragmented than has been the experience since 1945. However, the continued inability of both the Conservative and Labour Parties to win an absolute Commons majority would probably produce a coalition involving the Liberal Democrats. That in turn would result in Liberal ministers for the first time since 1945 and, should an electoral pact between Labour and the Liberal-Democrats emerge, a prolonged period of Labour-Liberal dominance might ensue. The impact on career patterns would be significant for the parties, but no more than a mirror image of the period of Conservative dominance since 1979.

1 This excludes the by-election at Bristol South-East in 1961, when Tony Benn was re-elected to the House of Commons but disqualified because he had inherited a peerage. Under the Peerages Act 1963 he was able to disclaim his peerage and was re-elected at a further by-election that year.
2 Pippa Norris and Joni Lovenduski, *Political Recruitment: Gender, Race and Class in the British Parliament* (Cambridge University Press, 1995).
3 One Labour MP, the late Bob Cryer (elected for Bradford S. in 1987) had previously served as MP for Keighley from February 1974 to 1983, when he was defeated and then elected to the European Parliament in 1984.

4   The proportion of union-sponsored MPs tends to increase when Labour has fewer MPs because of the relative concentration of union candidates in safer Labour seats, but in 1992 the number of sponsored MPs rose to its highest ever — 157 (53% of all Labour MPs).

5   See M. Rush, 'The Professionalisation of the British Member of Parliament', *Papers in Political Science*, Department of Politics, University of Exeter, 1989.

The Civil Service:
From the 1940s to 'Next Steps' and Beyond

BY GAVIN DREWRY

THE fifteen years since Mrs Thatcher first became Prime Minister, in 1979, have seen a transformation in both the structure and the culture of UK central government. The process of change continues, and the increasing fragmentation and privatisation of departmental functions casts doubt on whether the civil service can still be said to exist in any coherent sense. This article examines recent trends in civil service reform and considers the constitutional significance of changes that have profound implications for the future of parliamentary government.

Civil servants, ministers and Parliament: constitutional ground rules

The Index to Volume I of *Parliamentary Affairs* (1948–49) contains five entries for the 'civil service'—all of which turn out to be very peripheral references to the subject. This meagre attention by the journal of a then recently formed Society for promoting the cause of parliamentary government in the postwar world symbolises the gap that has traditionally existed between Parliament and the civil service. That gap is largely attributable to the stubbornly enduring doctrine of ministerial responsibility. In its pure form, this doctrine holds that ministers, individually and collectively, are the sole conduits of explanation and accountability between executive government and the Parliament to which those same minister's belong. The minister speaks publicly on behalf of his or her department; civil servants are anonymous ministerial advisers, lurking silently in the background and largely shielded from public criticism (though the civil service itself, as a corporate aggregation, is not immune from attack). Any public blame for failures of policy or administration falls, according to this constitutional orthodoxy, upon the minister.

The constitutional doctrine of ministerial responsibility is complemented and reinforced by the traditionally sharp dividing line that has existed since the early part of the nineteenth century between political/ministerial and civil service careers. Both ministers and civil servants are servants of the Crown; but ministers, in whom the prerogatives of the Crown are vested, are dominant. And the traditional orthodoxy remains, to quote the 1987 version of the Armstrong Memorandum on *The Duties and Responsibilities of Civil Servants in Relation to Minis-*

ters, that 'the civil service as such has no constitutional personality or responsibility separate from the duly constituted government of the day'.

Civil servants are politically neutral and are expected to serve ministers of any government currently in office with non-partisan loyalty (not at all the same thing as *enthusiasm* for particular ministers and their policies—a quality which by definition is inconsistent with neutrality). It has been noted that: 'When Attlee succeeded Churchill as Prime Minister in 1945, and returned to the Potsdam peace conference, he was accompanied by the same team of civil servants (including the same principal private secretary) that had made up his predecessor's delegation. This continuity surprised the Americans and the Russians, but the officials concerned made the transition without apparent difficulty and the Labour leader himself had no doubts about the impartiality of his staff. Out of office in the 1950s, Attlee would boast to international socialist conferences that the British career civil service was unequalled in the world, one of the strongest bulwarks of democracy, and that the same officials who had worked out the details of Labour's programme were now busy pulling it to pieces for their Conservative masters.'[1]

Thus the political world (and for more than a hundred years, the party political world) of Westminster has been a world apart, culturally and constitutionally, from Whitehall. But there is a vast gap between this version of constitutional theory (still proclaimed as current by ministers and civil service managers) and modern-day reality. For one thing, 'pure' ministerial responsibility has long been rendered illusory by the growth and the decentralisation of government activity, and the Next Steps civil service reforms (noted below) have recognised and reinforced this.

Parliament's procedures are still substantially founded upon minister-ial responsibility. But there have been important changes. Since the substantial reform of the House of Commons select committee system in the late 1970s, Parliament has begun to engage in regular, face to face, dialogue with civil servants[2] (sometimes in front of television cameras)—though the so-called Osmotherly rules remind official wit-nesses that they appear on behalf of their ministers. Those same select committees—in particular the Treasury and Civil Service Committee—have, through their inquiries into public sector reform—become a major quarry for academic study of the changing civil service. Next Steps has short-circuited ministerial responsibility for the service-deliv-ery functions of departments by encouraging MPs to take up matters relating to the operation of executive agencies directly with chief executives: and the latter's written replies to parliamentary questions are printed in *Hansard*.

The anonymity of officials—particularly in Next Steps agencies—has been substantially reduced by the requirements of the Citizen's Charter.

Some of the traditional assumptions about the non-political nature of the civil service have been called into question—not least by the length in office of the Conservative Party since 1979. Quite apart from the Next Steps programme, episodes like the Westland and Ponting affairs in the 1980s and the Matrix Churchill case in the 1990s have raised important concerns about the relationships between ministers and civil servants.

In recent years, the contents of *Parliamentary Affairs* have included many items on the civil service, and this article—starting from the premiss that the remaining gulf between Parliament and the civil service, inadequately bridged by ministers, is both artificial and inappropriate—maintains that pattern by looking at some of the main features of civil service development since the first issue of this journal appeared. Some of those changes have themselves been the subject of select committee inquiry. We will begin with an outline of some of the structural contrasts between the civil service of the 1940s and its counterpart in 1994—transformed by the public sector reforms of the Thatcher-Major years.

The civil service in the 1940s

In the preface to his study of the Higher Civil Service (completed a few months before the outbreak of the second world war but not published until 1941), H. E. Dale observed: 'If we can judge from the experience of the last war, it is probable that when the tempest is over, the permanent civil service will emerge from the waters not fundamentally altered from what it was before the floods covered it. In that event, my account will still retain some part of any value that it might have possessed if the war had not broken out. In the contrary event, it may have an historical value as a description of a state of things which has passed away, written just before the passing.'[3] The 'contrary event' did not occur (had it done so, it seems unlikely that we would now be celebrating the anniversary of the Hansard Society), and the civil service emerged after the War 'not fundamentally altered'.

Wars have always been great watersheds in administrative history, bringing in new people (known in 1939–45 as 'Whitehall irregulars'), breaking down old rigidities (while perhaps creating new ones) and changing the culture. One expects there always to be a ratchet effect—in the sense that things never quite revert to their pre-war state; but in the case of the post-1945 civil service, the ratchet did not work very effectively. Peter Hennessy suggests, tongue-in-cheek, that the last person truly to reform Whitehall was that well-known expert in public administration, Adolf Hitler who obliged the British government to find new men and new methods almost overnight. However, he then goes on to deplore the postwar failure to build upon the reforms forced upon Whitehall by the exigencies of war as probably *the* greatest lost opportunity in the history of British public administration.[4]

As we shall see, the nineteenth century civil service escaped radical changes at the hands of the postwar government of Clement Attlee (already seen to be an admirer of the professionalism and neutrality of the service) in the early years of *Parliamentary Affairs,* and then escaped the Fulton Report of 1968, but succumbed to the radicalism (some would say iconoclasm) of the Thatcher-Major years.

By the end of the Attlee era, in 1951, there were 1,075,00 civil servants—of whom 400,000 (37%) were industrial staff—a species whose numbers decreased sharply during the Thatcher years of privatisation and contracting out (particularly of naval ship repairing and ordnance manufacture). But the 1951 figure is swollen by staff of the Post Office, who then accounted for about one-third of the total; in 1969 the Post Office became a public corporation and its staff ceased to be civil servants. In 1979, Mrs Thatcher inherited a civil service of 732,000; by 1994 the figure was about 550,000, of which only about 3% belong to the policy-making grades of Principal and above. As we will see, most civil servants now work in semi-autonomous Next Steps executive agencies. In referring to statistics such as these, it should be remembered that in the UK the term 'civil servant' has a very narrow definition; civil servants comprise only about 10% of the public sector workforce. It should be borne in mind that many of the changes and tendencies described here are mirrored by similarly radical transformations that have been occurring elsewhere in the public sector.

Auguries of change: the Fulton Report

The Fulton Committee, 1966–68, was set up to undertake the most wide-ranging inquiry into the civil service since the middle of the nineteenth century. Its attack on the 'amateurism' of the generalist civil servant caused much controversy at the time, but few of its 158 recommendations made much headway: its most tangible monument, the Civil Service Department, was abolished by Mrs Thatcher in 1981. At that point, most observers would probably have accorded it little more than a respectful obituary notice in the administrative history textbooks.

But, from the standpoint of the mid-1990s, Fulton merits significant attention on at least three counts. First, because its establishment was a reflection of scepticism on the part of some members of a new Labour government, out of office for thirteen years, about the disposition of the higher civil service—dominated by Oxbridge generalists—towards a socialist programme. Justified or not, a similar scepticism might well be expected to afflict the minds of incoming ministers when the present long era of Conservative rule comes to an end.

Secondly, there is a lesson to be drawn from the failure of most of the Fulton proposals to make much headway—which can be explained substantially by the fact that the Wilson government that had commissioned the inquiry and endorsed most of the Report's recommendations

fell from office two years after it was published. This is in sharp contrast
with the public sector reform programmes undertaken by the Thatcher-
Major governments, which have not only not only given those reforms
very high priority, but have been continuously in office for long enough
to push them through. It should be added that Mrs Thatcher was not
one to waste time (as she would no doubt have seen it) by referring such
matters to an independent committee of inquiry, like the Fulton
Committee.

The third area of interest lies in the fact that some parts of the Fulton
Report anticipated changes that were destined to resurface, in a new
disguise, during the Thatcher years. In particular, Fulton's recommendations that steps should be taken to introduce management by objectives
and accountable management, and for there to be an inquiry into the
desirability of undertaking the selective hiving off of departmental
functions, anticipated future developments—in particular, the Next
Steps initiative, launched twenty years later.

The Thatcher-Major reforms

The election of the first Thatcher government in 1979 heralded a period
of revolutionary change throughout the public sector, including the civil
service. The reforms were driven by New Right ideas about the inherent
inefficiencies of public sector service provision as compared with the
provision of services through the play of market forces, and were
manifested both in terms of numerous variations on the themes of
privatisation and contracting out and in a crusade for greater efficiency,
effectiveness and economy (the '3Es'). They also gained impetus from
the government's determination to diminish the power of the trade
unions—including of course, the civil service unions, with which the
Thatcher government came quickly into conflict. The early phase of the
reform programme featured rhetoric about 'deprivileging' the civil
service and plans to cut civil service numbers and peg back pay
increases.

After the 1979 general election, Mrs Thatcher recruited Sir Derek
(now Lord) Rayner, joint managing director of Marks and Spencer, as
her special adviser on efficiency and the first head of a new Efficiency
Unit, located initially in the Prime Minister's Office but later moved
to the Cabinet Office (in 1992 it was one of several units brigaded
together in a new Office of Public Service and Science, under William
Waldegrave).

The Rayner Efficiency Unit undertook a series of small-scale efficiency
scrutinies, identifying areas of waste, inefficiency and duplication in
government departments; it also used such scrutinies to promote more
permanent changes in management procedures. One of the first of
these—given the acronym MINIS (Management Information System
for Ministers)—involved the enhancement of internal managerial
accountability in the Department of the Environment, with a view to

giving civil servants a clearer definition of their responsiblities and to giving the minister in charge of a very large department better access to information about what was going on. The then Environment Secretary, Michael Heseltine, took MINIS with him when he moved to the Ministry of Defence in 1983. MINIS was strongly endorsed by the Treasury and Civil Service Committee of the House of Commons, and in 1982 the government launched a new Financial Management Initiative (FMI), involving major changes in management of all central government departments, including substantial moves towards devolved budgetary authority and accountable management. Its aims were to promote in each department an organisation and system in which managers at all levels have: (a) a clear view of their objectives and means to assess and, wherever possible, measure outputs of performance in relation to those objectives; (b) well-defined responsibility for making the best use of their resources, including a critical scrutiny of output and value for money; and (c) the information (particularly about costs), the training and the access to expert advice that they need to exercise their responsibilities effectively.

Although the FMI had a considerable impact both upon the financial processes and the working culture of Whitehall, its impact on the the traditional style of central administration was limited. In the words of two commentators on the Next Steps initiative: 'Giving managers "the right to manage" was the next challenge—how to make sure that budgets really were delegated. This would necessitate "letting go" by top department officials and the Treasury. While civil servants undoubtedly became more cost-conscious and more managerially minded as a result of FMI, the real devolution of financial management, the development of targets and the switch from inputs to outputs never happened. The idea lived to fight another day.'[5]

Thus, while the FMI appears to have improved financial monitoring, it was widely felt that more needed to be done to modernise the traditional culture of the civil service and to stimulate managerial initiative. It was these perceived deficiencies that led to the launching of the Next Steps programme.

From FMI to Next Steps

In November 1986 the Efficiency Unit (then headed by Sir Robin Ibbs of ICI), at the instigation of the Prime Minister, embarked upon a new, service-wide scrutiny exercise 'to assess the progress achieved in managing the civil service; to identify what measures had been successful in changing attitudes and practices; to identify institutional, administrative, political and managerial obstacles to better management and efficiency that still remain; and to report to the Prime Minister on what further measures should be taken.'

The outcome of this review, building upon the experience of the FMI, was a programme for radical changes in the structure and culture of the civil service. After a lot of Whitehall infighting (the Treasury, in particular, was concerned about the prospect of a possible weakening of central financial control) a version of the Ibbs Report was eventually published, in February 1988, under the title, *Improving Management in Government: the Next Steps*. Based on extensive interviews with ministers and civil servants, it found, among other things, that most civil servants concerned with the delivery of government services (about 95% of all staff) welcomed the movement towards more clearly defined management tasks and devolved budgetary responsibilities. It also found widespread concern about the fact that senior management was dominated by people with policy skills but little experience of managing service delivery.

The radicalism of its diagnosis and of its prescription for change is summed up in one key paragraph: 'The aim should be to establish a quite different way of conducting the business of government. The central civil service should consist of a relatively small core engaged in the function of servicing Ministers and managing departments, who will be the "sponsors" of particular government policies and services. Responding to these departments will be a range of agencies employing their own staff, who may or may not have the status of Crown servants, and concentrating on the delivery of their particular service, with clearly defined responsibilities between the Secretary of State and the Permanent Secretary on the one hand and the Chairman or Chief Executives of the agencies on the other. Both departments and their agencies should have a more open and simplified structure.'

The centrepiece of the Ibbs recommendations was a formula for institutionalising the crucial but elusive distinction between ministerial support and policy functions on the one hand (performed by, at most, some 20,000 civil servants, working in close proximity to ministers) and executive or service delivery functions on the other. The latter would progressively be transferred to semi-autonomous executive agencies. These agencies, headed by chief executives, would be managed, within an agreed policy framework (which would normally be published), operating at arm's length from day-to-day ministerial control.

On the day of publication (18 February 1988), the Prime Minister made a House of Commons statement endorsing the recommendations. She said that the new agencies would generally be within the civil service, and their staff would continue to be civil servants, though she later conceded that the word 'generally' did not rule out the possibility of agencies being set up outside the civil service in some cases. She said that the convention of ministerial responsibility would still apply to agencies, which would remain within the purview of parliamentary select committees, the National Audit Office and the Parliamentary Commissioner for Administration.

Twelve areas of departmental activity were identified initially as candidates for agency status: most of the new agencies were very small (the one exception was the Employment Service), and most of them covered specialised, and in some cases commercial, aspects of departmental work that were already more or less semi-detached (e.g. the Meteorological Office, HMSO and the Queen Elizabeth II Conference Centre). By January 1991, another 22 agencies had been added to the total—but the total proportion of civil service staff employed in agencies at this point was only about 14%.

However, the picture changed very radically when most of the operational divisions of the Department of Social Security—one of the largest Whitehall departments—were designated as Next Steps agencies. The biggest of these, the Social Security Benefits Agency, then employing 70,000 civil servants (about 15% of the entire civil service) in around 500 local offices, and with a budget of around £50bn a year, was launched in April 1991; at the same time, a Social Security Contributions Agency, with 9,000 staff, became responsible for the administration of National Insurance contributions. Also in April 1991, another very large department, Customs and Excise (25,000 staff) was reorganised into 30 executive units on Next Steps lines; and the Inland Revenue (63,000 staff), subdivided into 34 executive offices, followed a year later.

By December 1993 there were 93 Next Steps agencies (plus customs and Excise and the Inland Revenue, both operating through Executive Units/Offices) employing some 60% of the civil service; 44 more activities had at that point been identified as candidates for agency status, the largest being the Court Service with 10,000 civil servants, due to become an agency in April 1995. There have been parallel deveopments in the much smaller Northern Ireland civil service. It is reckoned that about three-quarters of all civil servants will be working in agencies by the end of 1995.

Agency chief executives

In the upper echelons of many parts of the public sector there has been a significant movement away from permanent career appointments, automatic salary increments and internal promotions, towards recruitment by open competition, performance-related pay and short-term service contracts whose renewal depends upon proven capacity to achieve performance targets. Traditionally, graduate entrants into the higher civil service (particularly those allocated to the 'fast-stream' of career progression), having passed through a very tough recruitment programme, have been handed the golden key to a lifetime career, with incremental pay scales, index-linked pensions and the expectation of promotion to higher grades. These expectations have been changing for some time (they are part of what Mrs Thatcher had in mind as the targets of her 'deprivileging'), and the Next Steps has markedly accelerated the process of change.

The Next Steps Agency Chief Executives (ACEs) have been appointed on three to five year contracts; most have been recruited by open competition, and have come from outside the civil service. The position, as summarised by the Office of Public Service and Science to the Treasury and Civil Service Committee in June 1993, was that: 'Of 94 Chief Executive and Chief Executive-designate appointments made so far, 63 have been appointed by open competition, 23 are internal civil service appointments, and 8 [heading various Ministry of Defence agencies] are armed forces appointments. Of those recruited by open competition, 34 have come from outside the civil service. Chief Executives have a wide variety of backgrounds including civil service, local government, the NHS and the private sector.' Thus Michael Bichard, Chief Executive of the flagship Benefits Agency, has a local government background. Ros Heppelwhite, Chief Executive of the controversial Child Support Agency, was national director of the mental health pressure group, MIND, before which she served as a health administrator.

Historically, open competition and security of tenure—products of the civil service reforms of the mid-nineteenth century—have substantial constitutional significance, in signalling the neutrality and the independence of a minister's senior official advisers and the rejection of an American-style spoils system based on political patronage. Of course running an agency is different from being a top ministerial adviser, but the distinction is far from absolute: the powerful Chief Executive of a large agency may be expected to have lines of direct communication with ministers, and the latter may turn to ACEs for 'advice', but the minister's top policy adviser is still the traditional upwardly-mobile fast-stream high-flier.

Even this may change. Towards the end of 1993, a group headed by John Oughton, head of the Efficiency Unit, published a document called *Career Planning and Succession Planning Study*. The Oughton Report, which concentrates on the 626 civil service jobs in the top three senior open structure grades, is highly critical of many aspects of the current system. Among other things, it recommends that at least some vacancies at this level—including Permanent Secretary posts—should be publicly advertised. However, it also says that there should be a clearly stated expectation to appoint from within and that the civil service should continue to 'grow its own timber'.*

Beyond the next steps

It is quite clear that the Next Steps programme is not destined to be the final step in civil service reform. We have already noted one possible avenue of further change in the senior open structure. And then there is the Citizen's Charter. Launched by John Major in 1991, and proclaimed in the 1992 Queen's Speech to be at the centre of decision making, the Charter has been described by the Director of the Citizen's Charter Unit (*The Independent*, 7 October 1991) as: 'the next stage after Next Steps.

Next Steps gets management sorted out and now we are saying with greater clarity what we want management to deliver.'

Another, potentially even more important, development has been a growing emphasis on market testing, signalled in the white paper *Competing for Quality*, published in November 1991. Market testing requires civil servants, in effect, to compete for their own jobs. In the year ending September 1993 the government was planning to market test activities to the value of £1.5bn, and covering 44,000 civil service jobs. Areas affected include accountancy, audit and finance functions; information technology; estate management; office services and reprographics.

And the story does not stop here. In November 1992, Stephen Dorrell, Financial Secretary to the Treasury, told the Centre for Policy Studies that the Government was: 'initiating a new review of the activities of government to develop the successful privatisation programme of the last decade. This privatisation initiative involves a 'long march' through Whitehall ... In every department of state, we must apply the 'back to basics' test to every area of government. We are no longer simply looking for obvious candidates for privatisation. The conventional question was "what can we sell?" That question must now be turned on its head. Now we should ask ourselves "what must we keep?" What is the inescapable core of government?'[6]

More recently (see *The Independent*), 23 March 1994), the same minister has signalled the government's continuing commitment to privatisation of many agency functions: 'As agencies develop their specialisms, they will be temptd increasingly to ask why they should continue to live with the undoubted constraints that are employed by public sector ownership'.

The civil service in crisis?

Not long after the 1992 general election, the Treasury and Civil Service Committee (which had already been taking a close interest in the Next Steps reforms) embarked upon a wide-ranging inquiry into the role of the civil service. Having taken oral evidence from an array of ministers and top officials, it published an Interim Report in July 1993.[7] The Report identified at least five separate elements of current concern about the civil service: '(i) Concern about whether the management changes in the civil service in recent years, most notably the Next Steps initiative, have had fundamental implications which were not anticipated at the time the reforms were initiated; (ii) concern about the impact on the civil service of the market testing initiative and the possible privatisation of some civil service functions. (iii) concern about whether the formation of a higher civil service is suitable both for its management tasks and for the provision of good policy advice to ministers; (iv) concern about an alleged deterioration in standards of conduct in the Civil Service; (v) concern about the implications for the civil service of a fourth successive election victory by the same political party.'

One big constitutional issue (still under consideration by the Committee at the time of writing) is whether recent developments such as Next Steps and market testing, taken alongside recent controversies such as the Matrix Churchill affair, require a fresh look to be taken at the conventions surrounding the relationship between ministers and civil servants—where, for instance, civil servants feel that ministers are instructing them to do things that they consider ethically wrong, such as conniving in the deliberate misleading of Parliament. As already noted, the tensions and ambiguities in the relationship have been exacerbated by the fact that one party has been so long in office. Fresh impetus was given to this area of discussion when, in March 1994, William Waldegrave told the Committee that there were circumstances in which ministers might properly be less than truthful to Parliament.

The First Division Association has called for the promulgation of a Code of civil service ethics, supervised by an independent figure such as the Parliamentary Commissioner. There has also been discussion about the desirability of enacting a Civil Service Act—so far resisted by government on the grounds (dubious ones in this writer's view) that it would lead to 'inflexibility' and perhaps to litigation. At times of such rapid change, the shortcomings of an uncodified constitution are starkly exposed. An ex-prime minister (once a tax officer), Lord Callaghan, told the Committee that he was 'more worried about the civil service than I have ever been in the 60-odd years from when I first joined it and have been associated with it'.

The increasing fragmentation of the civil service is a particularly signficant issue in this context. The authors of the Ibbs Report cast doubts upon the traditional notion of a unified civil service. This concept of unity had grown up a century or more ago when the service was much smaller, less organisationally complex, and much less physically dispersed than it is now: 'In our discussions it was clear that the advantages which a unified civil service are intended to bring are seen as outweighed by the practical disadvantages, particularly beyond Whitehall itself. We were told that the advantages of an all-embracing pay-structure are breaking down, that the uniformity of grading frequently inhibits effective management and that the concept of a career in a unified civil service has little relevance for most civil servants, whose horizons are bounded by their local office or, at most, by their department.' The Cabinet Secretary, Sir Robin Butler, has used the cryptic phrase 'unified but not uniform' to describe his vision of the future shape of the civil service.

Arrangements relating to civil service pay and conditions of service have been increasingly decentralised under the Next Steps programme. Since April 1991, departments and agencies have been free to recruit their own staff for all posts except grades 1 to 7 (Permanent Secretary to Principal) and fast stream entrants. The Civil Service (Management Functions) Act 1992 removed legal impediments to the the devolution to departments and agencies of many detailed aspects of staff management. By April 1994, all agencies with 2,000 or more staff were required to be ready to implement their own pay and grading structures.

Lord Bancroft, a former Head of the Civil Service, and his former deputy, Sir John Herbecq—both forced into early retirement in 1981 when Mrs Thatcher decided to axe the Civil Service Department—wrote recently to *The Times* (25 February 1994), expressing concern about the long-term effects upon the efficiency and integrity of public administration, and the weakening of accountability, consequent upon 'the accelerating break-up of the home civil service'. They concede that 'with the ever-growing pervasiveness of of central government, ways should be sought to limit the burden of responsibility on ministers and to devise new methods, such as market testing, of enhancing efficiency'. But they warn that: 'This should not be carried to the point at which standards of service, of conduct and accountability are put at serious risk ... the permanent civil service of the state is self-descriptive: it has no autonomous existence, it is there to serve the state. If the fastidiousness of all its standards is perceived to decline, all citizens are diminished.'

The Treasury and Civil Service Committee probed Mr Dorrell about his references to continuing privatisation in the speech cited earlier. He explained that the rationale of privatisation was still, as it had been with previous privatisation exercises, 'to introduce greater flexibility into the supply side of the British economy, that is to say, to move away from a world where key management decisions about large sectors of economic activity in Britain were made by an over-centralised and over-politicised process'. His replies threw little light on the possible answers to his own interesting question—what is the inescapable core of government?

John Garrett, a member of the Committee, suggested to Mr Dorrell that: 'We are heading towards a core of government which is ministers surrounded by a nest of mandarins, untouched more or less, and below them 100 or more agencies, farming out about—shall we say for the sake of argument 100,000 contracts? How is that a civil service any more and is what I envisage for the future of the civil service right, in your views?' To which the minister replied, gnomically: 'No, I do not think it is. It is certainly not a representation of the world in language that I would choose.'

Parliament, the constitution and the 'new' civil service

The last few years, and perhaps the next few, may one day be seen with hindsight as a golden era of civil service accountability to Parliament. Framework agreements, and the other documentation relating to the operations and performance targets of Next Steps agencies, are a potentially invaluable starting point for parliamentary monitoring and scrutiny. The recent interest shown by select committees in civil service reform and in agency performance is an encouraging development. The direct contacts that have been been developing between MPs and executive agencies are also to be welcomed.

However, if this *is* a golden age, it may prove to be a transient one. The government's continuing (though recently qualified) commitment to market testing, and to the privatisation of many civil service (and agency) functions, will inevitably take many services now provided by central government out of the range of parliamentary scrutiny. As the public sector diminishes, so too, ipso facto, does the role of Parliament, whose roles and procedures are still largely founded upon the mythology of ministerial responsibility.

A central objective of government policy continues to be a reduction in the scope of state activity. As we have seen, recent ministerial statements suggest that the future pattern of reform will involve the privatisation of some agencies (at the time of writing there are reports about the impending privatisation of government laboratories, currently operating as agencies), and the contracting out of a lot of civil service jobs. Consequently, the scope of ministerial responsibility and of ministers' answerability to Parliament will diminish. More seriously, Parliament seems to have been slow to recognise, what government itself has never admitted, that the rolling back of the state and the dismemberment of the civil service are essentially constitutional matters, transcending superstructural considerations like value for money and organisational efficiency. These processes may prove difficult, if not impossible, to reverse. By the time that realisation dawns, it may be too late.

1 K. Theakston, *The Labour Party and Whitehall* (Routledge, 1992), p. 1.
2 This statement needs to be qualified in respect of the long-standing accountability of Permanent Secretaries, in their capacity as departmental accounting officers, to the Public Accounts Committee.
3 H. E. Dale, *The Higher Civil Service of Great Britain* (Oxford University Press, 1941). p. v.
4 P. Hennessy, *Whitehall* (Secker and Warburg, 1989), pp. 88 and 120.
5 A. Davies and J. Willman, *What Next? Agencies, Departments and the Civil Service* (IPPR, 1991), p. 10.
6 'Redefining the Mixed Economy', cited in *Sixth Report from the Treasury and Civil Service Committee, The Role of The Civil Service: Interim Report*, 1992–93, HC 390. Vol. I, para. 11.
7 Ibid. The Committee has continued to take evidence and is expected to produce a final report during the 1993–94 session.
* In July 1994 the government published a white paper that, with modifications, adopted some of these proposals and signalled important changes in the market testing programme.

Changes in Electoral Behaviour and the Party System

BY DENNIS KAVANAGH

THERE have certainly been changes in the party system and the bases of electoral behaviour in the fifty years since 1945. Change is to be expected, but, overall, it is the continuity that stands out, certainly when compared to the changes during the previous fifty years.

There is a the case for considering 1945 as a turning-point in the party system. Universal suffrage and a competitive party system are the hallmarks of a modern democratic political system. One possible starting point for Britain achieving this position is 1918, the year when Labour first presented itself as a national party fighting seats across the country, when the suffrage was extended to all adult males and many women, and when the Irish Nationalists withdrew from the House of Commons. But 1945, or more specifically the election result, is also a plausible date, for several reasons.

- It clarified the party system. A result of the split in the Liberals in 1916 was that the party system was confused for the next 29 years. After the 1945 general election two parties clearly predominated in Parliament and in the country until 1974 (Table 1).
- It produced a competitive two party system. In the inter-war years the Conservatives had dominated the Commons and the first Labour majority government was not elected until 1945. But in the 34 years to 1979 the two parties were in office for equal lengths of time (Table 2).
- It inaugurated an era of one party majority government. Between 1916 and 1945 there had been only one clear period of one party

1. Changes in the Party System 1918–1992 (% Vote)

1918–1934	
Conservative	44.8
Liberals	19.9
Labour	31.5
Other	3.8
1945–1970	
Conservatives	45.2
Liberals	7.1
Labour	46.1
1974–1987	
Conservatives	41.0
Liberals + Alliance parties	19.5
Labour	34.4
Others	5.1

2. Changes in Party Government 1918–1995

1918–1945	
Coalition/National government	18 yrs
One party majority (Cons)	6 yrs
One party minority (Lab)	3 yrs
1945 (Feb)–1974	
Conservative Majority	17 yrs
Labour majority	12 yrs
1974 (March)–1995	
Conservative majority	16 yrs
Labour majority	2 yrs
Labour minority	3 yrs

majority government (1924–29); the rest were coalition (1916–23, 1931–45) or minority Labour government (1924 and 1929–31). Since 1945 one party has had a majority of seats except for a few months in 1974 and again in 1977–79.

Electoral change

Voting behaviour alters as a consequence of social as well as political change. Britain has become a very different society in the post war period. The age of full employment has passed and there is more part-time and female employment; transportation by private car has replaced reliance on buses and trains; private home ownership (up from 26 to 66%) has replaced renting as the main form of housing; rationing has ended and Britain is a much more affluent society, reflected not least in the widespread ownership of consumer durables like televisions, fridges, washing machines and VTRs, as well as the increase in car ownership and foreign holidays.

There have been several symptoms of electoral instability. The electoral decline of the Labour Party in the 1970s and 1980s occurred on a scale greater than that of any other major party of government in Western Europe. The Conservative Party lost four out of five general elections between 1964 and 1974, then won four in succession and has been in office continuously for a longer period than any other party since Lord Liverpool's time. In 1981 the Social Democrats emerged as a major new party, only to self-destruct in 1988 and be absorbed in the new Liberal Democrat Party. The Green Party came from electoral anonymity to win 15% of the vote in the 1989 European elections, then to disappear again.

Some voting guidelines have changed. Class voting has declined. That is, fewer of the working class vote Labour and a diminishing proportion of the middle class vote Conservative; in the 1983, 1987 and 1992 general elections less than half of the electors voted with their 'class' party. The Conservative Party struggles to gain more than half of the middle class vote and Labour cannot gain that share of the working class. By contrast, in general elections between 1945 and 1970 there was a high degree of class voting; some two-thirds of the middle class regularly voted Conservative and some two-thirds of the working class voted Labour.[1] Some part of this decline is due to the changes in the composition of the social classes. The larger middle class today is less homogeneous, divided between those employed in the public and private sectors, and many of its members are first generation, coming from working-class backgrounds. On some definitions of class, the working class is now the latest minority and is divided between the 'old' and the 'new'. The old working class is diminishing; it draws on those who work in heavy manufacturing, belong to trade unions, live in council houses or are wholly reliant upon public transport. But some part of the weaker relationship between class and vote is also a consequence of the rise of the Liberal or centre parties.

Voters have also become more volatile. In the 1940s and 1950s the electorate seemed almost becalmed. Swings at general elections between Labour and Conservative were modest, although the aggregate figures between elections disguised a good deal of individual change — often movements between abstaining and voting from one election to another. Since 1979, general elections seem to show a similar stability in one respect at least, as the Conservative share of the vote has varied only between 41 and 43%. Again, although panel studies reveal a good deal of individual vote switching, during the election campaign many of the changes have been to and from a centre party or into and out of abstention. The main shifts in voting behaviour have occurred outside the Conservative Party — the decline of Labour, the growth of a secure base of support for Nationalists in Scotland and Wales, and the rise of a major third party vote.

These movements have been accompanied by big changes at by-elections and in opinion polls. In the first ten years after 1945 there was great stability of party support in the opinion polls, a contrast to the huge shifts in the 1970s and 1980s. In the 1983 Parliament, the Conservative, Labour and Liberal-Social Democrats each reached 50% or more levels of support in opinion polls. In over a hundred by-elections between 1945 and 1955, only one seat changed hands between the parties. In the thirty years since 1965, more than a third of over 150 by-elections have resulted in change, often with swings in excess of 20%.[2] A good part of this instability has been a response of voters to changing behaviour by the parties. Labour moved sharply left in 1983, and many voters abandoned it. A new Social Democratic Party was set up in 1981, formed an Alliance with the Liberals and then broke up. The Liberals in 1950 contested only one sixth of seats; since 1974 they have fought virtually every seat. As has been noted, much of the turbulence has been a 'party-led destabilisation'.[3]

The regional bases of party voting have altered. Since 1959 there has been a growing north-south split, with the north moving steadily to Labour and the south moving to the Conservative Party. This regional-isation of voting has meant the decline of uniform swing across the

United Kingdom. By 1987, for example, the Conservative share of the two party vote in Scotland was some 20% below what it would have been if Scotland had moved in line with Britain as a whole since 1959. The Conservative vote in the average southern England was some 9% higher than a uniform trend would predict.[4] To some degree the variation has been due to the different social class balance between the more working-class north and more middle-class south, but some is also due to the influence of class environment, in which members of a minority social class vote with the dominant social class in the constituency. For much of the period, these regional trends correlated with economic prosperity; compared to northern Britain, the south suffered less unemployment, enjoyed more buoyant house prices, and its households had higher incomes. 1992 produced a modest reversal of the political and economic trends and Labour actually improved its position in the south.

The breach in the popular standing of the two-party system was most clearly marked in the two 1974 elections. Those two elections mark something of a post-war turning point. In post-war general elections until 1974, Labour had averaged 46% of the vote, Conservatives 45%, and in 1951 and 1955 the two parties gained a combined 96% of the total vote. But the two 1974 elections saw the breakthrough of the Liberals (19% of the vote in February) and Scottish Nationalists (30% of the Scottish vote in October), and since then the Conservative and Labour Parties together have rarely exceeded 75% of the vote at a general election. Instead of gains and losses in votes being exchanged between Labour and Conservative, both lost to other parties. When the Social Democratic Party was formed in 1981, the prospects seem promising for a realignment of the system. Both Labour and Conservative Parties were divided and deeply unpopular, and the new party performed impressively in by-elections. In alliance with the Liberals, the new grouping gained around a quarter of the vote in the 1983 and 1987 general elections, but then broke up. In fact, the change in party support has been a half-way house, for the disproportionate effects of the electoral system have failed to translate the impressive growth in centre-party support into an equivalent number of seats. Popular support at general elections of between 25 and 30% for 'other' parties than Labour or Conservative has produced only some 5% of seats in Parliament.

Finally, as Table 3 shows, the fragmentaton of party loyalties has concided with a decisive shift in the relative position of the two major parties. The 1980s saw the rise of a considerable centre vote, as well as a big Conservative lead over other parties. Among the electorate the competitive two-party system has evolved into a three-party one and Conservative dominance. There are many indicators of this imbalance. One is that Conservatives now have a larger share of identifiers than Labour: in 1992 the respective figures were 39 and 35%, in contrast; by 1964 Labour led by 5% (43 to 38%). The table shows that in

3. Normal Vote 1945–1992 (%)

	Con	Lab	Lib	Other
	%	%	%	%
Mean, 1945–1970	45.2	46.1	7.1	1.6
Mean, Feb 74–1992	40.7	34.4	19.5	5.5
Range, Feb 74–1992	39.8	33.4	19.6	5.5
	+−4.1	+−5.8	+−5.8	+−1.1
Actual Result 1992	41.9	34.4	17.8	5.0

general elections between February 1974 and 1992 the Conservative vote has varied from a high of 43.9% (1979) to a low of 35.8% (October 1974), Labour's from a high of 39.2% (October 1974) to a low of 27.6% (1983). The Conservative mid-point in these elections was 39.8%, 6.4% higher than Labour's 33.4%, giving proximate normal votes of some 40 and 34%. In 1992 both parties (Con 41.9%), Lab 34.4%) just managed to exceed their normal vote.[5]

The figures clearly show that over the past two decades the Labour and Conservative Parties do not enter an election with equal levels of baseline support. Labour is second best and its strategy of the 1950s and 1960s of 'getting out the vote' is no longer sufficient for election victory. It has to build up support from outside the working class and attract voters from other parties. There is nothing new in this recommendation. It has been a lesson of every Labour election defeat since 1959 and was pointed out at the time in *Must Labour Lose?*[6]

In spite of these changes in society and electoral behaviour, Britain retains the same first-past-the-post electoral system. University representation and two-member constituencies were eliminated in 1950, but since then the system has remained largely intact. The method of voting has, of course, long been justified in terms of its ability to deliver strong stable government—when apologists really mean majority government by a single party. Britain has had this for all but 43 months since 1945. But critics of the system have gained in strength over time. The rise of a considerable third-party vote, which is hardly reflected in seats, has produced disproportional results of a new order in parliamentary representation. In recent years, critics have concentrated more on the presumed policy consequences of the two-party system, one-party government and the election rules that manufacture them. They claim that in terms of the quality of policy or economic performance, it is difficult to make a case for the superiority of the distinctive British party and electoral systems in Western Europe. It is only fair to add that disappointment with the policy record—particularly on the economy— has prompted criticism of many other distinctive features of the British political system.

Party system change

The idea of the two-party system as not only the norm but as desirable for parliamentary government has a long history, growing out of the old struggle between the House of Commons and the Crown. Part of the attraction of the model is that it connects with a tendency towards dualistic thinking about the working of Parliament in which *the* government is faced by *the* opposition, notions of responsible party government, and assumptions of the class basis of the vote. It goes without saying that this model has become distinctly frayed in the post-war years. But its hold is strange, given that it only accurately describes the period from 1945 to the 1974, together with a decade of Gladstone-Disraeli rivalry in the 1870s.

Imbalance

The most significant post-war change has been from a competitive to a dominant party system. Since 1918, the Conservatives have been in government alone or in coalition for 50 of the subsequent 75 years, since 1945, for 33 of the subsequent 50. The present period of Conservative ascendancy is a result of four successive general election victories and poses problems for the conduct of politics. In such a centralised political system, the dominant party has a major opportunity to shape the political agenda, and in the 1980s the Conservatives grasped it. The Labour Party has steadily moved since 1983 to compete on ground defined by its opponents; it is no longer a party of public ownership and is re-examining its commitment to universal welfare state benefits. On policies concerning the European Union, industrial relations, sale of council housing, role of markets, and defence it has made significant accommodations to the initiatives of successive Conservative governments. This shift is a far cry from the complaint of Sir Keith Joseph in the middle 1970s that the Conservative Party had always acceded to the ratchet effect of socialism. Another consequence is that the significant political debates take place within the dominant party. This was true of appeasement in the late 1930s and has been so again in the debate over Maastricht, Britain's membership of the ERM since 1992, as well as the financing of the welfare system.

Analyses of dominant-party systems in other countries suggest that over time interest groups, local government and the civil service gradually adapt to working with the dominant party. Since 1979, Conservative ministers have divided interest groups into the 'acceptable' and the 'selfish', and treated them accordingly. The last group includes virtually all trade unions, particularly those in the public sector, and most groups making a claim on the public purse. The powers of local government have been drastically pruned and the traditional culture of the civil service has been challenged with a view to rewarding these with a more businesslike outlook and managerial and accountancy skills. Quangos or non-governmental organisations have also become more responsive to the government, as their boards are often chosen on quasi-political grounds. In health and education, in particular, the Conservatives have established a range of appointive bodies to implement government policies. It is worth noting, however, that this Conservative dominance since 1979 has been achieved with the support of just over two-fifths of the electorate.

It is understandable, given the traditional British admiration for the two party system, that such a lengthy period of one-party dominance has caused unease. It is worth noting, however, that the dominance of one party has been normal in post-war Japan, West Germany, Sweden and Italy, and for much of the twentieth century in the United States. Critics in Britain might fairly add that in these countries the dominant party usually governs as part of a coalition, or the power of the central government is qualified by a written constitution, separation of powers or federalism, or a mix of all of these. But periods of one party dominance have been more usual in Britain than we think—notably in the inter-war years. Attention has been drawn to the rarity of the electoral pendulum swings among European and Anglo-American democracies. Among 20 of 21 democracies, one party has held power either alone or in coalition for at least two thirds of the post-war period to 1981. The exception was Britain.[7] By 1995, however, that ceases to be the case, for the Conservatives will have reached the two-thirds threshold.

Marginalisation

Graham Wallas's pre-1914 claim in *Human Nature in Politics* that a political party is 'something that can be loved and trusted' reads strangely today, in the light of studies of electoral behaviour, party loyalty, membership, and political values. In some respects the parties may have fewer roots in society today than fifty years ago. In spite of most people now enjoying more affluence, education and leisure, as well as universal suffrage, it is doubtful if the level of public interest in politics (about 15% of people claim to be very interested) or attachment to parties is any higher today than it was when Wallas wrote. The old homogeneous council estates, trade unions, large factories and working-men's clubs—solidly Labour in orientation—have been casualties of social and economic change. Popular identification with the parties has declined. The proportion of voters who identify very strongly or strongly with Labour and Conservative Parties has fallen, from over 40% in 1964 to a quarter today, with the big decline occurring in the mid-1970s. A MORI poll conducted in January 1993 found that only small numbers of people were willing to carry out demanding political activities for the party they supported. For example, only 2% expressed their willingness to canvass by telephone for the party or stop strangers in the street and discuss their party's merits, and only 4% would speak out for it at another party's meeting.

Political party membership has also steadily shrunk over the post-war years. Compared to the 1950s, individual membership in the Conservative Party has fallen to about 500,000 or a third of what it then was, and for Labour it has fallen to 250,000 about a quarter of what it was. Party membership is falling in a number of other countries also, but it has been particularly steep in Britain. The parties do not represent contrasting values or issue preferences among their supporters, In general, there is a widespread agreement among voters of the main parties on many values[8] and a MORI survey in 1988 found that a third of Labour voters held what the researchers regarded as Thatcherite values, and a quarter of Conservatives held socialist values.[9]

Interest groups are reluctant to associate closely with political parties. The trade union connection with Labour has not inspired others to follow it, and group spokesmen are now more likely to seek direct access to government rather than operate through a political party. Similarly, people concerned over a local bypass, school, or housing development, are more likely to work through a pressure group than a party. Some interest groups appear to be better supported and financed than political parties. The parties lack effective control over the mass media; parties cannot purchase broadcasting time; Labour's connection with the *Daily Herald* ended long ago, and all the evidence is that there is no popular market for a party newspaper, as Labour and Conservative ventures in this field have found.

These trends have affected the parties' approaches to electioneering. In particular, campaign managers have had to take account of the following.

- Social change, particularly the growth of a more middle class society and the weakening of the 'simple' working class/middle class split, as a growing number of voters have mixed social class characteristics.
- Changes in the technology of communications, particularly the spread of television, advertising, opinion polling and other tools of market research. For most voters television is the main source of information about politics and they are familiar with consumer goods being advertised on television.
- Political change, particularly the decline in voter's allegiance to the parties and the growth of instrumentalism towards parties.

The parties have recruited technical experts to assist with campaign publicity, media presentation, opinion polling and advertisments. They also place a greater emphasis upon the coordination and orchestration of the parties' communications with the electorate. Much of the leading politician's campaign day—the morning press conference, afternoon walkabout and afternoon and evening rally—is shaped by the requirements of the media, and campaign managers more self-consciously try to set the agenda. Party managers also commission public opinion polls to study the mood of the voters and shape their campaign communications.[10]

To call this process Americanisation is an exaggeration. But the trends do follow, although in a weaker form, what has been happening in the United States. The new methods have been a particular culture shock for Labour. Before 1959 most of the party's leadership knew that it spoke for the working class and knew what that class wanted. Politicians did not need pollsters to tell them. It was their job to lead public opinion. Many in the party were also uneasy about using public relations and advertising, both of which cast doubt on the above claims. The adoption of public relations seems to have been part of a larger agenda to reassure middle of the road voters and financial markets that Labour is a competent party of government and not tied to any class or interest. Not surprisingly the new methods have been opposed by the left.

These trends have meant that the parties are less reliant on local party activists and policy documents for communicating with voters. The key stages in the professionalism of campaigning have been:

1957, Conservative recruit the advertising agency Colman, Prentis and Varley to prepare advertising.
1962, Labour makes intensive use of private polls and begins national press advertising.
1970, Conservative breakthrough in party election broadcasts.
1978, Conservative appoint the advertising agency Saatchi & Saatchi to handle all the party's electoral communications.
1986, Labour Party appoints a Shadow Communications Agency to handle all its communications.

The parties have also become more serious about policy preparation and, again, been willing to look outside for ideas. The post-war political agenda of full employment, welfare, public ownership and fair shares, which prevailed until the late 1970s, could trace its origins to the inter-war years. The so-called Mixed-Economy Welfare-State consensus is often associated with the 1945 Labour government. But many of the ideas were first borrowed from policy entrepreneurs like the Webbs, Beveridge and Keynes. This borrowing has continued. Such post-war innovations as incomes policies, monetarism, opting out of schools from local authority control, student loans, comprehensive education, internal health service markets and budget-holding GPs, and market testing and the agency principle in the civil service, have all developed outside the parties. Of course the party must embrace the idea for it to gain momentum, and to be effective the ideas must address real world problems, be consistent with the value goals of the party and pass the test of administrative practicability posed by civil servants.

Where do ideas come from, if not the political parties? Royal Commissions have been killed off since 1979—Mrs Thatcher regarded them as classic consensus-mongering devices. But in recent years Labour has used a quasi-commission device to handle sensitive topics on constitutional change, electoral reform and the relationship between taxing and public spending. The party's working group on electoral systems, headed by Professor Plant, and the IPPR Commission on Welfare and Social Justice were means of bringing fresh (non-Labour Party) minds to the debate on contentious issues. Think tanks, often drawing on the lessons of foreign experience, have been important in 'thinking the unthinkable', and the Centre for Policy Studies, the Adam Smith Institute and the Institute of Economic Affairs were significant sources of support for Sir Keith Joseph and Thatcherism from the mid-1970s. The Institute for Public Policy Research has played a similar role for Labour. If the immediate post-war agenda was, in significant respects, egalitarian, paternalist and statist, most of the ideas since the mid-1970s have come from the free-market right. They appear to have had a more ready acceptance among the policy-making community than among the public. Public opinion polls suggest that some of the core ideas—more privatisation of services, less public spending on services in favour of tax cuts and less reliance on government action to promote employment—are supported by only a minority of voters.

Life inside the parties

There have been some modest changes within the parties. In 1945 few doubted that the Conservative Party was hierarchical in its organisation. The party leaders made no pretence that its structure was democratic; the party conference was a handmaiden to the leadership in Parliament; and MPs acquiesced in the leader who had 'emerged' as a result of soundings by senior figures (1937, 1940, 1955, 1957). It was the controversial 'emergence' of Lord Home to replace Macmillan in 1963 which discredited that recruitment system. Since then there have been changes, notably the formal election (1965) and re-election (1975) of the leader by MPs. Although Conference does not make policy, it has not always proved to be a deferential body. It has generally voiced populist, authoritarian sentiments, giving Ted Heath difficulties over immigration, John Major embarrassment in 1992 over Maastricht, and it was pressure from the floor in 1987 which led to the introduction of the poll tax in one stage.

In 1945 Labour took pride in being an internally democratic party—in contrast to the authoritian Tory party. It was, for example, pressure from the floor of Conference which resulted in the ambitious national-isation proposals for the 1945 general election. Although the party leader, Clement Attlee, repudiated the instruction of the party chairman, Harold Laski, that he should not accept the King's commission to form a government before the National Executive Committee had expressed a view, it is interesting that Laski was confident enough to issue the instruction. Conference delegates and party leaders all appeared to assume that Conference was sovereign. Hence the explosive impact of Robert Mackenzie's claim in his *British Political Parties* (1955) that the internal relations in the Labour Party closely resembled those of the Conservative Party. In spite of the parties' portraits of themselves and each other, Labour's parliamentary leadership in practice was as autonomous in relation to the external party as was the Conservative leadership. The party's claim that Conference was sovereign was incompatible with the sovereignty of Parliament; the constitutional conventions of collective Cabinet responsibility and ministerial responsibility meant that Labour MPs and ministers could not be instructed by an outside body. The party's claims about inner democracy was a myth or, more brutally, a 'living lie'.

However, the authority of the parliamentary leadership always depended upon the support of the trade union block vote. From the late 1960s onwards, that support was no longer forthcoming and Conference regularly defeated platform. But the Wilson governments between 1964 and 1970 treated Conference cavalierly, its authority declined, and the McKenzie thesis seemed to be confirmed. The job of a Labour government, Wilson lectured Conference, was to govern, and it would not be instructed by any outside body. But the left took its revenge when the party returned to opposition between 1970 and 1974. It increased the power of Conference and the NEC in relation to the Parliamentary Labour Party, forced through radical changes in the party constitution and the PLP adopted left wing policies. The inner-party democracy model was reinstated and the left's power was reflected in the choice of leader and manifesto in 1983. The pendulum swung again after the crushing election defeat in 1983, and Neil Kinnock managed to recover a good deal of authority for the party leadership. Conference and NEC followed the leadership and, where they did not, were ignored. Policy-making power is being transferred from Conference to a Policy Commission in whch front-bench spokesmen in Parliament have the major say. In 1993 the trade unions agreed to reduce their voting strength at Conference and their influence in the selection of parliamentary candidates. Finally, a leadership-initiated policy review after 1987 trimmed back left-wing policies on defence and industrial relations and virtually abandoned public ownership.

Another aspect of McKenzie's thesis has been vindicated. Labour leaders may lead unruly parties but they seem pretty safe from dismissal. Wilson, Callaghan and Kinnock each resigned the leadership in his own time and (apart from the 'gesture' challenge by Tony Benn in 1988) never faced a personal leadership contest. Conservative leaders, however, have had a less certain tenure. Heath and Thatcher were forced out as a result of MPs' votes and Sir Alec's resignation in 1965 was an acknowledgement of the weakness of his position. Before 1940, this had been the experience also of Balfour and Austen and Neville Chamberlain. The possibility of an annual election for the leadership makes any leader feel vulnerable. Conservative leaders may enjoy more power over the party than a Labour leader but their hold on office is less secure.

Parliament is a deeply frustrating experience for some five-sixths of

MPs. At any time a half of the membership belongs to the defeated parties and some two-thirds of the governing party's MPs do not hold office. The House of Commons in recent years has reformed its procedures, introduced specialist committees, improved Members' pay and facilities and probably includes more full-time and career members than ever. But it has failed to dent the government's control over its business. Non-members of the government usually deplore the way in which the executive treats the House—until they are in office themselves. Within the House of Commons there have been spectacular rebellions against Heath, Thatcher and Major. Some commentators have attributed these variously to the arrogance of Heath and Thatcher, the weakness of John Major, and the rise of new and more divisive issues.

But perhaps the animal itself has also changed. If there are fewer aristocrats, old Etonians and knights of the shires on the Tory benches, there are also fewer former trade union officials and members of the working class on Labour benches. MPs are more middle-class, career-minded, and perhaps less willing to follow the party line. In the 1945 Parliament Labour could point to Dalton, Cripps, Crossman, Gaitskell and Attlee as political heavyweights drawn from elite public schools. Conservatives similarly could draw from a social elite, one strongly connected to the Establishment. That is less so today, given the rise of the middle class in both parties. The change may also stem from the way in which the values and procedures of establishment institutions (Church of England, BBC, Oxbridge and the professions) were regularly assaulted by a more market-oriented Conservative government in the 1980s). MPs may now be less deferential to their leaders and more willing to defy the whips. But one needs to keep the rebelliousness in perspective. The discipline imposed by the whips is still important. The average MP defies the whip only once a year in divisions in the Commons.[11] The MP's position is very different from the United States where members of Congress can use their votes, the local media and the resources of Congress to build up a personal electoral support, and be independent of the party and its whips.

There have been some changes in the position of MPs within their parties. Conservative MPs achieved the right to elect the leader in 1965 and then in 1975 the right to elect (and therefore deselect) annually. The withdrawal of support by Conservative MPs in 1922 and 1940 had effectively led to the resignation of the party leader in one case and resignation of the Prime Minister in the other, but they had no say in the sucessor. But MPs now have effectively not only voted out the last two leaders but also elected their successors. The Conservative procedures for leadership election now resemble those of the 'old' Labour party.

Labour has, meanwhile, moved the goalposts again and MPs have lost their exclusive right to elect the leader. As a result of the changes in 1981 to the party constitution, an electoral college of MPs, trade unions and constituency parties now elects the leader. Even though (since 1988) candidates for the leadership have to be nominated by at least 20% of MPs, there is still the potential for a leader to be elected who lacks the support of a majority of MPs. The creation of the college, added to the system of 'open' voting and mandatory reselection of MPs, was a device by the left wing to chastise the parliamentary party. But in another respect MPs have gained. Under the party's standing order, an incoming Labour Prime Minister must choose the Cabinet from those who held office in the Parliamentary Committee (elected by MPs) immediately before the dissolution. And the Cabinet and appointments to junior government posts have to be approved by Labour MPs.

Cause for concern

The two-party system was for much of the post-war period widely regarded as a jewel of the political system. It presented clear choices for the voters, the majority party was able to form a government and implement its programme, and the government could then be held accountable to voters at the next general election. This was responsible government in action and was held up as a model against which the complexities and irresponsibilites of the party systems of continental Europe and the United States were found wanting.

But concern about the negative consequences of the two party system surfaced in the mid-1970s. It was prompted both by the bitter divisions between the major parties and their decline in popular support. Lord Hailsham in *The Dilemma of Democracy* and S. E. Finer in *Adversary Politics* pointed to the undesirable effects of power being wielded by a government backed by less than 40% of the voters. The critique of the party system was of course related to such features as the sovereignty of Parliament and the first-past-the-post electoral system. Critics claimed that what might have been tolerable in the consensual 1950s and 1960s was damaging at a time of the breakdown of consensus, when the parties, driven by ideologically motivated activists, were becoming more extreme. In opposition, each party was committed to radical policies which, in government, it tried to implement but was soon forced by circumstances to abandon or moderate. Massive discontinuity in key policies were a consequence of extremism, more interventionist government and a greater turnover of parties in government.

Another point of view is that British parties actually lack sufficient resources to direct government effectively. Other forces seem to have been more important when it comes to shaping macro economic outcomes, for changes in party control of government have rarely made much difference to the big picture. An examination of such major economic turning-points as the application to join the European Community (1961), devaluation (1967) coping with the public spending and inflationary pressures from the sharp rise in Arab oil prices (1973), International Monetary Fund intervention (1976) and British withdrawal from the ERM (1992) point to the decisive impact of international factors.[12] Limits on the government's autonomy in managing the economy are limits on the party in government.

It is also possible to question the presumed policy strengths of the parties. The Labour Party from 1964 was deadlocked over such crucial issues as incomes restraint, industrial relations and Britain's membership of the European Community. The party's links with the unions and the split between left and right produced something akin to paralysis in some policy areas. The Conservatives since 1979 have also lacked cohesion on the European Community: the issue created Cabinet instability in 1989 and 1990 and among backbenchers since. The sharp contrasts in the programmes adopted by the Labour Party for the 1983 and the 1992 general elections, or the Conservative manifesto in February or October 1974 and that of 1983, show a certain flippancy with regard to policy, one more regularly associated with American parties. Labour's changes reflected the lessons of successive election defeats, public opinion research and the reformism of the party leaders. In the case of the Conservative Party, the changes were driven largely by the new leader. The Thatcher governments demonstrated that governments could change the agenda in other areas—in education, industrial relations, public ownership versus privatisation, and health provision. In retrospect, however, the 1980s may represent less a case of the strength of party government than of Prime Ministerial government.

Concerns over the party system in recent years have concentrated on the lack of competitiveness in the party system; this has prompted renewed concern among commentators and centre-left politicians about the dangers of one-partyism, just as it did in the 1930s. Some of the post-war satisfaction with the British constitution was due to the existence of a competitive party system. A strong opposition and a reasonable prospect of it replacing the government at the next general election provided a sense of restraint on the government and reduced the incentive for the opposition to limit the power of the executive. Both could expect to gain from the electoral system and the sovereign Parliament. But since 1987 many in the Labour Party, disillusioned by the working of the electoral system, have broken ranks and expressed interest in constitutional reforms to limit the executive and the introduction of a more proportional electoral system. The problems posed by the long-standing constitutional imbalance have been compounded in the 1980s by the lack of a competitive party system and one-sided Parliaments. No doubt some part of Labour's interest in electoral and constitutional reform, and support for a larger role for the European Community, is a tactical response to impotence at Westminster.

Conclusion

In Britain it is the continuity in the party system since 1945 which stands out, particularly in comparison with the changes elsewhere in Western Europe. West Germany, Italy and Austria had to invent new party systems after 1945, and a new party system emerged in France after 1958. But in Britain, Labour and Conservative have been the two leading parties in votes and seats in all general elections, as indeed they have since 1922. In the past fifty years there has been no coalition, less than four years of minority government and no significant support for an anti-system party. The social bases of voting have changed, in large part because the traditional contours of social class have changed.

The electoral system continues to be a formidable barrier against a breakthrough by centre or extremist parties. It has reduced the effect in parliamentary seats of the growth in centre-party support. A 4% swing from Conservative to Liberal at the next election would only bring the Liberals an extra 14 seats. At the same time, Labour strongholds, particularly in the north, protect the party's parliamentary strength, even if there is a sharp fall in its vote. Earlier commentators noted how many European party systems had been 'frozen' since the granting of universal suffrage, as the parties socialised new voters into allegiance.[12] In Britain, for all the weakening of the class bases of voting and the rise of considerable support for the centre, there has been no realignment.[14] The electoral system has been important not so much in political socialisation but in political engineering.

There are always dangers in extrapolating from the present. After Labour's third successive election defeat in 1959 there was much discussion along the lines of 'Can Labour Win?' and 'Must Labour Lose?'. In both cases the answers were broadly pessimistic. Social and cultural changes, particularly 'embourgeoisement' in the working class, seemed to be weakening Labour's long-term prospects. But Labour after 1959 won four of the next five general elections, *Political Change in Britain* showed how in 1969 the combined effects of political socialisation and demography (notably the larger size of the working class) were weakening the position of the Conservatives. Labour was the 'natural' majority party.[15] The Conservatives, however, won the 1970 general election. Since 1983, the view has developed that the forces of demography and party identification now make the Conservative Party the natural majority party. Calculations of the voting effects of the decline of the working-class and trade-union membership, growth of house ownership (all anti-Labour) and the growth of ethnic groups and secularism (both pro-Labour) indicate a net gain for the Conservatives of 2.7% and a fall of 4.5% for Labour. The outcomes of the 1987 and 1992 elections did not dent that view.[16]

What of the future? One prospect is for Conservative dominance to continue, a situation which allows for occasional non-Conservative governments. There may be swings of the pendulum, in which long periods of Conservative rule are punctuated by brief spells of Labour government. After all, something similar has happened this century. For reasons already discussed, the most likely alternative to a Conservative majority in the near future appears to be a hung Parliament. Conservative dominance is likely as long as the party has a 40–42% 'lock' on the electorate and some 55% of the electorate divides between Liberal and Labour. Such a situation might force some tactical cooperation or an arrangement even more far-reaching between the Labour and Liberal Parties. A problem with this strategy is that surveys have long shown that the second choices of Liberal supporters are evenly divided between the Conservative and Labour Parties, and Lib and Lab voters may not agree with the deals arranged by the leaders. Social change is, if anything, helping the Conservative Party and working against Labour. At the next general election Labour will need a 4.2% swing from 1992 to secure an overall majority, a higher swing that it has achieved in any election since 1945. Labour may be running up a downward-moving escalator.

Electoral reform would be a lever for change in the system. At present, reform is not in the interest of the Conservative Party and the leadership is adamantly opposed to change. Labour is divided between those who think that the party is unlikely to get a majority again and those who believe in 'one last heave'. If electoral reform comes, it will ironically be passed by a House of Commons elected under the present system. But this would almost certainly require a Lab-Lib majority in the Commons. The most likely consequence of proportional representation is the end of one-party majority government.

Where else, then, might change come from? One possible avenue of change might be a split in the government party. Historically, this has been the main means through which changes in the party system has been achieved. The Conservative split over the Corn Laws in 1846 and tariffs in 1903; the Liberals over Ireland in 1886 and again in 1916. In each case, the divided party was punished electorally and spent a considerable time out of power. Historically, it has usually been Britain's external relationships—Ireland, India, the retreat from Empire and now Europe—which has proved most troublesome for Tory party managers.

1 There is some controversy over the decline of class voting. See the exchange between A. Heath et al, 'Trendless Fluctuation: A Reply to Crewe', *Political Studies*, 1987, and I. Crewe, 'On the Death and Resurrection of Class Voting', *Political Studies*, 1986.

2 P. Norris, *British By-Elections* (Oxford University Press, 1990).

3 R. Rose and I. McAllister, *The Loyalties of Voters: A Lifetime Learning Model* (Sage 1990).

4 M. Steed and J. Curtice, Appendix in D. Butler and D. Kavanagh, *The British General Election of 1987* (Macmillan, 1987)

5 R. Rose, 'Structural Change of Electoral Fluctuation', *Parliamentary affairs*, 1992.

6 M. Abrams and R. Rose *Must Labour Lose?* (Penguin, 1960).

7   M. Punnett, *Alternative Governments: The Inefficient Secret of British Politics?* (Centre for Study and Public Policy, University of Strathclyde, 1981).

8   R. Rose and I. McAllister, *The Loyalties of Voters*, A. Heath et al, *Understanding Political Change* (Pergamon, 1991) ch. 11.

9   R. Worcester, 'Polls Apart', *New Socialist*, Summer 1988.

10   D. Kavanagh, *The Professionalisation of Campaigning: Polls, Advertising and Media*, forthcoming.

11   R. Rose, 'British MPs: More Bark than Bite' in R. Rose and E. Suleiman (eds), *Parliaments, Parliamentarians and Democratic Politics* (Holmes and Meier, 1986).

12   R. Rose *Do Parties Make A Difference?* (Macmillan, 1982).

13   S. Lipset and S. Rokkan, *Party Systems and Voter Alignments* (Free Press, 1967).

14   P. Mair, 'Myths of Electoral Change and the Survival of Traditional Parties', *European Journal of Political Research*, 1993.

15   D. Butler and D. Stokes, Political Change in Britain (Macmillan, 1970).

16   A. Heath et al, *Understanding Political Change* (Pergamon, 1981).

The Cabinet System Since 1945: Fragmentation and Integration

TODAY, of course, we have a huge advantage. In 1945, unless you were either a government minister or a pretty senior civil servant, you could have virtually no idea of what went on in the Cabinet room. Ministers did not leak much, and the general assumption was that what went on there was rightly confidential.

There was a literature, of a kind. Ivor Jennings' magisterial *Cabinet Government* expounded the principles of government in pallid, mechanistic terms, but gave little sense of the reality behind the forms: an author who declares 'Conflict between the Prime Minister and a colleague is a rare occurrence' has, to put it politely, a chilly political touch. Laski had written a bit, and there had even been a rather vapid discussion of the idea propagated by Leo Amery and Clement Attlee (separately) that an inner Cabinet was needed because the scope of government had broadened beyond the Cabinet's grasp. Otherwise, there was little: Bagehot was still a key text (granted, he still repays reading today) and not the least of his observations that still held true in 1945 was 'The most curious point about the Cabinet is that so very little is known about it'.

Today, evidence is not the problem. In 1992 the government made public some of the inner workings of the Cabinet system. We have ministerial diaries, a voluminous 'grey literature' of speeches and articles by participants and—often at a lower level of accuracy—leaks and ministerial memoirs. In our era it is rather analysis that is scanty, with few up-to-date books on the Cabinet and none on the Prime Minister.

What has changed behind the circumspect façade of No. 10? 1945 was one of the big dates in the history of Cabinet government, when Attlee decided to transplant into peacetime government the committee system that had been necessary to run the war. The growth of those committees has combined with ministers' increasingly heavy workloads to cause a discernible fragmentation of the Cabinet system, raising question marks over the collegial nature of central government, the purpose of the Cabinet and the role of the Prime Minister.

Cabinet committees

Before the second world war, committees had been rare beasts. The Committee of Imperial Defence dated from the turn of the century and

© Oxford University Press

its clerks had elaborated an extensive network of sub-committees. A committee on future legislation existed in some form throughout the inter-war period. Otherwise committees were occasional, transient bodies, set up to address a passing issue and then allowed to lapse. A few, notably on India and foreign policy in the 1930s, achieved some longevity, but up to 1939 ministers spent little time in committee.

Total war changed that. Between 1939 and 1945 the Cabinet Office serviced some 400 committees, which between them held over 8000 meetings.[1] Had Churchill won the 1945 election, he might have tried to dispense with them (he made a brief and fruitless attempt to do this in 1951). As it was, the practical Attlee perpetuated the system. He and his colleagues had become used to working through committees in the wartime coalition. It mirrored the way the Labour Party and trade unions ran their affairs, and it was an efficient means of implementing their massive programme of reform. The essentially Gladstonian system that had served Mr Baldwin's modest purposes could never have coped with the task of reconstruction, economic management and inauguration of a welfare state. Committees have been with us ever since: in the words of *Questions of Procedure for Ministers* to 'relieve the pressure on the Cabinet itself by settling as much business as possible at a lower level'. Mrs Thatcher disclosed in 1979 the existence of four main committees—foreign and defence, economic, home and social, and legislative—and these, with their attendant sub-committees, form the core of the committee system whose composition and membership was finally made public by John Major in 1992.

As pressure of work has caused committees to proliferate, increasingly they have taken decisions on their own authority, without seeking Cabinet ratification and often not reporting their deeds to it. Indeed, appeals to Cabinet by ministers defeated in committee increasingly came to be seen as something of an imposition on its time: Wilson introduced a rule in the 1960s forbidding appeals unless the committee chairman agreed to them, and the current version of *Questions of Procedure for Ministers* warns: 'If the ministerial committee system is to function effectively, appeals to Cabinet must clearly be infrequent. Chairmen of committees are required to exercise their discretion in advising the Prime Minister whether to allow them. The only automatic right of appeal is if Treasury ministers are unwilling to accept expenditure as a charge on the reserve, otherwise the Prime Minister will entertain appeals to the Cabinet only after consultation with the Chairman of the committee concerned.'

Furthermore, over time there has been further and deliberate downward pressure on the level at which decisions are taken. The volume of business has grown to such a degree that it is now a working presumption that ministers should not only avoid taking to Cabinet what can be settled at committee but avoid taking to committee issues that can be settled by discussion between ministers. In particular, a convention of clearance by correspondence has grown up, under which a minister initiating a proposal writes to interested colleagues—usually the other members of the relevant committee—with a copy to the Cabinet office (which tracks all important decisions) and perhaps to No. 10. If there is no significant dissent, the proposal goes ahead.[2]

Much of the policy decided in this way will be fairly minor, and *Questions of Procedure for Ministers* still requires that ministers bring to committee 'questions which significantly engage the collective responsibility of the government, because they raise major issues of policy or because they are of critical importance to the public' and 'questions on which there is an unresolved argument between departments'. Nonetheless, a lot of business is cleared by correspondence; this device has become a significant part of the Cabinet machinery.

The consequence of these changes, then, is that the term Cabinet government can no longer be taken literally: at the centre of government there is rather a Cabinet system, a highly articulated but diffuse organisation of which the Cabinet is only the pinnacle.

The problem of fragmentation

Fragmentation through committees. As ministers have been forced increasingly to resort to the use of committees, a partial fragmentation of the Cabinet system has become apparent. This phenomenon can be detected in an impressionistic sort of way in the diaries and memoirs of ministers from the 1960s and 1970s: for example, Michael Stewart confirmed that, as Foreign Secretary, he saw far more of the Prime Minister, the Defence Secretary and the Chancellor than of other colleagues, and he clearly did not see much of economic or social affairs. This fragmentation is confirmed by an analysis of the Cabinet committee memberships published by the government (using the February 1994 edition). Harold Wilson makes it clear that in his administrations, while most members of a committee were chosen because they had a departmental interest in the business under discussion, he also appointed members to give the committee political balance, so that it reflected the shades of opinion in the Cabinet. By the end of the Callaghan government, Shirley Williams was serving on some twenty committees, most of them covering issues outside her departmental remit.[3] Today, that does not seem to happen: ministers are almost invariably allocated to committees on a functional basis, attending only those directly relevant to their departmental business.

This has two effects. Firstly, ministers only get to discuss a proportion of government business. The February 1994 list contains 27 committees. Of these, four are made up mainly of junior ministers and two others—on legislation and the Queen's speeches—deal essentially with process rather than policy. Of the remaining 21 committees, the number on which each Cabinet minister serves is:

Chancellor of the Exchequer	14
Foreign Secretary	13
Home Secretary	13
President of the Board of Trade	13
Environment Secretary	12
Chancellor of the Duchy of Lancaster	11
Chief Secretary to the Treasury	11
Defence Secretary	10
Transport Secretary	10
Leader of the Commons	9
Prime Minister	9
Employment Secretary	8
Leader of the Lords	8
Northern Ireland Secretary	8
Welsh Secretary	8
Education Secretary	7
Minister for Agriculture	7
Health Secretary	5
Social Security Secretary	5
National Heritage Secretary	3
Lord Chancellor	1

From this simple listing it would be misleading to draw conclusions about the relative roles of individual ministers within the committee system. The figures are distorted by the greater use of small, specialist committees in the overseas field; they also fail to reflect the frequency with which committees meet. They conceal the fact that, since the Treasury must be represented on almost all committees, the Chancellor of the Exchequer and the Chief Secretary box and cox; and that the Prime Minister, although he attends only nine committees, is kept in touch with developments in other spheres by the Cabinet Office. The Leaders of the Lords and Commons are more important players than the simple listing would suggest, since between them they chair ten committees. For all the limitations of this breakdown, however, one fundamental point is obvious: ministers on average attend less than nine committees, which makes them an active party to only a proportion of collective decisions.

Furthermore, the pattern of membership suggests a Cabinet fragmenting into three policy areas. Committees tend to operate in one of three broad policy spheres: overseas and defence policy, economic and industrial issues, and home and social affairs. Ministers tend to serve on committees in only one or two of these spheres and see little of the issues being discussed in the others. Of the 21 committees covered in the list above, 18 can be categorised in one of these three spheres. The committees on public spending (the famous 'EDX'), science and technology, and public sector pay, by the nature of their subject matter cut

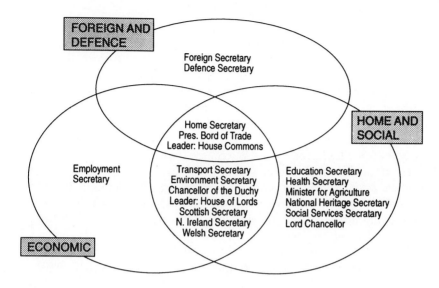

Figure 1

across these boundaries. Omitting the Prime Minister and Treasury ministers, for the reasons given above, the pattern is shown in graphic form in figure 1.

There is relatively little overlap between the overseas group of committees and the other two spheres (for simplicity, the presence of some domestic ministers is omitted in the figure from two committees whose business touches on refugees and economic aid). There is more substantial overlap between the economic and home spheres, since six ministers serving on economic committees also serve on many home committees. Nine members of the Cabinet serve exclusively (or near-exclusively) in one sphere: the Foreign and Defence Secretaries in the overseas sphere; the Health, Education, Agriculture, Social Security and National Heritage Secretaries and the Lord Chancellor in the home affairs sphere. There is a noticeable overlap between committee memberships in the economic and home affairs spheres; seven ministers serve on committees in both: the Transport, Environment, Welsh, Scottish and Northern Ireland Secretaries, the Leader of the Lords and the Chancellor of the Duchy of Lancaster. As to the rest, the President of the Board of Trade, the Home Secretary and the Leader of the Commons serve on committees across all three spheres: in the case of the first two, although most of their committee memberships are explicable on functional grounds, there is probably in some cases an element of 'ad hominem' appointment, given the seniority of the ministers involved (Michael Heseltine and Michael Howard).

Circumstances combine to discourage a minister engaged mainly in one sphere from showing too much of an interest in another. Indeed, a minister might even come to the conclusion that he has only a limited right to express an opinion on issues in a sphere in which he attends no committees. For example, when in 1966 the Cabinet discussed proposals to keep a military presence east of Suez and to buy the F-111 aircraft, Crossman recorded: 'It soon became clear that all the details were now cut and dried . . . so the whole thing was fixed. All Cabinet could do was express opinions and influence to some extent the general tone of the white paper by drafting amendments. Of course there were some ministers like Barbara Castle who took up postures of protest. But the rest of us felt that there was nothing we could do and that the procedure under which we had been excluded was not unreasonable. Fourteen of our twenty-three members of Cabinet are members of the Cabinet committee. To the preparation of this white paper this fourteen had devoted nineteen meetings and two Chequers weekends. After all this, it was natural enough that they should expect Cabinet to give formal authorisation to the recommendations that they had worked out.'[4]

This should not be exaggerated. It would be false to say that the Health Secretary has no right to speak on overseas affairs, or that the Defence Secretary may not chip in on housing or agriculture if the mood takes him. But circumstances combine to reduce a minister's opportunities to comment on developments in other spheres, to discourage him from intervention and, as practice solidifies into convention, to assume that his right to intervene is attenuated.

Ministerial overload. This significant, if often overlooked, fragmentation of the Cabinet system is abetted by other factors. One is the ever-growing burden of business on ministers. It is a commonplace observation that British ministers are grossly overworked. The interminable treadmill of meetings, policy discussions, paperwork, legislation, press interviews, Cabinet and Committee meetings, visits to Brussels, parliamentary questions, speeches around the country and party duties imposes on them a workload that the private sector would baulk at. Wilson reckoned that the economic traumata of the 1970s increased ministerial burdens by between 30 and 50%. The load on ministers is a problem highlighted by successive studies, including the original 'Next Steps' report by Mrs Thatcher's Efficiency Unit.

Which leaves ministers still in the position described in Barbara Castle's diary for Wednesday, 20 December 1967. At a time when departmental business might be expected to be winding down for Christmas, she spent until 2 a.m. that morning working on a speech for the second reading of the Transport Bill; then attended Labour's National Executive Committee at 10 a.m., prepared her parliamentary questions while the speech was being typed; then delivered it to the Commons.[5] Seen in this context, it becomes easy to sympathise with her complaint, 'How does one solve the problem of finding the time to equip oneself to be a fully effective member of Cabinet? I work sixteen to seventeen hours a day non stop and there is still not enough time.'

Expectations of ministers. There are other reasons for this departmental parochialism. There are the dynamics of departmental life: officials, who naturally are unconcerned with matters outside their own sphere, preoccupy their ministers with departmental problems, crowding out broader issues. As Barbara Castle complained in a lecture to civil servants in 1973: 'You control every single ten-minutes of the minister's day and night. I would have to plead with my private office to get half-an-hour with my constitituency secretary.'[6]

There are also psychological and political reasons. Ministers are, as a matter of occupational preference, absorbed in the affairs of their own department. An all too rare survey of ministers in the 1970s showed that they perceived their main duties as being departmental and parliamentary: of the 50 surveyed, only 19 mentioned representing their department's interests at Cabinet level, and only five mentioned participating in Cabinet debates as an 'all rounder'. Anecdote and the content of diaries and memoirs confirm this deliberate self-absorption in the affairs of the department.[7] And in the eyes of the public and backbenchers, ministers are first and foremost Secretaries of State for this or that: their political success will be judged primarily on their impact on their home ground. This is particularly true of ministers newly appointed to the Cabinet, who have been given their first chance to prove themselves; but it can never cease to be true of any minister. Ambitious politicians will therefore see Cabinet and its committees primarily as battlefields where they must fight their own corner and defend their budget. The Agriculture Secretary will gain little credit for showing interest in electric cars or north sea oil, nor does the Employment Secretary gain much from demonstrating a mastery of immigration law or export credit guarantees.

These pressures do not cause the Cabinet system to come apart at the hinges but there is, inevitably, a loss of articulation and a diminution of collegiate spirit. The sense of joint commitment to a policy must inevitably be attentuated if members of the government begin to drift out of touch with policies outside their 'sphere' even though, formally, they remain collectively responsible for them.

The impact on the Cabinet

What has been the impact of committees on the Cabinet itself? Ever since it took a recognisably modern form in Victorian times, it has never been able to discuss more than a few of the current main items of government business. As the scope of state activity has grown, so the proportion of business discussed at Cabinet has proportionately diminished; and since the second world war all but a tiny proportion of decisions have been taken by individual ministers, by correspondence, or by committees. What business, then, does the Cabinet transact, and to what extent is that business effectively 'precooked' in committee?

From 1945 until the arrival of Mrs Thatcher, Cabinet meetings followed a standard format: first came a standing item on parliamentary business, under which the Leaders of both Houses would detail business for the following week; then a report on overseas developments, in which the Foreign Secretary sketched out the dominant issues of the moment. The rest of the agenda consisted of items referred up by committees. Occasionally these came because, although the committee supported the proposal unanimously, the issue was so important that it was felt Cabinet should look at the subject. But in most cases ministers had disagreed at committee and the chairman had allowed an appeal. Most of these appeals were straightforward arbitration exercises: the ministers who had argued the issue in committee would rehearse their cases, and in effect appeal to the judgement of their colleagues who had not been there and who were asked to screen the proposal, not from an expert point of view but for its good sense and public acceptability in a sort of political litmus test.

Although the Cabinet's court of appeal role gave it a say on some key decisions, the system had serious faults. The Cabinet became almost entirely reactive to the proposals of ministers and committees. There was little discussion of general political developments. There was no item of 'any other business' to allow discussion of other issues that might be worrying ministers. The Cabinet's role was essentially negative: it could block, amend or qualify proposals, but of itself did not inititate policy. It was a brake, not a dynamo. Furthermore, by the time an issue reached it, it had often gained irreversible momentum. Hailsham observed, after serving under Macmillan and Heath: 'The ground has usually carefully been prepared by discussion between civil servants, correspondence between ministers, in formal meetings, Cabinet committee meetings ... By the time the Cabinet is brought in as a whole, it may be that only one decision is possible even when, had it been consulted at the outset, the policy would have been unacceptable.'[8]

There were occasional instances of the Cabinet holding broader discussions. Wilson occasionally hosted all-day sessions at Chequers to discuss particular issues—notably EC membership—although he was careful always to take any conclusions back to a regular Cabinet meeting for ratification. Under Heath, the Central Policy Review Staff treated the Cabinet every six months to a review of overall government strategy. The Cabinet sometimes held political sessions, with officials absent, in the run-up to general elections. But these were exceptions (and infrequent at that) to the basic rule that it did to hold broad discussions of general policy issues.

So, as the post-war epoch progressed, much of the initiative and energy in the Cabinet system passed to committees, the more so since in the 1960s Wilson reduced meetings from two a week to one. And there developed a natural reluctance to see a subject reopened once it had been painstakingly agreed in committee. Increasingly in the 1960s and 1970s ministers came to regard the Cabinet as a forum to be informed of action taken but which should not necessarily question a decision within the remit of one of its committees. Indeed, for all that Mrs Thatcher's detractors bewailed the loss of collegiality in her administrations, it was a principle frequently breached by her predecessors. Sometimes they had bounced the Cabinet into decisions; often issues had been managed by secret committees. Barbara Castle's diaries record that for years Wilson prevented his Cabinet from discussing Rhodesia and devaluation; similarly the head of Callaghan's policy unit recalls his Prime Minister running economic policy through a secret committee called 'the seminar'.

Mrs Thatcher took matters further. Well advertised in the press at the time, and confirmed by participants as diverse as James Prior and Cecil Parkinson, was the overt downgrading of the collegiate ethos of the government. In the early years, Mrs Thatcher's Cabinet included many who disagreed with her economic and social views. She countered their opposition by moving the fight to different battlefields. Her Cabinet met less often, and those meetings were brief. Often, major issues never went to Cabinet or, if they did, were presented as decisions taken by committees in which it was invited to acquiesce, preferably without argument. Appeals from committee became infrequent. Even when the dissident wets left the government, Mrs Thatcher perpetuated this new dispensation. By the mid-1980s, hers was a government of Cabinet committees. The decline was not absolute: there were some classic, serious Cabinet debates — over Prior's proposals for a Northern Ireland Assembly, on public spending, on the Falklands expedition. But by the middle of the decade Sir Geoffrey Howe could openly acknowledge that 'There are very few discussions of government decisions by full Cabinet',[9] and commentators had begun to speculate whether the Cabinet had become, like the Privy Council, a decorative vestige, a 'dignified part of the constitution'.

The role of the Prime Minister

Oddly, these postwar upheavals have made comparatively little difference to the Prime Minister's job. They have not changed what might be termed the Prime Minister's key organisational duties, those tasks necessary to keep the mechanics of government running: appointing and removing ministers, ensuring that they observe the obligations of collective responsibility, and reporting on the conduct of the government to the monarch. His additional function of appointing Cabinet committees and chairing them, or appointing chairmen, is an extension of his function of chairing the Cabinet and ordering the distribution of functions between ministers: a different way of doing the same things.

Nor, broadly speaking, has there been any change in the Prime

Minister's national political role, at least as it impinges on government. The advent of television may offer the opportunity to project a more forceful image, but it offers opportunities to other ministers, and exposure to what Churchill mistrusted as 'that pitiless, probing eye' can be as damaging as it is advantageous. Nor has the Prime Minister's relationship with his party changed very much: indeed, it is one of the surprises of the British system that once a party takes office, its party organisation has minimal influence on government policy. Instead, the impact of the fragmentation of the Cabinet system lies in the three other main facets of the prime minister's functions: his duty to cultivate collectivity; his duty to provide strategic leadership to his government; and his ability to intervene in any policy issue that he chooses.

The myth of presidentialism. At this point it is necessary to clear out of our path the debris of the most misleading and yet tenacious theory to have been propounded about post-war Cabinet government: the argument that the Prime Minister has effectively become a president. This simplistic allegation was propagated in 1963 by Richard Crossman in his introduction to Walter Bagehot's *The English Constitution*, and was elaborated rather more subtly by Professor John Mackintosh in *The British Cabinet*. The gist of the argument was that the Prime Minister had become the focal point of public attention and governmental power. He was effectively irremovable. He hired and fired ministers, dominated Cabinet by determining its agenda and formulating its decisions, created and dissolved committees and chose their chairmen. He controlled the civil service, patronage and publicity. Other ministers' desire for office was so great that they would be reluctant to stand up to him.

Crossman made his claim against the background of the skilful exploitation by Macmillan and Wilson of television and the institution of Prime Minister's Question Time. In the absence of much evidence to the contrary—sources were meagre at the time—the theory took hold. On the academic plane, George Jones methodically demonstrated Crossman's theory to be simplistic and unreal, and the outpouring in the 1970s and 1980s of memoirs and diaries—not least Crossman's own—provided ample evidence that the truth was more subtle. But the myth obstinately survives in popular consciousness, and the personal ascendancy of Mrs Thatcher gave it a powerful fillip.

In a way, Crossman did Cabinet studies a favour by jolting the subject out of the dull rut in which it was lodged. But he damaged the subject by his simplistic generalisations: not only did he give public currency to a caricature of presidentialism that persists stubbornly today, but on the academic plane he muddied the waters. His flimsy arguments were so thoroughly exploded by his critics that the debate passed over the genuine point that the Prime Minister's influence over policy was greater than the legalistic textbooks of, say, Jennings, allowed.

Furthermore, Crossman laid out a restricted framework of analysis that constrained the debate for years to come. His critics set about refuting his arguments point by point (can the Prime Minister keep an issue off the cabinet agenda indefinitely, can he appoint and dismiss at will?) while implicitly accepting his basic premise that the Cabinet can be analysed in terms of a power struggle between Prime Minister and colleagues. The assumption, rather like the premise of mercantilist economics, was that there is a fixed amount of power and that there is a constant striving for this commodity between the Prime Minister and his colleagues.

This is untrue. Power may not be easily amenable to analysis, but it is a more subtle and elusive concept than this approach allows. And ministers do not, in practice, behave like that. For all the rivalries within any government, on matters of broad principle and gut instinct ministers are actually on the same side. They belong to the same party and share a fundamental core of beliefs. They are held together by a strong sense that 'you hang together or hang separately': the existence of an predatory alternative government on the opposition benches is a constant impetus to unity. And if ministers happen not to care for the Prime Minister under whom they serve, it still beats being on the backbenches.

Indeed, collegiality is an essential element of Cabinet government, and one of the Prime Minister's main duties is to cultivate a collegiate sense among his colleagues. The doctrine of collective responsibility holds all ministers jointly answerable for government decisions: if they are required to justify their colleagues' policies to the public — especially to their own constituents — ministers will want to have a say in at least the more important of government decisions. The Prime Minister, for his part, might superficially be expected to prefer a system with weak collegiality: it favours policy devised by a departmental minister and cleared bilaterally through No. 10, rather than through Cabinet and committees. But if ministers collectively are cut out of decisions, they can apply subtle and damaging sanctions: coded dissent, as practised by the 'wets' against Mrs Thatcher; mutinous silence, such as Lawson's refusal to defend the community charge (poll tax); leaking to the press; and, if matters become intolerable, explosive resignations like those of Heseltine and Howe. Failure to cultivate a sense of collegiality amongst her ministers was a substantial factor in the downfall of Mrs Thatcher, and it is significant that after her fall all three contenders for the succession committed themselves to what they described as the true traditions of Cabinet government.[10]

The leadership function. For all that, there is a strong expectation from both public and ministers that the Prime Minister should give strong leadership. Few Prime Ministers can be expected to be like Mrs Thatcher, but they are expected to give coherent shape and purpose to the government's efforts, just as Heath gave, first to the drive for free-market economics and, after his U-turn, for reflation and intervention. If the Prime Minister does not lead, ministers are critical. In his brief premiership, Douglas-Home failed both to give definite direction to the government or to tackle live problems such as profiteering by land speculators. An anonymous colleague at the time observed: 'When ministers discovered he really wouldn't do it, they began to huddle with each other, little groups of major figures. You would get from them enough agreement or accommodation to produce the main lines of a government position, something they could try to steer through Cabinet. Or if you couldn't get it, there was nothing to be done.'[11] Equally damaging was the paralysis of indecision that seemed to overcome Callaghan at the height of the 'winter of discontent'.

This is not to say that ministers crave leadership at any cost. It must be exercised within the parameters of political tolerability. The Prime Minister will not win any friends if he tries to lead ministers in a direction in which most of them do not wish to go: for instance, Wilson accepted the urgent need for an incomes policy by late 1974 but acknowledged that he could not hope to persuade the Cabinet—or the rest of the labour movement—of this necessity until an acute crisis made it unavoidable. Leadership is also more effective if exercised with tact and good humour. Eden's jittery meddling and Mrs Thatcher's famously peremptory manner irked their colleagues needlessly; the avuncular Callaghan and the deceptively relaxed Macmillan probably got more out of their ministers with less effort.

Leadership is not confined to the strategic plane; it extends to specific important issues of policy. One of the Prime Minister's most significant powers is his ability to intervene in any policy issue he chooses: asking questions, offering suggestions, suggesting that a different option be explored, or warning that this option is politically impossible. Such 'suggestions' cannot be ignored by ministers. Indeed, on the big issues, the Prime Minister is expected to get involved, as Attlee did over Indian independence, Wilson in innumerable strikes and Mrs Thatcher over the Falklands. The relationship between the Prime Minister and the minister in charge of the departmental policy can be tricky, however. A Prime Minister needs strong and capable ministers in those departments which he sees as crucial to the government's success. Weak ministers are a drain on his time: they need to be propped up, cosseted, and on occasion hauled out of the pits that they dig for themselves. The presence of a weak or inept minister debilitates the government and, by extension, the Prime Minister—as witness, for instance, the mess that Shinwell made of the 1947 fuel crisis.

Instead, the Prime Minister needs capable colleagues upon whom he can rely to give him good advice, run the department without gaffes, alert him to any impending problems, accommodate his suggestions if possible, stand up to him when necessary, and generally not make a mess of it. The minister, in return, needs Downing Street's consent, support and trust to see through his policies and, in moments of adversity, needs to be able to invoke the Prime Minister's support. The relationship between Castle and Wilson revealed in her diaries is a good example of this type of working alliance.

Problems arise, of course, when a Prime Minister and a strong minister end up at loggerheads over a policy. It will happen occasionally: any Prime Minister worth his salt will come up with his own views on policy, and decisive ministers will have independent viewpoints. If departmental ministers dig in their heels the Prime Minister, who will always have other fish to fry, will need to weigh the drawbacks of a row—he cannot afford to undermine good colleagues—against the importance he attaches to getting his way in this instance. So Mrs Thatcher, in her first year in office, was obliged by her Home Secretary to abandon immigration quotas and a register of immigrants' dependents, by her Foreign Secretary to abandon support for the Muzorewa regime in Southern Rhodesia, and by her Energy Secretary to drop plans to privatise the British National Oil Corporation.

Prime Ministers need to be particularly cautious because, although ministers will be wary of sticking their necks out on matters outside their own department, the possibility of defeat on their own ground may be countered by a threat of resignation. Since 1945 the most notable resignations—and, more numerous, threats of resignation—have come from ministers protesting at a reversal of their own departmental policy.

The frequency of such conflicts is reduced by the Prime Minister's control of the allocation of portfolios; he is not likely to appoint to a sensitive post a colleague with whom he knows he is likely to end up frequently at loggerheads. Colleagues' seniority and party standing limit quite severely a Prime Minister's discretion to determine who joins the Cabinet and who stays out, but the power to decide who fills which post offers rather more discretion. For example, Mrs Thatcher was at pains to keep the key economic ministries in the hands of those who shared her views. When a minister persistently opposed her instincts, he was removed: the most blatant example of this was Prior's replacement at Employment by Tebbit.

This discretion may be less when dealing with the most senior two or three members of the Cabinet, who can more or less insist on one of the top jobs. For something like two-thirds of the postwar era, the Exchequer and the Foreign Office have been held by party magnates who were effectively irremovable. Once someone has reached that level in the Cabinet, there are few other places to which they can be transferred. For instance, once Mrs Thatcher fell out with her Chancellor, Lawson, and her Foreign Secretary, Howe, in 1989, she found Lawson 'unassailable' (her term) and only with inordinate difficulty persuaded Howe to move to the leadership of the Commons. In effect, the Prime Minister may find that on foreign and economic affairs—which absorb the majority of his time—he is dealing with colleagues he would not necessarily have chosen for the job, while in other key

	Weak Collegiality	Medium Collegiality	Strong Collegiality
Strong Leadership	11 Thatcher	1 Eden 2 Wilson 1964-1966	6 Macmillan 4 Heath 3 Callaghan
Medium Leadership		4 Wilson 1967-1970	4 Churchill 6 Attlee 2 Wilson 1974-1976
Weak Leadership			1 Douglas-Home
	Weak Collegiality	Medium Collegiality	Strong Collegiality

Figure 2

departments he will be dealing with colleagues who are likely to be in tune with his thinkings.

Leadership versus collectivity. Should we deduce from this that there is a conflict between the Prime Minister's need to give leadership and his duty to maintain collegiality? There is an obvious tension between the two, as Mrs Thatcher's government showed, but they are not incompatible. The relationship, together with the duration of each Prime Minister's tenure of office, is shown in figure 2.

This is very much a freehand exercise, dependent as it is on this author's historical assessment. It aggregates Prime Ministers' characteristics both over time (except for Wilson, who clearly passed through three distinct stages) and over all policy spheres. Only broad conclusions can be drawn from it, but it does suggest quite strongly that a simultaneous combination of medium to high levels of collegiality and leadership has been the predominant characteristic of the postwar era. A low level of leadership is rare: its only exemplar is the ill-starred Douglas-Home government. Generally, a low level of collegiality is politically intolerable: the only example of such a trend is the Thatcher government, and her admirers and detractors alike will concede that there was something wholly exceptional about Mrs Thatcher's premiership. And although she got away with it for an exceptionally long time, her neglect of collegiality was one of the reasons for her downfall. A combination of weak leadership and weak collegiality is unknown (indeed, such a combination cannot be discerned in any government since the preposterous Rosebery administration).

Forces for integration

In the face of the strong forces working against collegiality—fragmentation into a committee based system, ministers' preoccupation with their departmental work, the potential tension between collegiality and prime ministerial leadership—what are the forces that hold the system together?

There are certain institutional forces. The entire administrative apparatus of Whitehall acts in a sense as a centripetal force, especially central agencies like the Cabinet Office and organised networks like the weekly meeting of Permanent Secretaries. But there is a limit to what institutional arrangements can achieve: the Central Policy Review Staff, created to brief the Cabinet as a whole, lasted little more than a decade, and its briefings for the Cabinet on overall government strategy were abandoned after only three or four years.

More potent is the political will of Prime Minister and Cabinet colleagues. Despite all the forces discouraging ministers from involving themselves in issues outside their immediate remit, there is a recognition that if ministers are to be shackled to collective responsibility, they must have some opportunity to discuss the more important government initiatives. Nigel Lawson records that at the Cabinet meeting at which he resigned over the Westland affair, Heseltine declared that he was not bound by collective responsibility because Mrs Thatcher had not allowed a proper collective discussion of the issue. This, and the debacle that ensued, is a cautionary tale to Prime Ministers that the enforcement against ministers of the rule of collective responsibility implies an obligation on the Prime Minister, as coordinator of government business, to ensure that colleagues are consulted, at least on major issues.

The revival of the discursive Cabinet. In the mid-1980s, as the debate on the Cabinet's seeming debility was well under way, ministerial interest in broader policy issues was given an outlet. Perhaps in reaction to the Westland affair (the timing is unknown), the Cabinet's role was altered by a change in its agenda. As described above, its decision-making function had diminished further under Mrs Thatcher and appeals from committee had become rare. But quite early in her premiership Mrs Thatcher had supplemented the oral reports on foreign and parliamentary affairs with a regular slot for European Community affairs. Since these matters now bulked so large in governmental life, this merely formalised a developing practice. But, far more significant, in the middle of the decade home affairs were added as a further oral item. Home affairs are usually the most politically lively issues the government faces, and this allowed a discussion in which, in Nicholas Ridley's words 'one could raise any matter that troubled one, or that one thought one's colleagues should know about'.[12] It strengthened the cabinet's influence on current political developments and held out the prospect that the Cabinet might come to hear about issues earlier than was previously the case. Major has retained this arrangement.[13]

Even when the Cabinet acted primarily as a court of appeal, pressure of time prevented it from considering more than two or three issues a week, and these had been predigested at length in committee. In its new guise, as a sounding board for a whole range of government policy, its role is widened. Its more flexible agenda allows ministers to bring up matters that concern them at an early stage rather than wait until the point at which policy has developed to a point at which it is irreversible. And the new arrangements are not only a logical consequence of devolution to committees but are also a reversion to a much older tradition. Today's Cabinet now resembles the Cabinets of the nineteenth century, in which ministers met as a group of political colleagues to discuss the issues of the moment, not often promulgating decisions as such but shaping the development of policy.

The 'inner circle'. The other factor which may, to a degree, act as a collegiate force in the Cabinet is the existence of an inner circle of ministers who share with the Prime Minister the taking of key decisions and formulation of a strategic impulse for government policy as a whole. This should be distinguished from an inner Cabinet. A formally constituted inner Cabinet has flitted only once across the Whitehall landscape since the war: Wilson, amid much publicity, set one up in the late 1960s, but to judge by ministerial diaries it was a toothless seminar that talked much and decided little—another product of Wilson's love of gimmickry.

Instead Prime Ministers—whose eminence is, after all, rather lonely—tend to share their burden either with one or two trusted colleagues, or with an inner circle of senior colleagues. Churchill had cronies; Mrs Thatcher had a series of single confidants—notably Parkinson and, later, Tebbit—while Heath leant on the official William Armstrong. But there is a discernible pattern of inner circles: Attlee's consultations with Bevin, Cripps and Morrison; Eden's informal talks with Macmillan, Salisbury and Butler; the flexible grouping—always including Butler—with whom Macmillan discussed matters before they came to Cabinet; the troika of Wilson, Brown and Callaghan in Wilson's early premiership; and in Callaghan's government his reliance on Foot, Healey and—to a lesser extent—Rees. If newspaper reports are to be believed, a similar group has existed since Major took office, including Hurd, Heseltine and Clarke.

What do such groupings do? This will depend on the circumstances of the moment and the personalities involved—especially the Prime Minister's sense of self-reliance. But as a general rule an inner circle will discuss the main issues of the day, do some of the fixing and dealing necessary to keep any government working, and give some strategic shape to the government by thinking ahead and pulling together the strands of policy. If a Prime Minister feels the need to discuss policy with such groupings of colleagues, it is out of respect for their standing, or because he values their judgement.

Given the privacy of their work, the extent to which such groups counteract fragmentation is not easy to gauge, but potentially it must be significant. They must at least have the capacity to act as a sounding board for the Prime Minister's ideas; to sound warning bells about misgivings amongst their colleagues; and to act as intermediaries and allies when the prime minister faces his full Cabinet. Nigel Lawson reckoned that if Mr Thatcher had gone through with her professed intention to create a group, of this kind in 1986 it would have restrained her from becoming domineering and isolated in her final years.[14]

Conclusion

The tensions remain. Some element of conflict between central leadership and collective management is inevitable in any organisation whose ultimate power is vested in a collegiate body, be it a company board or a public authority. Within the Cabinet system the problems of excessive workload and the need for delegation to committees are unlikely to be reversed; the consequent fragmentation seems set to remain a permanent feature of the system. The mid-1980s change in the Cabinet's agenda — and the profound consequences of this on the Cabinet's modus operandi — is a substantial institutional change that entrenches collegiate practice; the intermittent phenomenon of the 'inner circle' of ministers reinforces this to some (immeasurable) extent. But in the end, governments must rely on the personal characteristics of the Prime Minister for a regime that reconciles leadership with collectivity. For the past half century, despite moments of danger under Mrs Thatcher, Prime Ministers contrived to do this, however irksome it has proved; the price of collegiality, as seen from No. 10, is eternal patience.

Simon James is author of *British Cabinet Government* (Routledge, 1992).

1   S. Wilson, *The Story of the Cabinet Office to 1945* (HMSO, 1975).
2   Lord Wakeham, 'Cabinet Government', lecture at Brunel University, 10 November 1993.
3   S. Williams, 'The decision-makers', in Royal Institute of Public Administration, *Policy and Practice* (RIPA, 1980), p. 87.
4   R. Crossman, *Diaries of a Cabinet Minister: Minister of Housing 1964–66* (Hamish Hamilton and Jonathan Cape, 1975)(, pp. 455–6.
5   B. Castle, *The Castle Diaries 1964–70* (Weidenfeld and Nicolson, 1984), p. 324.
6   B. Castle, 'Mandarin Power', *Sunday Times*, 10.6.73.
7   B. Headey, *British Cabinet Ministers* (Allen and Unwin, 1974), pp. 58–60.
8   Lord Hailsham, *The Dilemma of Democracy* (Collins, 1978), p. 206.
9   *Daily Mail*, 6.2.84.
10 *The Times*, 23/27.11.90.
11 R. Neustadt, 'White House and Whitehall' in A King (ed.) *The British Prime Minister*, (Macmillan, 1985), p. 165.
12 N. Ridley, *My Style of Government* (Hutchinson, 1991), p. 30.
13 Wakeman, op. cit.
14 N. Lawson, *The View From No. 11* (Bantam, 1992), pp. 128–9 and 680–1.

Parliament, Ministers and the Law

BY DAWN OLIVER

ONE of the major developments over the fifty years since the Hansard Society was formed to promote the study of parliamentary government has been the growing recognition of the limitations on the ability of Parliament to control government. This has spawned a succession of attempts by the House of Commons to increase parliamentary influence over government, for example through Richard Crossman's reforms of the select committees of the House of Commons from 1966–68 when he was Leader of the House, and the St John Stevas reforms establishing departmental select committees in 1979. Recognition of the limitations of parliamentary control and the weaknesses of the conventions of individual ministerial responsibility (and other conventions) has also led to a search for alternative, non-parliamentary methods of improving the quality of government, both in order to improve policy-making and to provide enhanced redress of grievance mechanisms for individuals affected by government activity. One of the resources that has been employed has been the law.

This sense that alternatives are necessary and Parliament cannot, unaided, control government has led to important measures to develop alternative or complementary statute-based systems of control in the years since 1945. For example, a system of tribunals has been established to hear appeals from decisions by officials relating to the eligibility for and calculation of the amount of welfare benefits. Inquiries which report and tender advice to ministers are now a well-established means of investigating proposals for land development and such matters as disasters and scandals. The Parliamentary Commissioner for Administration may inquire into complaints of maladministration in government. The office of Comptroller and Auditor General and the setting up of the National Audit Office represent improved mechanisms for monitoring public expenditure by central government and its offshoots.

This article focuses on the increased role that the law has come to play in the control of government in recognition of the limitations of the conventions of individual ministerial responsibility in providing a system of control. Its concern is with a triangular relationship between Parliament, ministers and the law.

Ministerial responsibility

In the immediate post second world war period much faith was put in individual ministerial responsibility to Parliament, both by Parliament itself and by the courts. Indeed, recognition of its importance goes back to Dicey's *Introduction to the Study of the Law of the Constitution*, published in 1885, and even before. In the Crichel Down affair in 1954 the House of Commons seemed to affirm the importance and assume the effectiveness of ministerial responsibility as producing a system of control of both ministers and the civil servants in their departments: Sir David Maxwell Fyfe, the Home Secretary, laid down the then understood convention that 'Where an official makes a mistake or causes some delay, but not on an important issue of policy, and not where a claim to individual rights is seriously involved, the minister acknowledges the mistake and he accepts the responsibility although he is not personally involved. He states that he will take corrective action in the department'. But 'Where action has been taken by a civil servant of which the minister disapproves and has no previous knowledge, and the conduct of the official is reprehensible, there is no obligation on a minister to endorse what he believes to be wrong or to defend what are clearly shown to be errors of his officers. He remains however, "constitutionally responsible to Parliament for the fact that something has gone wrong" but this does not affect his power to control and discipline his staff'.[1] The point is that at the time of Crichel Down the position set out here seemed to be perfectly satisfactory. If there were not alternatives or complementary mechanisms to ministerial responsibility in the 1990s to deal with errors by civil servants, the position would be regarded as entirely unsatisfactory. (In that affair, the minister resigned when an inquiry by Sir Andrew Clark QC found that there had been muddle, inefficiency, bias and bad faith on the part of officials in his department. But there were suggestions that the minister himself knew about some of this maladministration, and he was not prepared to abandon the unpopular departmental decision, and this personal involvement probably accounted for the resignation.)

Looking back over ministerial resignations and ministerial failures since then, we can now see that there is no obligation to resign even if the minister is personally at fault or his own policy is shown to have been defective. Whether a minister resigns has more to do with the support he has from the Prime Minister and colleagues in government, his own sense of honour, the question whether he has lost credibility and whether he is an embarrassment to his party and government than with any clear 'obligation' to do so.[2] Theoretically, there remains a duty on ministers to explain and justify departmental actions when questions are asked and to make amends when errors are disclosed but in practice this duty is often unenforceable politically — and it has been delegated, for example to Chief Executives of Next Steps agencies.

The courts and ministerial responsibility

In the post-war period the courts accepted ministerial responsibility as a constitutional principle which, because it was widely assumed to be effective, provided a justification, though not the only one, for non-intervention by the courts in alleged mismanagement—to use a neutral term—by ministers and civil servants. There were a number of cases to this general effect in the late nineteenth and early twentieth centuries, but the most famous is the now notorious case of *Liversidge v. Anderson* ([1942] AC 206). A minister had made a detention order under the wartime Defence (General) Regulations 1939 in respect of a person whom he said he had reasonable cause to believe to be of hostile associations. The detainee asked the court to order that the minister could not make such an order unless he had objectively reasonable cause for his belief. A majority of the Law Lords hearing the case found in favour of the minister, giving weight to the fact that he was responsible to Parliament—and, incidentally showing deference to ministers which it would be rare to find nowadays. Lord Macmillan emphasised that the statute had authorised the emergency power of detention to be conferred upon a Secretary of State 'one of the high officers of State who, by reason of his position, is entitled to public confidence in his capacity and integrity; who is answerable to Parliament for his conduct in office'. In a famous dissenting judgment which would now be regarded as reflecting more accurately the attitudes of judges to arguments such as those advanced for the minister, Lord Atkin insisted that the words 'if a man has reasonable cause' do not mean 'if a man thinks he has reasonable cause'. He accused the rest of the court of being 'more executive-minded than the executive' and found for the detainee.

In this wartime and post-war period not only did the courts hold back from supervising exercises of ministerial powers—unless they were plainly illegal—but there was generally a low level of statutory regulation of government conduct. Many of the powers of government were exercised in the name of the Crown, a constitutional abstraction which generates—or generated—a sense of the awesome dignity of the constitution and so deflects thought of legal regulation. The Crown possesses extensive residual common law powers that have not been conferred by statute and are not regulated by statute either. Many of these are known as 'prerogatives' and include, for example, the power to conduct foreign relations, to conclude treaties that are binding in international law, and prerogatives of mercy and pardon. The Crown also possesses legal personality and is thus able, without identifying a statutory basis or complying with statutorily-imposed procedures, to make contracts, acquire and dispose of land and so forth as ordinary individuals can. Here a contrast can be drawn with local authorities which are creatures of statute and do not possess these powers of general competence because they have not been granted in any of the Acts of Parliament which regulate local government. It was—and is—convention, custom and convenience rather than law which regulate matters internal to the Crown such as relations within the Cabinet, relations between government departments and most aspects of relations between ministers and civil servants. Conventions rely for their efficacy on an accepted political ethos. There are, as will be seen, signs that such an ethos is no longer strong.

The need to rely on convention, custom and convenience rather than law to regulate these relationships is partly due to the fact that the Crown is unitary, so that its different components can not have formal legal relationships with one another or contract with themselves. There are—until recently secret—guidelines about these matters, such as the *Questions of Procedure for Ministers* and the Osmotherly rules (*Memorandum of Guidance for Officials Appearing before Select Committees,* 1980) which lay down that civil servants appear and answer questions on behalf of and at the direction of ministers and not independently. These matters are regulated by law only to the extent that the Official Secrets Acts of 1911 and 1989 and the law of employment and confidentiality impose duties of obedience and non-disclosure on civil servants.

The power to order and reorganise the civil service derives either from the royal prerogative or the normal powers of a body recognised by law to enter into employment relations. It is detailed by Orders in Council, but these leave much leeway to ministers. It is this 'flexible friend' that has been used to establish Executive Agencies in the civil service and various other innovations over the years. All of this without the need for recourse to Parliament or law.

It is still the case that the exercise of ministerial powers is not subject to extensive and explicitly legal regulation, although the position has changed in important ways over the years. There was, and there still is, a presumption that statutes do not bind the Crown or, in contemporary terms, the government. But most statutes are expressed to bind the Crown. Until the decision of the House of Lords in *M* v. *Home Office* ([1993] 3 WLR 433) ministers could not be held to be in contempt of court if they disobeyed court orders. But a series of important Acts of Parliament since the 1940s has substituted statute-based, legal regulation of government for reliance on parliamentary control through ministerial responsibility in important areas of activity.

Legislating for the control of government

The introduction of the welfare state has necessitated giving officials the power to make decisions about entitlements to the social rights it involves. A gradual process has taken place since the late 1940s by which decisions of government and of civil servants have been placed under a greater degree of legal regulation than previously. Earlier mention was made of the system of tribunals separate from the Crown to deal with appeals against decisions by civil servants in government departments about eligibility for and size of award of welfare benefits or to promote government policy on rent control and employment protection. Dealing with this sort of grievance could have been left to MPs to raise in Parliament and internal complaints procedures within departments. But it was clearly preferable to provide a set of specialist, conveniently accessible, independent, informal and cheap tribunals to deal with such matters and this was done.[3] Parliament could not itself have dealt with the volume of cases generated by welfare state provision. Its role in dealing with such grievances was relegated to one of last rather than first or only resort.

With the need to regulate land development and to deal with matters of major public concern about the environment or disasters, a system was built up for the use of public inquiries to act as the eyes and ears of ministers before decisions about planning permission and controversial developments were to be authorised (e.g. the third London Airport, Sizewell B nuclear power station); and provision has been made for appeal against ministers' decisions on these matters to the courts, on grounds of illegality or failure to comply with procedural requirements. Again, technically these decisions could have been made by a minister subject only to a duty to account to Parliament, but this was not considered appropriate for many reasons, including the limited time available to Parliament and the level of expertise required for the decision to have a rational basis. It is significant that the solution to this problem has been a procedural one. Ministers must follow a procedure before making a decision, and thereafter a procedure is available for the courts to review it for legality and procedural propriety.[4]

A series of landmark statutes has incrementally increased the level of legal regulation of government activity. The point about statutory provisions is that they provide more clear cut limits to ministerial powers than the common law recognition of prerogative powers or legal capacities can do; they provide criteria against which action is to be judged; they may impose liability to civil or criminal proceedings where none existed before; and they may provide the procedures which must be followed before the powers in question may be exercised. Some examples will make this point. Until the Crown Proceedings Act 1947, the Crown — ministers in modern terminology — could not be sued for breach of the ordinary law of tort (negligence, for example) though individual civil servants could be. By that Act, liability in tort was extended to the Crown. The Interception of Communications Act 1985 put the authorization of telephone tapping for purposes such as the detection of crime on a statutory footing. Hitherto, an informal system operated under which the Home Secretary or the Attorney General authorised phone tapping by the police.

Other aspects of government activity which were until recently beyond reach of the courts, and also of Parliament, include the Security and Intelligence Services and General Communications Headquarters (GCHQ). In response to public pressure, the Security Service was put on a statutory footing by the Security Service Act 1989. At the time of writing, the Intelligence Services Bill is before Parliament which also puts the Intelligence Services on a statutory footing with some interesting new, hybrid, quasi-parliamentary controls. A Committee of nine members drawn from the House of Commons or the House of Lords is to be appointed by the Prime Minister; they will be removable in effect by the Prime Minister after consultation with the Leader of the Opposition (this is an interesting example of the statutory recognition of the existence of an Opposition with a leader, and gives statutory expression to what would otherwise be a convention).

The committee will report to the Prime Minister (the reverse of the orthodox position) who will lay the report before Parliament, subject to the right to omit certain sensitive material. It will examine the expenditure, administration and policy of the Security and Intelligence Services and GCHQ—which is what parliamentary select committees usually do. This is a veritable hybrid.

In each of these areas the mode of control of the exercise of power had, prior to legislation, been the development of internal or semi-independent systems of control within government and ministerial responsibility to Parliament. In each instance it had come to be recognised that ministerial responsibility was not a sufficient check against abuse of power and more formal, though imperfect, controls were introduced. But, typically for the United Kingdom, an incremental, trial and error approach has been taken to dealing with these problems.

The redress of grievances

Procedures for the redress of grievance have been considerably formalised in a legal framework in the last thirty years or so. Traditionally, the House of Commons has had an important role in securing the redress of grievances for citizens. The idea that the King or government should deal with and redress grievances before the Commons would consider a request for 'supply' was reflected in the House of Commons' Standing Orders providing for Supply Days on which the opposition could raise grievances, until these were replaced by less picturesque sounding Opposition Days in the 1980s. But by the 1960s it had become obvious that Members of Parliament could not, by invoking ministerial responsibility or flexing their muscles on Supply Days, effectively secure redress for individual constituents who had grievances. So in 1967 the Parliamentary Commissioner Act established the Parliamentary Commissioner for Administration, commonly known as the Ombudsman or the PCA.

The PCA has the right to investigate complaints of 'injustice in consequence of maladministration' and to recommend remedies such as the making of ex gratia payments to individuals if their complaints are upheld. In passing the Act, Parliament was careful to maintain the House of Commons' function in redress of grievance and required aggrieved individuals to refer their complaints first to an MP: MPs alone have the right to refer matters to the PCA. The latter reports to a House of Commons Select Committee for the PCA, which has the role not only of monitoring his performance but also of supporting his (they have all been male) recommendations and pressurising ministers to accept and implement them. But the point for this article is that the legislation placed the redress of grievance system in part at least on a statutory footing, recognising that MPs could not unaided secure remedies for grievances and giving an independent official a role in the process. But at the same time it maintained the parliamentary link. The courts have been involved very little in this process, though they have been willing to intervene in a few cases to ensure that the PCA acts lawfully in deciding whether or not to accept a complaint for investigation. (The system was extended to the National Health Service under the Parliamentary and Health Services Commissioners Act 1987.)

European Union law

The effect of membership of the European Community—or Union since 1993—on the regulation of ministerial activity and the operation of ministerial responsibility is profound. The passing of the European Communities Act 1972 gave legal effect to the United Kingdom's membership of the European Communities as from 1 January 1973. The 1972 Act has since been supplemented by the European Communities (Amendment) Act 1986 and most recently the European Communities (Amendment) Act 1993, which gave effect to the Treaty on European Union (Maastricht Treaty). The significance of this is, first, that it placed government policy and action in the sphere of Community activity—mainly in 1973 to do with trade and competition matters—under the jurisdiction both of the UK courts and of the European Court of Justice at Strasbourg. It expanded greatly the areas of government action subject to legal regulation, in particular in the field of contracting or procurement in which, as indicated above government, has been substantially entitled to the same freedom of action as individuals.

European law also, of course, limits the freedom of member states and their governments in economic, commercial and even political fields in order to facilitate the creation of a single internal market and ultimately a political union. In practice, it is not possible to isolate commercial from political matters and so, for example, passport controls within the Union are being dismantled. And under the Treaty on European Union political rights are to be extended to nationals of member states residing in the Union outside their own states: they and their family members will be entitled to vote in local government and European Parliament elections, for example.

European Community law places on governments of member states the duties to give effect to Community law, and it gives rights to individuals affected by government failure to implement Community law to have it enforced and obeyed. This has resulted in, for example,

Acts of Parliament being held to be unlawful (see the *Factortame No. 2* case, [1991] 1 AC 603 on the registration of fishing vessels, and the *Equal Opportunities Commission* case, March 1994, on part-time workers). Governments of member states are exposed to being sued for damages if they do not give effect to European directives which are sufficiently precise in their wording to give rise to a cause of action for an individual who would have benefited if the directive had been properly implemented. The former freedom of governments to push through their parliaments any legislation they wished has been substantially limited by membership of the European Union, and the liability of governments to other governments and persons whose interests are damaged by breach of Community Law (in the European Court of Justice and their own courts) is a strong incentive to implement that body of law. Ministerial responsibility—political pressures on government via Parliament (or from other sources)—is not surprisingly regarded by the European Court of Justice as insufficient safeguard of the due performance of the obligations of Union membership and hence the law—the European rule of law—has come to play a central role.

And, finally in this brief consideration of the impact of membership of the European Union on Parliament and ministerial responsibility, the Single European Act of 1986, the 1993 Act and the Maastricht Treaty impose decision by majority voting in the Council of Ministers in many areas for decision, with the result that British ministers cannot be held 'responsible' by Parliament for decisions in the Council which they were not in a position to veto, as was previously the case.

The House of Commons and legislative control

The House of Commons itself has been instrumental, and even taken the initiative, in some of the reforms to the accountability of government through legislation. Here it has insisted on a parliamentary link, thus maintaining a degree of ministerial responsibility. The National Audit Act of 1983 placed the audit and control of public expenditure on a more secure statutory basis, making the Comptroller and Auditor General an officer of the House, independent of government and enjoying security of tenure. He reports to the Public Accounts Committee of the House of Commons, and he and the National Audit Office have coercive powers and access to documents in the course of their work of investigation. This Act represents a triumph by the Treasury and Civil Service Committee and the Public Accounts Committee, who combined to press the government to make provision for better parliamentary scrutiny of public expenditure. Eventually, a backbench MP introduced a bill which the government reluctantly took over, and which emerged from Parliament as the National Audit Act.

Sunlight is a powerfully effective disinfectant. Under Section 2 of the Official Secrets Act 1911 it was an offence for anyone to disclose, without authority, any information at all about central government.

Only ministers could authorise disclosure and they defended this position on the ground that it would undermine their responsibility to Parliament if information could be disclosed by others—civil servants, for example, or other individuals who came by it. This is but one example of the excessively secretive nature of British government and the way in which ministerial responsibility to Parliament can be invoked to avoid control rather than to promote it.

Section 2 of the 1911 Act came into increasing disrepute in cases such as *Ponting* and *Tisdall,* and in others where harmless but embarrassing information had been disclosed by civil servants and they were prosecuted. Finally, under pressure, the government introduced the Official Secrets Act 1989: this decriminalises the disclosure of information without authority save in specified circumstances, mostly to do with defence and national security. But, very importantly, it does not itself authorise disclosure of any information and it does not touch non-criminal legal sanctions against disclosure of information by ministers and civil servants or even sometimes third parties who come into possession of government information without authority. So the terms and conditions of service of civil servants still require non-disclosure of 'official information' and the common law rules relating to confidentiality forbid disclosure of confidential information. And the government continues to claim the right to 'public interest immunity' in respect of documents it does not want disclosed in court proceedings—the matter at the heart of the Scott inquiry into the Matrix Churchill case.

Finally in this review of legislation to enhance the accountability of government by putting it on a legal basis, the Supreme Court Act 1981 put the jurisdiction of the courts in judicial review of the public activities of public bodies or of the exercise of public functions—often, therefore, affecting government—on a statutory footing, endorsing reforms to procedure that had been introduced by Rules of the Supreme Court in 1977. These provisions simplify the procedure of the application for judicial review in some respects and enhance the powers of the courts in relation to procedural matters.

The Supreme Court Act provides a convenient link with the next part of the article, which is concerned with the steps taken by the courts in the exercise of their inherent common law powers to enhance the legal control of government. But before passing on to that topic some general comments need to be made about the way in which Parliament—sometimes at the instance of government but more frequently in response to other pressures—has progressively increased the statutory regulation of government powers. It would be wrong to assume that the landmarks identified in this process in this part of the article mean that there is now anything like a satisfactory system of legal regulation of government. The royal prerogative, which empowers government to act in many important areas such as defence, foreign policy, treaty making, the granting of pardons, the granting of passport and many aspects of the management of government, remains largely unregulated by statute. Ministers possess many of the powers of 'natural persons', notably powers to make contracts for the supply of goods and services to departments and the public, and (subject to certain requirements of European law relating to the fairness of the procurement process) these powers are still largely unregulated. The Acts referred to above are subject to strong criticisms in many important respects which cannot be explored here. But the point remains a valid one, that there has been a process of subjecting government to statutory controls in the last fifty years or so, and that this has taken place largely in response to the realisation that other methods of control — ministerial responsibility to Parliament are ineffective and inappropriate in modern conditions.

Some of the more important reasons for this search for alternatives to parliamentary control are: the need for specialists and experts to monitor government in a way that the MPs can not do; the immense increase in government activity which an overloaded Parliament can not scrutinise; a changing political culture which is no longer deferential to government; and a degree of breakdown in the comity between the political parties that used to act as a brake on some government excesses (this was particularly acute in local government in the 1980s which saw considerable statutory regulation of political relations and reduction of discretion in local government). And of course the operation of the party system, producing the well-known phenomenon of the 'elective dictatorship', which marginalises opposition MPs and undermines Parliament's ability to exercise independent control over government.

Parliament, ministers and the courts

To consider the changing attitudes of the courts to the efficacy of ministerial responsibility as a check on government, and the part that they have played in the last forty or fifty years in promoting good government or protecting the individual against encroachments by government, it is necessary to return to *Liversidge* v. *Anderson* (1942), the low-point in judicial deference to ministers and ministerial responsibility. The Law Lords were probably influenced by the fact that the country was at war and concerns about national security. But it is at those times that individuals most need legal protections against arbitrary state action.

At that period, the only generally recognised ground on which the courts could review the acts of ministers and other public bodies was that it was unlawful, and this was conceived as a technical question of statutory interpretation. Since then, and particularly from about 1964, the courts have become increasingly willing to 'review' the decisions of ministers and other public bodies on a broader range of grounds. Grounds now include, as well as illegality (which is now more broadly construed), breach of procedural requirements for fairness when individuals are adversely affected by a decision, and 'irrationality', which includes the decision-maker being influenced by irrelevant considerations, failing to take into account relevant considerations, acting unfairly or frustrating legitimate expectations.

The grounds for judicial review are not codified and it is not easy to paint an accurate picture of the range of cases in which the judges are willing to quash a decision, requiring the minister or other decision-maker to reconsider the matter in accordance with the requirements of the law. Broadly, the courts will intervene if the way in which a decision was made breaches rules of fairness and rationality, but they will not interfere on the merits — they will not quash a decision just because they consider it unwise or wrongheaded. Fairness includes duties, depending on the circumstances, to give those affected by decisions an opportunity to put their own views before they are made, sometimes a duty to give reasons for decisions, duties not to act in a discriminatory way, to consult, not to bring illegitimate pressure to bear on individuals or punish people who have done nothing wrong. Irrationality includes acting in breach of accepted moral standards or being influenced by party political considerations such as seeking to avoid embarrassment in Parliament.

From time to time the judges are pressed to accept arguments on behalf of ministers to the effect that it would be inappropriate for the courts to exercise their supervisory jurisdiction in judicial review because the minister is accountable to Parliament or because Parliament has expressed a view on the matter. In some recent cases the courts have refused to quash as irrational a ministerial decision made under a regulation that had been laid before Parliament, on the basis, in effect, that it is unlikely that Parliament would authorise irrational decisions or alternatively that ministers are accountable to Parliament and this is sufficient check against abuse. Perhaps the real reason has been a desire not to find Parliament itself irrational for fear of breaking the truce with it which is discussed briefly below.

Among the unspoken assumptions in these arguments are that ministerial responsibility is (a) effective and (b) more appropriate than judicial review. The courts are now less willing than they were in *Liversidge* v. *Anderson* to accept ministerial responsibility as an effective check on government. In *R* v. *Parliamentary Commissioner for Administration, ex parte Dyer* ([1994] 1 A11 E.R. 375), the judge observed that 'many in government are answerable to Parliament and yet answerable also to the supervisory jurisdiction of this court.' As the role of the courts has developed, it has become clear that legal accountability and ministerial responsibility operate according to different criteria and are suitable in different situations and for different purposes, though both may apply to the same set of facts. A minister who disobeys the law may face trouble in Parliament both because he has been found to act unlawfully and on the ground that he acted unwisely or oppressively.

A quite different aspect of the relationship between the courts and Parliament is to do with the courts' willingness to take account of proceedings in Parliament and to regard these as relevant to their decision whether to exercise their supervisory jurisdiction. There has been a longstanding truce between Parliament and the courts under which the latter will not question proceedings in Parliament, accepting that it is mistress of its own procedures. This goes back to the Bill of Rights 1689 and to a series of conflicts between the courts and Parliament in the nineteenth century (for example, *Stockdale* v. *Hansard* in 1839). So the courts will not listen to arguments that an Act should not be given effect because Parliament did not follow the correct procedure in the course of its passage, or that Parliament was misled about the effects of its legislation (*Edinburgh and Dalkeith Rly* v. *Wauchope* in 1842; *Pickin* v. *British Railways Board* in 1974).

The courts have recently tried to buttress Parliament against government when deciding how to interpret statutes that are ambiguous, obscure or even absurd if given their natural meaning, by modifying their previous unwillingness to have regard to parliamentary proceedings. In *Pepper* v. *Hart* ([1992] 3 WLR 1031) the House of Lords was concerned with a taxpayer who complained about the way in which a perk or fringe benefit had been treated for tax purposes. He was a schoolmaster at a fee-paying school and his children were being educated there at a much reduced fee on the basis that the marginal cost to the school of educating them was small. The Inland Revenue sought to tax him as if he had received as part of his salary the whole of the cost of educating each child, roughly the full fee, less the small contribution he was making. The point that troubled the court was that while the bill in question was being read in the House of Commons, the minister had made a statement that teachers in this position would be treated as receiving only a small benefit and would thus be taxed lightly. The majority in the House of Lords broke with established case law and decided that it was legitimate to look at *Hansard* to discover the intention of Parliament, and thus they could take into account minister-ial statements made to Parliament about the government's understand-ing of the meaning of clauses in bills.

One implication of this decision is that the courts are more astute to find Parliament's true intention in applying statutes, a position which, it might be assumed, should enhance the influence of Parliament. But in practice it may mean that ministers will make a point of either saying nothing or putting their own views plainly to Parliament in the hope that this will in due course carry weight in court. (It would also increase the costs of litigation because litigants or their advisers will have to look up ministerial and even other statements in *Hansard* and Standing Committee proceedings, which are not at all accessible.)

Government and Parliament

What are government's own perceptions of the difficulties in control-ling its activities and its attitudes to the respective roles of Parliament and the law in imposing controls? A number of statutory provisions which replace ministerial responsibility or supplement it with a statutory framework, and the possibilities of judicial supervision or remedies have already been noted. Most of these have come on to the statute book in the face of opposition by the government of the day, and this explains many of the exceptions and limitations which have been introduced by it into the provisions, designed to mitigate the effects for government of being subjected to legal control.

A set of reforms to government operations that is currently being introduced merit — all too brief — consideration. Under the 'Next Steps' initiative in the civil service the greater part of civil service activity is being placed under Chief Executives in Executive Agencies. The Citizen's Charter initiative of 1991 seeks to give individual 'customers' of government and other services rights to complain and a set of expectations about such matters as the time within which applications for benefits or hospital appointments should be dealt with, together with the promise of lay adjudicators to deal with complaints independently (the first one, the Revenue Adjudicator, was appointed in 1993). The *Open Government* White Paper of 1993 establishes an informal framework of 'rights' of access to information, and the right to complain to the Parliamentary Commissioner for Administration (via an MP) in the usual way if access is refused and this refusal is alleged to involve maladministration (see earlier discussion). And the market testing of government services seeks to determine whether they could be provided better and more economically by the private sector.

A number of points emerge from this set of initiatives. First, none of them raises issues about the quality or merits of ministerial decision-making; they are concerned with the activities of civil servants. How do they affect ministerial responsibility? The government insists that the convention remains unaffected by the Next Steps initiatives. But the reality is that grievances are almost always addressed by the individual or the MP to those in the Executive Agency who are charged with complaints procedures and ultimately the Chief Executive before they will be substantively dealt with by the minister. In practice, ministerial responsibility will be a last resort.

Although it is not openly admitted to be a departure from the normal operation of ministerial responsibility, the appointment of the Revenue Adjudicator represents an acknowledgement by government that recourse to the department (the Board of Inland Revenus is a quasi-independent non-ministerial department) or to the PCA, with its tie with ministerial responsibility, is ineffective. The appointment seeks to plug this gap by introducing a degree of independent non-parliamentary accountability. In effect changes such as these do undermine ministerial responsibility and they leave — or expose — lacunae in accountability whch need to be plugged.

Secondly, these 'reforms' in public administration have almost without exception been implemented without resort to legislation, so they maintain the old tradition of preference for non-legal methods of control of government. They all implicitly acknowledge the deficiencies of ministerial responsibility in the old-fashioned sense as a means for controlling government. They provide alternatives but do not seek to give them new teeth. Quite the reverse.

Ministerial responsibility, it is suggested, has become a governmental defence against accountability instead of a weapon against government and a mechanism for accountability. Civil servants remain for the most part anonymous, without personal responsibility to members of the public with whom their departments deal or, most importantly, to Parliament and its select committees. They can never express their own views about government action, for which ministers alone are 'responsible'. Nor do ministers have to answer questions about these matters, because they are Members of Parliament and MPs cannot be compelled by select committees to answer questions. Hence Parliament encounters barriers against the effective investigation of areas of government activity because of the doctrine of ministerial responsibility and its flip-side — parliamentary government.

Parliament is effectively excluded from input into decisions about how government is to operate. For example, the Executive Agencies' framework documents, which lay out the policy they are to implement, are drawn up in a process of negotiation between Chief Executives, the Permanent Secretary of the department and the minister. Parliament has no input into their content at all. They are not laid before Parliament and Parliament does not have the right to comment, or to reject — or accept — them. Nor does it have a role in identifying functions which may be suitably transferred to Executive Agencies or in approval of the terms of appointment of Chief Executives.

The Public Accounts Committee, the Treasury and Civil Service Committee and the departmental select committees may decide to inquire into the performance of Agencies under the framework documents and this may lead them to question the practicability of the content of those documents. But the House of Commons has no input at all into their content, no say over who is appointed as Chief Executive, no role in any board or consultative body to whom the Agencies are accountable apart from the select committees of the House, whose functions are general. They have had no influence in the drawing up of the Citizen's Charters, no say on market testing and none on the *Open Government* White Paper.

Parliament, in sum, has virtually no role in important questions about the design of the machinery of government. Nor does the law. These subjects are conceived by the Conservative Party and often by the public as managerial rather than constitutional or democratic in nature. This is not surprising to those who are accustomed to the modus operandi of British government, but a Martian landing in the United Kingdom on a whistle-stop tour of advanced democracies would notice stark differences between our way of doing things and how things are done in, for instance, New Zealand, the United States or Sweden.

Thinking the unthinkable

A picture of ministerial responsibility as an ineffective check on government or method for the redress of grievances has been sketched. Moreover, statutory and judicial regulation have evolved largely in response to the perception of the weaknesses of the traditional mechanisms. Yet ministers and MPs cling to the idea that ministerial responsibility is crucial to the constitution. It is suggested that the time has come to dare to think the unthinkable and accept that ministerial responsibility can only offer a marginally effective, last resort, solution to problems of bad government. Indeed, it actually inhibits the targeting of criticism and thus enables bad government and bad decision making to be perpetuated.

We need to face up to the fact that alternatives are needed, are possible, are being devised and could be developed, as far better checks on government than ministerial responsibility can ever be. This is not to argue for an end to parliamentary government (though the Liberal Democrats' 1993 paper *Here We Stand: Proposals for Modernising Britain's Democracy* suggested relaxing the requirement that all ministers be members of one or other of the Houses of Parliament: perhaps even this constitutional principle is not immutable?). Nor is it to exonerate ministers from responsibility for their own acts and policies or those of their departments. It is an argument for accepting explicitly the need to supplement existing arrangements with legally based, non-parliamentary mechanisms of control and accountability, and acknowledging that there are situations where ministerial responsibility can be involved inappropriately to protect government against accountability rather than to expose government to it.

There is not the space here to develop a programme for a set of supplements to or alternatives for ministerial responsibility. Much work needs to be done on the subject. But the possibilities can be mapped out. There are civilised countries in the world with comparable levels of development and sophisticated political cultures (and the British political culture is sophisticated, even if part of the sophistication lies in the scepticism of Britons about government, anti-intellectualism and deep indifference to matters of governance) which manage, indeed are relatively effectively governed, without our level of reliance on this convention, our rejection of legal regulation in central government (local government is quite another matter in the UK) and our tendency to reject fully-fledged or full-blooded alternatives.

In New Zealand[5] for example—the closest relative of the United Kingdom system—much of the public sector has been corporatised in State Owned Enterprises independent of ministers, thus breaking the unity of the Crown. Almost the whole of the remaining civil service is organised into Executive Agencies and ministers are responsible for formulating the policy within which these operate. Ministers, not chief executives, are responsible to Parliament. Appointments of chief executives and staff are on the recommendation of the State Services Commission, which is independent of the government department, by the Governor General in Council—effectively the Cabinet; the chief executive is the employer of agency staff. There is an Official Information Act 1982 and a Bill of Rights Act 1990. In Sweden[6] executive agencies are independent of government, they have representative boards, they report directly to Parliament and they are subject to audit by a range of independent auditing agencies. Ministers are not responsible to Parliament for them, although Sweden has a parliamentary executive. Sweden has a freedom of information regime. The United States, without a parliamentary executive, adopts a quite different model for controlling government, with regulatory agencies concerned with rule-making and adjudication, and functions conceived quite differently from our framework of policy making, administration and management. There, too, is a government in the sunshine act.

In a typically Jourdainian way—unwittingly—we may be moving away from the parliamentary executive and ministerial responsibility in the UK. Clearly, with majority voting now widely provided for in the European Union Council of Ministers, ministerial responsibility cannot operate in relation to Union matters. The statutory initiatives discussed above establish the beginnings of non-parliamentary mechanisms of accountability. The Executive Agencies remove much administration, in practice if not in theory, from the scope of ministerial responsibility save as a last resort. The link between Parliament and redress of grievances is almost broken in appointments such as the Revenue Adjudicator, and the government has promised a number of lay adjudicators under the Citizen's Charter to deal with grievances which will further weaken these links. If such officers proliferate and are successful, the redress of grievance function of Parliament can be expected to atrophy. And we can expect alternatives to develop as the ineffectiveness of Parliament over what both ministers and their departments do creates problems for which solutions are essential.

The absence of a parallel mechanism to ministerial responsibility in local government has led to the creation of alternatives there which may provide models for central government—rights of access to official information, regulation of political relationships within authorities and of the relationships between officials and elected members, regulation of procedures. The principle of access to official information has been conceded by the government's *Open Government* White Paper and in local government. The step to a statutory regime of access to central government information in the UK would not be so large. And the courts, developing their own rules about public administration, are increasingly imposing duties of rationality and fairness on ministers and civil servants. The British approach is instinctively a Heath Robinson one.

But where would this leave the aspects of ministerial responsibility that the law can not reach—the parliamentary and party-political accountability of ministers for their own policies and their own actions? This is another enormous subject which opens up questions to do with the electoral system and the unitary nature of the country which can not be considered here.

1   HC Deb., 20 Jly 1954, cc. 1286–7.
2   See e. g. S. E. Finer, 'The Individual Responsibility of Ministers', *Publication Administration*, 1956; G. Marshall, *Constitutional Conventions* (Clarendon Press, 1984) D. Woodhouse, *Ministers and Parliament: Accountability in Theory and Practice* (Clarendon Press, 1994).
3   See the *Franks Committee Report*, Cmmd. 218, 1957.
4   See M. Chen and Sir G. Palmer, *Public Law in New Zealand*, 1993.
5   See O. Macdonald, *The Future of Whitehall* (Weidenfeld & Nicolson, 1991) and Institute for Public Policy Research, *Swedish Models: the Swedish Model of Central Government* (IPPR, 1992).

The Changing Commons

BY MICHAEL RYLE

THIS is a very personal piece. It attempts to tell the story of the workings of the House of Commons in the past half century based on the impressions, feelings and judgements of one man who was privileged to work in the Clerk's Department of the House for 38 years and who has observed the House and its Members, and their achievements and failings, for a still longer period. It also happens to cover the period of the writer's membership of the Hansard Society. Norman Gibbs, a wise Politics tutor, persuaded me in 1948 to part with the five shillings that was then the entrance fee to a life-long involvement with parliamentary affairs (and *Parliamentary Affairs*). I am glad to have been able to assist throughout that time in the work of the Society. For at the heart of my description of the House of Commons in the post-war period lies a profound affection for a great democratic institution. Of course it has its faults, and reform of its procedures and ways of proceeding are much needed, but without a central sense of respect, perception of the House of Commons will either slide into ignorant and easy cynicism or will lapse into lazy complacency with little care for reform. Either attitude is the enemy of parliamentary democracy.

My central themes are simple. The basic functions of the House of Commons have remained constant. As Gladstone is said to have reminded it: 'Honourable Members are summoned to this place not to legislate or govern, but to be the constant critics of those who do govern.[1] To put it another way, the principal function of the House is to call ministers to account and to do so publicly, so securing, as Leo Amery once wrote, 'full discussion and ventilation of all matters'. Publicity must be at the heart of this process, for it is by speaking for the public that elected them and at the same time speaking to the public and so influencing public opinion, that MPs can influence the government.

The Commons is therefore best portrayed as a communications medium or as a critical forum, not as a decision-taking body. Most decisions are essentially taken by the government—at various levels—but ministers still have to present those decisions to Parliament and, in the case of legislation, to secure its approval; and ministers are always liable to have to explain and justify anything they have done under the powers that Parliament has given them. The government governs—but it must govern through Parliament. And it is by these tests—how it performs its critical functions—that the effectiveness of the Commons should be measured; it is its critical processes and influence, not its formal powers over the government, that are of central importance.

Although the essential functions of the House of Commons have remained constant, the procedures of the House—and consequently the use that Members make of the opportunities those procedures provide—have all changed significantly. The first half of this article looks at changes in or affecting the Commons, the second asks whether such changes have made it more influential. In a few areas practices have got worse, but, by and large, I believe the House of Commons is a much more lively and politically significant body than it was fifty years ago and, in particular, is far more effective today as a critical body than it has been for a very long time.

CHANGES

The constitutional framework

Even the constitutional setting of Parliament changes from time to time. There have been some important changes in the period under review, which have had procedural consequences at Westminster.

The former Northern Ireland Parliament at Stormont has been suspended and responsibility for legislation and executive authority in the province has reverted to Parliament at Westminster and the government in Whitehall. One consequence was that the number of seats in the House of Commons for Northern Ireland was increased from 12 to 17 for the 1983 election onwards. Acts of the Stormont parliament have also been replaced by Northern Ireland Orders laid before Parliament by ministers and subject to approval like any other affirmative statutory instrument (except that an extra hour may be allowed for their debate in committee), with no procedure for their amendment. A Northern Ireland Committee was empowered to look at proposed Orders, but seldom met. However, a Northern Ireland select committee is currently being set up which would also be able to examine proposed legislation of this kind.

It is worth remembering that proposed constitutional changes in the government of other parts of the United Kingdom were rejected when legislation brought forward by the Labour government in 1977 and 1978 for Scottish and Welsh Assemblies failed to become law. The only procedural fall-out at Westminster was the inclusion, among the new select committees set up in 1979, of the Scottish Affairs and Welsh Affairs Committees. The Scottish Grand Committee has also been given leave from time to time to sit in Edinburgh.

Not everyone can stand for or sit in Parliament. Some changes affecting the membership of the Commons have been adopted. Until 1975, anyone who held an 'office of profit under the Crown' was disqualified from sitting in Parliament. The House of Commons Disqualification Act 1975 now lists specific disqualifying offices. The Act is frequently brought up-to-date to include newly created bodies.

Much the most important constitutional change affecting Parliament in the last fifty years was Britain's entry into the European Communities on 1 January 1973. Under the Treaty of Rome and the European Communities Act 1972, Community law has effect in all member states, and, for the first time in history, it is now possible (as the Factortame case showed) for an Act passed by the United Kingdom Parliament to be held by the courts to be of no effect. In practice, although the issue remains of hot political concern, there has been remarkably little difficulty in the working of Parliament as a result of this limitation of sovereignty. Successive governments have sought to ensure that Britain is not in conflict with Community obligations, and legislation has often had to be introduced to achieve this; much of our legislation is now Community-inspired. However, there remain many matters affecting UK citizens in which the European Union (as it now is) plays no part and in respect of which the powers and authority of Parliament are undiminished.

As a result, although the United Kingdom has to abide by the rules of the Community it has voluntarily joined, Parliament in no way behaves as a subordinate or constricted body. The main consequence of British membership for the practices and procedures of the Commons has been the creation of opportunities for the scrutiny and debate of Community law and other matters. The new procedures are described later.

Composition and MPs' approach to work

In some ways the most notable change in the Commons over the post-war years has been in the nature of its membership. This has had a significant effect on how the House has worked. New types of Member have tended to perform their political and parliamentary functions differently from their predecessors and to favour procedural changes, such as the extension of select committees, which expand their opportunities. Some of these changes, in their turn, have made membership of the Commons more attractive to these same types of politician. Cause and effect have been interactive and a spiral of change has been set in motion.

In the 1940s and 1950s a great number of backbench MPs had come into politics relatively late and were not particularly active in the House or committees. They usually had no great political ambitions. Such Members, if Conservative, were often landed gentry or retired army officers. They were loyal voters and rarely openly criticised their leaders. On the Labour side, many manual workers and former trade union officials filled much the same roles. They were good political litmus paper whose opinions must be heeded, but most of them accepted that they would not sit at the Cabinet table.

The present composition of the Commons is notably different. On the Conservative side, the number of university graduates (if service colleges are excluded) has risen substantially; more Members have a business background; and there are more career politicans who have started their careers as research assistants to MPs working in the party's offices or as political advisers. The proportion of Labour Members who have graduated from institutions of higher education has risen even more, while the number of manual workers has correspondingly fallen. There has been a marked increase in the numbers of teachers and college or university lecturers, which now comprise more than a quarter of the Parliamentary Labour Party.

Socially, the two main parties have moved a little towards each other, with fewer from public schools on the Conservative benches and still some in the Labour ranks. However the Conservative Party is still strongly middle-class in its outlook while the Labour Party still claims to be a working-class body. In some ways the two main parties are remarkably similar in their make-up. For example, about 40% of the Members of both parties after the 1987 election were identified as professional. The main differences were that 37% of Conservative Members came from the world of business and commerce (10% for Labour), while 29% of those on the Labour benches had a manual workers background (1% of Conservatives).

Two other changes should be noted. First, Members are retiring earlier (no doubt encouraged by the introduction of a pension scheme in 1964). Second, there are now considerably more women in the House — 60 at the time of writing, including the first woman Speaker.

For an increasing number of Members on both sides today, words and figures were the tools of their trade before they entered Parliament and this is clearly reflected in their approach to their work. They want to use their skills; they want to be involved; they want to be active on committees, or tabling Questions or motions. They spend much more of their time on their parliamentary — and especially constituency — duties than most MPs did forty or fifty years ago. The great majority of MPs are now working full-time at Westminster.

The consequence of these changes in approach have been twofold, and apparently contradictory. On the one hand, backbenchers are much more politically ambitious today. When they first enter Parliament, they nearly all want to make a mark and to become ministers. This has led, especially on the government side where the prospect of early ministerial office or promotion more clearly beckons, to overt and public attempts by backbenchers to curry favour with the Whips or to demonstrate their support for the Prime Minister and his or her government.

On the other hand, willingness to dissent has also increased. This is not entirely a consequence of large government majorities (in the 1974–79 Parliament, for example, there were 44 divisions when 50 or more Labour backbenchers cast a vote against their own government), although that clearly makes it easier for government side backbenchers to rebel. The newer types of Member are more willing to think for themselves or to take an independent stance on issues. This may also reflect the increasing radical and therefore controversial nature of government policies since 1979, compared with the much more 'conservative' and cautious approach of Conservative governments in the 1950s and early 1960s.

Whatever the causes, in recent years there has been a regular pattern—particularly on the government backbenches—of Members voting against their own party, or abstaining, or at least of speaking openly against the official line on selected but key issues. This is a novel and important development. Studies made by Philip Norton show that in the years from 1945 to 1970 the percentage of divisions in which there was any dissent was normally recorded in single figures for each Parliament. Since 1970, some dissent has occurred in about a third of the divisions. To take one session, in 1983–84 there were 62 divisions in which 137 Conservative Members (one third of the parliamentary party) cast a total of 416 votes against the government; and, as recent experience of the Maastricht bill and other legislation shows, the practice continues. The Whips, particularly on the government side (where it counts most), can no longer rely on almost automatic support in debates in the House or even in the lobbies as they usually could in the first half of the post-war period.

Declaration of financial interests

For many years, Members were expected, by a long-standing convention, to declare in debate any relevant pecuniary interest they might have in the matter before the House. In 1974 this requirement was spelt out in a formal resolution, which also extended to Members' dealings with ministers and civil servants. As a result, failure to declare a relevant interest could be found to be a contempt of the House and punishable.

The rules for declaration were reinforced by the establishment of a public Register of Interests, maintained by a Registrar, and policed by a Select Committee on Members Interests. Nine classes of outside financial interests are required to be included in the Register, but not the sums received. The great majority of Members have registered their interests, although a few have challenged this. The requirements for registration have recently been tightened up and clarified, but proposals for requiring the registration of the sums paid were rejected.

Occasionally, complaint has been made, and examined by the committee, that a Member has failed to declare or register an interest. No further action is usually taken, but in one case—John Browne in 1990— a Member was found to have failed to declare a substantial interest and was suspended by the House from its service for twenty sitting days, with corresponding loss of salary.

Volume of business

Two factors have combined to cause substantial growth, ever since 1945, in the amount of work in the House of Commons. The first is the extension of the areas of government which has required increased — and increasingly detailed and complex — legislation and more and more activity by ministers and their civil servants for which Parliament demands accountability. The second factor is the greater desire by Members to be involved in the debates on legislation or in enforcing accountability through Questions and select committee work. More government business and increased willingness to scrutinise it has meant a substantial increase in the amount of business conducted in the House of Commons.

The volume of government business is roughly indicated by the thickness of the statute book which has increased about fourfold in the period under review; the amount of delegated legislation has also doubled. In both cases it is significant that the increase results from the amount of matter and detail included in the legislation rather than the numbers of Acts and statutory instruments, which have remained remarkably constant.

The increased activity of Members is something to which all who work in the House of Commons — Members and staff — could testify. To give one example: when I was in the Table Office vetting Questions and giving procedural advice to Members at the end of the 1950s, we thought we had had a busy day if we received a hundred Questions; in 1989–90, over 66,000 Questions appeared on the Order Paper — an average of nearly 400 Questions a day.

Other figures measure the activity of Members off the floor of the House. The number of meetings of standing (mainly legislative) committees rose from 152 in the 1945–46 session to 562 in 1989–90; and the number of select committee meetings (including sub-committees) rose from 253 to 748 over the same period.

Although most of the increased work has been done in committees, more Members have been more active on the floor of the House. In 1951–52, 155 backbenchers (out of some 500) spoke five or more times in major debates; by 1971–72 the corresponding figure had risen to 249. Competition for limited time means that today most Members are only called about four times a year in such debates.

Services and facilities

The changes described above have been accompanied by improvements in the services and facilities available to Members to enable them to do a professional job. Members' salaries have increased significantly in real terms and since 1972 a clear distinction has been drawn between the salary and expenses. Also important has been the extension of free travel on parliamentary business, and free postage and telephone calls.

The most valuable advance was the creation, in the late 1960s, of a secretarial and office allowance. The effect has been dramatic. In 1945, few Members had their own secretaries and almost none employed research assistants. Today, the average Member employs about three staff for parliamentary work and about half the Members have full-time research assistants.

The massive increase in the constituency work of MPs, as well as their enhanced interest in Questions and committee work, is reflected in their growing use of the research services provided by the Library. These have greatly improved over the last fifty years. Individual Members, when preparing for a debate or other parliamentary activities, can now turn to the Library of the House for research and information, and the Library produces a steady stream of factual briefings on bills going through the House and other matters of current interest.

The growing numbers of staff in the Library and other departments must have places to work, and most Members now wish to have their own offices. In the 1940s and 1950s very few backbenchers had offices—they had to keep their papers in a small locker and take them out each day to work in the Library or on benches in the corridors—and all the staff in the Clerk's and other departments of the House worked in the Palace of Westminster. Today, every Member who wants one has an office of his own or shares an office with one or two other Members, and his personal staff all have offices to work in with modern equipment such as computers, photo-copiers and fax machines. These advances have only been made possible by extension of accommodation. A new parliamentary building across the road from the House of Parliament has been opened, with a branch of the Library, and many of the staff in the departments of the House are located in other buildings around Westminster.

Despite the extension of the parliamentary estate, Members still tend to spend much of their time working near the Chamber in committee rooms or in the Library, or looking after constituents and other guests in conference rooms, in the corridors or in the bars, or relaxing—and discussing current issues (politics never ceases)—in the Tea Room, the Smoking Room and the dining rooms. However, the need of some Members to go to offices outside the Palace for much of their time, and the dispersal of staff, has undoubtedly broken down, to some extent, the close collegiate ethos of the old House of Commons.

The House has also become more outward looking. A Public Information Office now answers public enquiries and publishes regular information about the business before Parliament and the work of committees, etc. As recommended by the Hansard Society, there is also an Education Officer providing material and advice on Parliament for use in schools, and a Parliamentary Bookshop at the foot of Whitehall for sale of *Hansard* and other parliamentary papers to the public.

The Commons is increasingly affected by outside pressures and public influence. The House of Commons is no longer—if it ever was—a closed 'workshop', getting on with its legislative and other business in its own way and in its own time, and largely blind to public interest or influence, as it was sometimes portrayed in the 1950s. As already said, the Commons today is a great communication medium and must organise itself accordingly.

Two organisational changes have brought about improvements in services for Members to help them in their work. The first was the creation of the Select Committee on House of Commons (Services), which has recently been replaced by a set of domestic committees covering accommodation, information, administration, catering and broadcasting, co-ordinated by a Finance and Services Committee. These committees have, since 1966, provided a forum for backbench Members to look critically at services and facilities and to advise the House, the Speaker and the relevant officers.

The second change was the passage of the House of Commons (Administration) Act 1978, under which the House of Commons Commission, chaired by the Speaker, plans and controls the House's own services and expenditure. Prior to 1978, the Treasury had to approve the House's Estimates and could control every detail of Parliament's expenditure (even the appointment of a part-time cleaner needed the approval of some civil servant), and therefore the level and nature of services provided for the House to assist the scrutiny of the government was directly determined by ministers themselves. Today, the Estimates for the House of Commons Administration are laid before Parliament by the Speaker after examination by the Commission. Subject to Parliament's approval of the total, the expenditure, staffing and services of the House are therefore now decided by the House itself and controlled by the Commission on behalf of the House. Six heads of separate departments, chaired by the Clerk of the House, are responsible for advising the Commission and implementing its policies and decisions.

One other innovation has been of value to many Members. The office of Parliamentary Commissioner for Administration (commonly called the Ombudsman) was created in 1967 to examine complaints of maladministration by government departments referred to him by Members of Parliament. He reports regularly to the House.

The use of time

There has been little change in the number of sitting days per session in the period under review. Apart from a slight rise in the length of sittings, total parliamentary time (excluding committee work, which has expanded enormously) has remained broadly constant. There has, however been one welcome reform for many Members. After the war, when much controversial business was being pushed through, the House sat late night after night and often all through the night. Since the

1960s, changes to standing orders have limited late debate on some types of business, the Whips have been willing to agree to avoid late sittings on other business and really late sittings are now relatively rare.

With one exception, the division of time on the floor of the House has not changed significantly. 50–55% of business is initiated by the government, 10% is initiated by the official Opposition and 35–40% is initiated by backbenchers[2]. Exceptionally, in the first few sessions after the war no time was allowed for private Members' bills and motions. Since 1951, however, at least twenty Fridays, have been allotted in each normal length session for these proceedings and in recent sessions this has been increased to the equivalent of 24 Fridays by taking some private Members' motions on Mondays.

A formal change in the rights of the Opposition was achieved by the creation in 1982 of Opposition days—at present 20 each session—when the matter for debate is chosen by one of the opposition parties. Until then, the Opposition were able to choose the subject for debate on Supply days when, technically, the government's Estimates were before the House, but until 1967 even this was limited by the exclusion of various matters, especially legislative questions. The creation of Opposition days with almost no restrictions on the matters of debate is another change of constitutional significance. In the last century the opposition parties as such had no specified opportunities to initiate debate.

Legislation

The essential features of the legislative processes in the Commons have not changed during the period under review, but the growing volume of legislation, greater controversy and increasing activity by Members has resulted in changes in the procedures for debating bills and delegated legislation.

One of the first things the Labour government did in 1945 was to accelerate the House's handling of the legislative programme. The first step was to appoint standing (i.e. debating) committees of about 45 Members for the committee stage of many government bills, and to require those committees to sit more often and longer. In practice, quite a number of more important bills were still taken in committee of the whole House, but over the following years the procedures and their use have been further developed. More and more bills have been committed to standing committees of about 20 Members, and the number of their sittings has steadily grown. In session 1947–48, five committees considered 21 bills at 125 sittings; in 1989–90, ten committees dealt with 38 bills at 454 sittings. Since 1969, most clauses of the Finance Bill have been considered in a standing committee.

One change that could have proved important, but in practice has been so little used that it hardly counts as a change, was the creation in 1980 of special standing committees, with power to hear evidence before debating amendments and the clauses of bills. Initially experimental, the procedure has only been used on five bills, and not at all since 1984. However, the procedure has been strongly supported by the Procedure Committee and, having been incorporated in standing orders in 1986, it could yet be used again.

The procedures and practices for restricting and time-tabling debate on bills by the use of guillotines have also been developed. In 1946 the procedure was extended to the time-tabling of proceedings in standing committees, and in 1967 debate on allocation of time orders was restricted to three hours. Until recently, however, the guillotine has not been extensively used — guillotine of the committee stage of some two or three bills a session being typical — but since 1987 governments have resorted to it more often: ten bills were guillotined at one stage or other in 1988–89, four in 1989–90 and six in the short session of 1991–92. However, more time has usually been allowed for their debate in recent years.

Some floor time has been saved by transferring to committees the second reading debates on less controversial bills: six such bills in 1988–89 and five in 1989–90. Less controversial Scottish bills are also debated at this stage in the Scottish Grand Committee consisting of all the Members sitting for Scottish constituencies.

There have been several significant procedural changes in respect of delegated legislation. Until 1973 all delegated legislation was debated — if debated at all — on the floor of the House. Since then, in order to reduce business on the floor of the House, the debates on the merits of many instruments — indeed, now, most — have been transferred to standing committees. Second, to improve parliamentary scrutiny, all instruments are examined by the Joint Committee on Statutory Instruments to ensure that there has been no misuse of the powers given to ministers to make legislation in this way.

European legislation

Members of Parliament are able to debate European Community (now European Union) legislation, although not to amend or reject it. The Commons has appointed the Select Committee on European Legislation, which examines every week all documents that have been presented to the Council of Ministers and decides whether they raise questions of legal or political importance and, if they do, whether they ought to be debated by the House. Since 1973, there have been many debates, often late at night and restricted in time. More recently, debates on documents have been held in standing committees and recently two semi-specialised committees have been appointed for the regular debating of the merits of European legislation. Uniquely, these have power to question ministers before debating the merits of the documents. Select committees also pay occasional attention to European legislation.

In the House there are nowadays periodic full-scale debates on

European business, such as before (until recently, after) European summit meetings. And of course no one can forget the highly controversial legislation to authorise the UK's ratification of amendments to the European Treaties, such as the bills for ratification of the Single European Act and the Maastricht Treaty.

Expenditure and taxation

In no area is parliamentary practice further separated from theory than that of control of expenditure. For many years the House has made little use of its formal powers to control the totals, balance and detail of expenditure (no Estimate has actually been cut by the House since 1919), but, as Gladstone said, expenditure flows from policy and real parliamentary 'control' has been achieved by the House's influence in the evolution of policy. Since 1945, this reality has been increasingly reflected in the procedures of the House, and today even the formal opportunities to debate expenditure as such have been almost eliminated.

In the 1950s and 1960s a number of Supply days were allotted each session when the government's Estimates could be considered; in practice Supply days became opportunities for debates on policy issues of the Opposition's choosing. Since 1982, when Supply days were abolished, the only formal opportunities for debating the actual Estimates have been on three Estimates days each session, when the Estimates to be discussed are chosen by the chairmen of select committees, and the debate of Scottish Estimates in the Scottish Grand Committee. All other Estimates are now approved without debate. Nor, since 1982, has debate been permitted on the annual Consolidated Fund and Appropriation Bills which give statutory authority for government spending.

In practice, closer scrutiny of expenditure has been transferred from the floor of the House to the departmentally-related committees, most of which carry out systematic reviews of the departments' Estimates and, more important, of the government's longer-term expenditure plans. Since the 1960s, these have been set out in Public Expenditure White Papers or, more recently, in the Chancellor of the Exchequer's Autumn Statement and in the annual reports of all government departments.

In 1993 the Budget was brought forward in the session from April to the end of November and we had, for the first time, a unified Budget, covering both expenditure and taxation. This change, which is to be permanent, has potential affects on the government's legislative programme and could, as the Procedure Committee has argued, open up opportunities for a more systematic scrutiny of expenditure plans. It is too early, however, to see how the new unified Budget will work in practice.

The Public Accounts Committee continues to examine the Appropriation Accounts with the assistance of the Comptroller and Auditor General and of the National Audit Office. Since the passage of the National Audit Act 1983, the Office and the Committee have been increasingly concerned with economy, efficiency and effectiveness, as well as with ensuring that money has been spent on the purposes authorised by Parliament.

Lastly, there was a major simplification of the details of financial procedures in 1966 and 1967. The old Committees of Supply and Ways and Means were abolished and all formal financial business is now done on the floor of the House itself. This has had little effect on the actual scrutiny of expenditure or taxation, but it has saved a little time and reduced duplication of debate.

Other opportunities for scrutiny

In addition to their Opposition days, the official Opposition choose the subject for debate on all but the first of the five or six days debate on the Queen's Speech at the beginning of each session. They have debates — in practice, less than one a session — on motions of censure. They can have debates on 'prayers' to annul statutory instruments on the floor of the House or in standing committees. They can apply for emergency debates (in recent years the Speaker has only allowed one or two such debates each session). Scottish and Welsh matters of the Opposition's choosing have, since 1957, been debated in the Scottish and Welsh Grand Committees. Opposition front-bench spokesmen are asking an increasing number of private notice Questions on urgent matters. And Prime Minister's Question time is used increasingly by Leaders of the Opposition to give a public airing, at prime time for media attention, to matters of their choosing. In a wide range of ways, the opportunities for the Opposition to set the agenda have increased to some extent over the past fifty years.

Opportunities for backbenchers have expanded considerably more. Time for private Members' bills and motions has been increased. Backbench Members choose which European documents to debate. They can raise any matter for which ministers are responsible on numerous adjournment motions. They choose the subjects for Estimate days. Backbenchers also bring in many more bills under the 'ten minute rule', which permits a short speech at prime media time, than they did in the 1940s and 1950s. Backbenchers also have many opportunities to raise matters without debate. Aided by their research assistants, Members have made fuller use of Questions for written answer to obtain information and to press ministers for action, and the back pages of *Hansard* are a mine of information on an amazingly wide range of matters; that was not the case forty or fifty years ago.

The conduct of Question time itself has changed markedly. Far fewer Questions are reached for oral answer: some 45–50 a day in the 1940s and 1950s; about 15 a day today. Oral Questions have become broader and more political and Speakers have been willing to allow more supplementaries; today they are really opportunities for Members on both sides to make political points rather than to seek for information as originally conceived. There has also been the development of the syndication of Questions, whereby Members—inspired, it may be thought, by their Whips—put down very similar Questions on arranged topics in the attempt to get as many Questions favourable to ministers, or hostile (as the case may be), high on the list and likely to be called.

Another development has been the adoption, since about 1977, of 'open' Questions to the Prime Minister which enable Members to raise whatever matters they wish. Again, the tabling is often syndicated. Prime Ministers Question time is covered live on television and Members—particularly the Leader of the Opposition—regularly seek to highlight current political issues of their choosing and hope to get coverage on the evening television news programmes. This is a far cry from the intimate, sometimes searching, sometimes lightly teasing, exchanges between Attlee and Churchill in the years after the war; quite often in those days there would be no Questions to the Prime Minister (they only came up after 44 Questions to other Ministers) or there would be no supplementaries.

Other expanding opportunities for backbenchers include almost daily applications for emergency debates when a matter which a Member considers urgent may be given publicity, occasional private notice Questions, and the right to table early day motions; little used until the mid-1960s, today up to 2,000 such motions are tabled each session. The Speaker tries to call as many Members as possible—certainly more than in the years up to 1983—to speak in debates and to ask supplementary Questions on ministerial statements. There has been one restriction of backbenchers' rights, however; because more and more Members want to speak in some important debates, it became necessary in 1984 to give the Speaker power to impose 10-minute limits on speeches for part of some debates.

Select committees

Standing committees are increasingly used to do work that could have been done in the House. Select committees are carrying out tasks that could not possibly be undertaken by the House itself. There has been a substantial expansion and improvement of the select committee system since 1945.

Soon after the war the Estimates Committee, consisting entirely of backbenchers, was revived to look at departmental spending and administration while not querying policy. The committee produced a lot of reports—some quite useful—but its sub-committees were non-specialised and the committee as a whole did not carry much weight.

A more influential committee, dating from 1956–57, was the Nationalised Industries Committee. This pioneered important procedural reforms, including the hearing of ministers as well as civil servants, the examination of witnesses in public (earlier select committees always sat in private) and the appointment of specialist advisers, and it made a number of substantial reports. Other committees, established by the 1966 Labour government, included committees on Race Relations and Immigration, Overseas Aid, and Science and Technology, all of which continued until 1979, and departmental committees on Agriculture, Education and Science and Scottish Affairs which were short-lived. In 1971 the Estimates Committee was replaced by a larger Expenditure Committee which was empowered to consider policy as well as administration; it worked through six subject-specialised sub-committees.

In 1979 the whole select committee system was revised. The Public Accounts and other scrutiny and domestic committees were untouched, but the Expenditure Committee, the Nationalised Industries Committee and all the other specialist committees were abolished and replaced by 14 departmentally-related committees covering nearly all aspects of government. Recently, the number has been increased to 16 following rearrangement of government departments. The Home Affairs Committee has also had its terms of reference extended to include the responsibilities of the Lord Chancellor's Department. All departments are now covered, although there is no specific committee scrutiny of the intelligence services.

These committees have wide terms of reference—to examine the expenditure, administration and policy of the departments and of associated bodies (such as nationalised industries)—which enable them to choose for themselves their subjects for inquiry. A Liaison Committee, comprising the chairmen of committees, oversees their operations and allocates funds for travel overseas. The committees travel frequently, both overseas and in the UK; they take evidence from many sources, including ministers; they have more staff than earlier committees; they appoint specialist advisers; and they take most of their evidence in public.

Overall, the new select committees have been highly active, each often making four, five or six reports a session on different matters and hence covering many aspects of departmental policy that would not otherwise be considered by the House.

Broadcasting and television

Sound broadcasting of the Commons was approved in 1977, and one of the most significant change that has ever occurred in the life of the House of Commons was brought about when the televised reporting of the House was launched in 1989. All proceedings in the House are televised although the choice of what is actually broadcast lies with the BBC and other broadcasters. The broadcasters also decide what proceedings in committees they wish to televise, and there is regular coverage, especially on special parliamentary programmes, of the work of select committees. On one day recently there were three items relating to select committees on the BBC's Nine O'clock News.

The effect of television on the business and proceedings of the House has also been important. Somewhat surprisingly, it has had little impact, now that it is part of normal life, on the way Members speak in debate (though front-bench speakers always include some carefully chosen quotable sentences which they hope may make the evening news programmes) or in the way they behave when listening to debates; even the notorious 'doughnuting' (gathering around the Member speaking) appears to have fallen out of fashion. On the whole, Members largely ignore the cameras and behave much as they did before they were brought in.

Collectively, as an institution, the House has, however, been changed by televising. Tactical and procedural jockying to get the most favour-able coverage has become important for all the parties and for some prominent individuals. There is now, for example, keen competition between the parties to get business of their choosing—perhaps a ministerial statement from the government side or a private notice Question or 'point of order' from the Opposition—before the House on Tuesdays, Wednesdays and Thursdays from after Questions at 3.30 till 4 p.m., when the House is covered live on BBC television. And select committees like to choose inquiries or hearings that will be of interest to the broadcasters.

More generally, both MPs and the viewing public have become increasingly aware of the bond between them that television has forged. Members are conscious that the electorate is watching and listening to what is going on in Parliament. The viewers are conscious that they are being shown their own Parliament in action, and what it says and does influences their own political judgements—and their votes at the next election.

EFFECT

The changing mood of the House

For this observer, it all seems a far cry from the time when he first sat in the gallery as a new young Clerk and looked down on the last sitting of the House before the 1951 election. Attlee, Dalton, Morrison, Gaitskell and other Labour ministers were slumped on the government front-bench like Disraeli's 'row of exhausted volcanos'. When the House next sat all had changed; jubilant Conservative Members were ready to cheer the new Prime Minister but almost gasped with horror as Churchill came in and proceeded slowly to to the left of the Speaker's chair as if to take his seat on the opposition front bench, where he had been sitting for the past six years. But half way along the Opposition benches he looked up, grinned broadly and walked back slowly and deliberately to take his seat on the government side. Then they cheered;

the point was made; the Conservatives were now the party in power. And a young Clerk had an experience he will never forget.

It is difficult to imagine anything like that happening today. No doubt there are still big men—and women—in the House of Commons, but their style and approach is different. Confrontation has long been the characteristic feature of the British House of Commons—those who remember the strongly held differences over nationalisation bills in the 1940s or the bitter differences over Suez will confirm that fierce party clashes across the floor of the House are not new—but the parliamentary confrontations today, exacerbated until recently by far wider doctrinal differences between the two major parties than in the 1950s and 1960s, seem shriller, and perhaps more contrived, than the differences between the two sides thirty or forty years ago. It is a personal view, but some of the fun and even pleasure seems to have been lost. With a few notable exceptions, there is less sense of humour in the Commons today.

Perhaps, in part, this is because parliamentary politics is a more serious business today. The whole Palace of Westminster—or at least the Commons end—is no longer anything like 'the best club in London'. The Central Lobby and the corridors are crowded; people lobbying Members and visitors of all sorts are going in and out all the time; Members and their staff are hurrying to and fro; the whole place is buzzing with activity. Again, it is a far cry from the time when many Members spent their time in the fairly quiet or empty corridors writing their letters in long-hand.

More effective scrutiny

In a more specific sense, work in Parliament is conducted more seriously today. As already shown, much more is done. The great growth in the use of Questions for written answer, although no doubt partly stimulated by research assistants wishing to be seen to be busy, is a very healthy development, opening up wide areas of government to public scrutiny. The use of oral Questions has also changed, particularly Questions to the Prime Minister, but while this may be offensive to the purists, the emphasis on making political points and highlighting the issues of the day makes a valuable contribution to the 'discussion and ventilation of all matters' that Leo Amery looked for.

One important advance has been the securing for the Opposition of guaranteed occasions for raising business of its own choosing, as already described. Whether the opposition parties always make the best use of these opportunities may be questioned, but a non-political outsider should not hasten to condemn; many of the Opposition day debates, which are often predictable in content and usually largely ignored outside Parliament, may still be valuable in internal party terms. And if nothing else is achieved, at least ministers are required to come to the House to defend their policies and actions on matters which they would usually prefer not to be debated at all. No changes in practice may result, the government may even have a good case, but it is all part of the process of calling minsters to account and avoiding government from behind closed doors.

For the backbenchers on both sides, the advances made are even more significant and represent a major reform. Apart from the increased opportunities for individual Members on the floor of the House, which the present Speaker and her predecessor have done much to establish and protect, the establishment of the departmentally-related select committees, enhanced by the increasingly effective use of the powers of committees to question witnesses in public, has represented the single most important increase in the effectiveness of the House of Commons in this century.

The value of the new select committees have been extensively discussed in books and articles. For me, the main benefits have been as follows. First, by being permanent for each Parliament (earlier committees were sessional); by being specialist; by covering all departments; by taking evidence much more widely (evidence to earlier committees came mostly from civil servants or other officials); by using their powers to inspect and hold informal meetings on site in this country and to seek for relevant experience overseas; by hearing evidence in public; by being better staffed; and, not least, by working hard, the select committees have ensured that a far larger sector of government is opened up to efective public examination than ever before. Some fifty reports a year from these committees, on separate topics, is evidence that every area of a ministers responsibilities has a reasonably high chance of being selected for scrutiny.

Second, the new committees have become increasingly confident and willing to take on controversial issues central to current politics, as evidenced by recent inquiries into the enlargement of NATO, Europe after Maastricht, the Pergau dam and aid to Malaysia, London's health services, the future of the BBC, VAT on domestic fuel, the operation of the Child Support Act, the sale of arms and related equipment to Iraq (in effect overtaken by the Scott inquiry), rail privatisation and the future of the railways, privatisation of the electricity industry, the market for coal and energy policy. This would never have happened in the past and, while not all such inquiries are successful, and while they often result in less than unanimous reports, they do indicate a willingness by the committees to act independently (these inquiries were often agreed on by the committees against the wishes of the government Whips). And, once again, ministers and their advisers are publicly examined, in ways that are far more searching than Question time or debate on the floor of the House, on matters of concern to many people.

Third, much wider hearings and consultation has meant that many affected interest groups and expert or experienced bodies have been given a public platform on which to make their views known. MPs have been put more directly in touch with the interested or affected public, and the public have been able to speak directly to MPs (I remember a committee on race relations taking evidence from young blacks in a café in Notting Hill). And the interest groups and lobbies, having to go public, have themselves been required to defend their case to their critics, including other interest groups. In addition to private lobbying of ministers and departments and private consultations on proposed bills or policies, the committees have brought about more public debate and scrutiny of the arguments. All this is a welcome advance towards a more open society.

The combined effect of these reforms has been that ministers have to be much more sensitive to parliamentary opinion or probable reactions when reviewing any policy or bringing forward new policies or legislation. A select committee report and its recommendations may well carry weight and have some influence (with affected bodies and experts, including civil servants, even if not with the minister). The very process of inquiry has more influence, not least by requiring the department or body involved to review its own policies and practices in order to defend them before the committee. The greatest influence, however, comes from the very liability of inquiry. Whenever decisions of any importance are being taken in a government department, the civil servants and the minister now have to ask themselves how the select committee is likely to react. A committee inquiry will almost certainly be more thorough, more persistent and more hungry for information than the House itself in response to a ministerial statement. A wise minister will certainly take the committee into account.

Select Committees, whatever the quality of their actual reports and whether or not their reports are debated formally in Parliament, have, by their very existence, done much to ensure that there is a proper parliamentary dimension to policy making in Whitehall. The increasing effectiveness of the National Audit Office and of the Public Accounts Committee, and the creation of the office of the Ombudsman, have added to this influence. The government cannot afford to ignore backbench and committee opinions at Westminster as I fear it did far too often in the past.

Parliament and the public

The other major beneficial change has been the further opening up of Parliament to the public. The increased concern of MPs with constituency problems and consequential contacts with constituents, often at Westminster, is one manifestation of this; another is the development of various services to inform the public about how the House of Commons works and what is going on there; another is the considerable increase in public contacts provided through the select committees. However, the most important advance has been the televising of the House and its committees.

Televising of the House of Commons will, in my view, prove to be a quantum leap in the evolution of Parliament. It is showing the public day by day not only how the House works (warts and all) but, more important, what it is considering. It is increasing the public's awareness of the policies and actions of the government and of the alternative policies of the opposition parties. It is making people aware of the the parliamentary reactions to those policies and actions. And it is showing how the party leaders and other Members perform at the dispatch box or before committees. It is thus both informing the electorate on the issues it will have to vote on at the next election and giving them a fuller awareness of the personalities who will be asking for their vote when that democratic test comes.

This is indeed a far cry from the time of the 'fourteen-days rule' (thankfully abolished long ago) which prohibited the coverage by sound or television broadcasts of any matter which was due to be debated in Parliament in the next two weeks. Today it is almost unbelievable that such a rule existed, yet it was made and tolerated by Parliament for a number of years in the 1950s. If the House of Commons is to influence government, it must be able to speak to the people and government must be aware of the effect of parliamentary debate on public opinion. Televised coverage of Parliament is essential to this process.

Reforms are still needed

These are some of the changes which have benefited the House of Commons. In other areas, reforms are still needed. The lack of formal consideration of expenditure by the House (although of course policies implying expenditure are often debated) appears a serious lacuna. The adoption of a unified Budget has provided the opportunity for more systematic debating and approval of expenditure, in particular of the balance of expenditure between major services, which is something with which the Cabinet has to wrestle each year but which the Commons as such never debates at all. The recent carefully thought-out recommendations of the Procedure Committee on this subject, and the evidence of the Study of Parliament Group and others to that committee, should be carefully considered by the House, and there should be a positive response from ministers. Ministers could only benefit from heeding a properly structured debate on expenditure priorities.

Second, there is a lack of opportunities for early debate of current issues. Emergency adjournment debates are rarely granted; private notice Questions serve to enable a few Members to let off steam or get a quote in their local paper but are no substitute for a proper debate; the abuse of points of order by frustrated Members who have no other outlet is highly unsatisfactory. In many other countries—in Australia for example—less time is spent on legislation but more time is available for debates on crises and matters of urgent concern to Members. Time could be provided (especially if legislation were properly time-tabled). The Procedure Committee should look at this again.

Third, I have a niggling worry about something which could become a serious problem. Concern is growing about the danger of some Members having conflicts of interest which they resolve by putting their private interests before their parliamentary duties. Members may properly declare the sources of all their outside earnings, but this does not stop them from using their membership of the House to add significantly to their earnings by sponsoring or advising various interests in return for fees. In many cases this may be harmless or even positively desirable (by enhancing a Member's experience, for example) but it does cause concern if the augmentation of the parliamentary salary in these ways becomes the main activity of the Member in Parliament or even his motive in becoming a Member.

The difficulty lies in having to judge motives, but it should be faced. The extent of some outside earnings points to a real danger. It might be helpful if the Committee of Privileges were first asked to examine this general problem (for abuse of the kind here envisaged would be a contempt of the House). It would also provide a salutary warning if, from time to time, specific cases where a Member appears to have pursued private interests in an undesirable way were to be referred to that committee.[3]

The final and most regrettable failure of the House of Commons to reform its procedures satisfactorily is in respect of legislation, which is one of the main functions of Parliament. I will not go into detail here as the whole legislative process, and Parliament's part in it, has been reported on at length by the Hansard Society Commission on the Legislative Process in its report, *Making the Law*, which was published in 1993.[4]

The Commission received evidence from a wide range of bodies and people which was strongly critical of the way legislation is handled in Parliament, especially in the Commons. The main complaints related to rushed legislation, the inability of those directly affected to give evidence to committees on bills, and the disgraceful lack of proper scrutiny of delegated legislation. The Commission made detailed recommendations on all these matters, including the the use of select and special standing committees to give more attention to the practicalities of government proposals as set out in bills and statutory instruments, and for more systematic examination of how Acts of Parliament have worked in practice.

The acceptance of these reforms depends on longer-term programming of legislation and the time-tabling of all legislation in the House of Commons. The government's business managers could not be expected to accept the taking of evidence and a more positive role for backbenchers unless there is certainty that this will not lead to unacceptable delay in the passage of bills. If Members want improved scrutiny of legislation, they must accept this package deal.

The Procedure Committee have made various proposals for time-tabling of most bills in committees which have all been rejected by the Government (with the support of the Opposition front-bench). The Jopling Committee on the Sittings of the House has accepted the need for time-tabling if more reasonable sitting times are to be adopted, but so far nothing has been done. The Hansard Society Commission goes further and recommends the systematic time-tabling of all bills and delegated legislation at all stages, to be agreed and imposed by all-party bodies (as is done in many other parliaments) rather than by the use of guillotines prepared and imposed by the government alone. If the legislative process is to be reformed, as is sorely needed, this issue must be confronted.

The final assessment

The House must be judged as a critical, not decision-taking, body and as a communications forum. The growing powers of the executive and the increase in the volume and complexity of business have challenged the working arrangements in the House of Commons over the past fifty years. The government has consistently sought to ensure the passage of its legislation without undue delay and has reformed procedures to this end. The response in Parliament has been to step up the scrutiny of the policies and actions of ministers by developing more effective critical machinery in some areas, though not, so far, on the legislative front. In effect, there has been a package deal by which the government, the Opposition and the backbenchers have been able to increase their effectiveness.

There have been other advances. Commons backbenchers are more active and increasingly willing to take an independent line when they have thought it right. They enjoy greatly improved resources, services and facilities to help them in their work. They have achieved growing influence, most notably through the select committees.

Still more notably, government backbenchers (aided in some cases by dissident voices and votes in an increasingly independent House of Lords which is no longer totally controlled by one party) have scented real power. Pressure from their own backbenches has forced ministers to revise or even reverse their policies (witness the poll tax, criminal justice policy and child support in the recent past) or have closely influenced other major policies, for example on Europe. Above all, it was backbench opinion which brought the downfall of one Prime Minister and is currently threatening another. Backbenchers have not enjoyed such continuing power or influence at any other time this century.

And all of this is witnessed by the electorate on television. This has undoubtedly encouraged the backbenchers to flex their muscles and reminded ministers that they must never fail to heed the views of Parliament. This in its turn conditions their policies.

The House of Commons is more effective today in its central critical and communication roles than it has been for many years. However, problems and further challenges remain. For example, the electoral system may be changed and Parliament has yet to come to grips with the consequences of British membership of the European Union.

The country and Parliament itself cannot afford to be either cynically neglectful or complacent. In my view, the basic weakness in the way the House of Commons faces the future is its failure to take itself seriously. Some things are clearly not right, but no serious attempt is being made to put them right — or even to debate them properly. For example, the Procedure Committee has made carefully thought out proposals for the time-tabling of bills in committee; its reports have been rejected by the government with only minimum discussion in the House. The Hansard Society Commission's detailed and radical report, *Making the Law*, has been supported in an early day motion by nearly a hundred backbenchers, who have urged early debate; there has been no debate or government response of any kind.

If we are to have the Parliament the country needs, Parliament itself must be closely scrutinised. The opportunities and procedures for reform are already there. It can all be done from within the House itself. It does not require a constitutional revolution. It only requires imagination and the will to accept change.

I sometimes feel ashamed that we take so little pride in our own House of Commons. Media obsession with the private lives of MPs does not help, and is largely irrelevant to the effectiveness of the Commons as a critical body. Allegations of hypocrisy and of deceit, and suggestions that ministers have deceived the House, must clearly be taken seriously, but these should strengthen the House's determination to ensure that there are parliamentary opportunities for exposing of such practices. These fashionable criticisms should not weaken the country's respect for Parliament as an institution, but should stimulate efforts to create a still more effective body to represent the people.

So to sum up, all my experience leads me to believe that not only is the House of Commons the best House we have (to paraphrase Rab Butler) but it is more effective, significant and influential today than it has been at any previous time in this century. This has been the achievement of the past fifty years. It is up to our MPs to ensure that further reforms are made in the years to come.

1   I have read from time to time various versions of this dictum, but have been unable to trace the source or the true wording. Perhaps some reader of this article knows the answer?
2   For explanation of how this is calculated and more details, see J. A. G. Griffith and M. Ryle, *Parliament* (Sweet and Maxwell, 1989), pp. 12–13.
3   Since this was written, two such cases have been referred to the Committee of Privileges.
4   I declare my interest; I was a member and Secretary of the Commission.

Select Committees and Parliamentary Scrutiny: Plus Ça Change

BY PHILIP GIDDINGS

'PLUS ça change, plus la même chose'. That there has been considerable growth in select committee activity at Westminster over the last fifty years no-one can doubt: there are now more committees, more system-atically organised, occupying the time and energy of many more MPs, receiving written and oral evidence from more ministers and officials (and others). But what does this growth in activity signify? In other — and arguably more fundamental — respects the Westminster scene is unchanged. The Chamber itself still predominates. Select committees perform an important function of scrutiny but they do not have real power over the things that matter to governments — the passage of legislation, the voting of taxation and expenditure, the continuation of ministers in office. The growth of select committee activity over the last three decades has not significantly altered the relationship between government and Parliament. The main focus of parliamentary activity in the 1990s as in the 1940s remains the struggle between Government and Opposition, reflecting and shaping their competition for the support of public opinion and those who influence it.

To begin an essay on select committees with such a point is not to diminish the significance of scrutiny or to minimise the changes which have taken place. Rather, it is to put those changes in con-text, a preliminary exercise made necessary by the exaggerated claims (and fears) of some advocates (and opponents) of committees as a means of 'reforming' Parliament. That those hopes and fears have not been fulfilled should be seen as evidence not of the 'failure' of select committees, but rather of a misperception of their purpose in Britain's post-war parliamentary system, a purpose determined by the adversarial nature of the political system within which Parliament operates.

The debate about committees

In 1954 Herbert Morrison, former Lord President of the Council, wrote that in Britain 'the function of examining and challenging important government policy is reserved to Parliament as a whole. This doctrine has, I imagine, been preserved for two reasons: the wish of Parliament not to weaken its own powers and authority, and the desire of governments not to become (to put it crudely) the victims or creatures of committees'. He went on to compare the British position unfavourably with that pertaining in the United States and France where committees 'would often appear to have even more decisive powers and influence than the parliamentary institution as a whole'.

Morrison was in part responding to proposals put forward before the war by, amongst others, Ben Jowett and David Lloyd George for a reformed Commons committee system. His five objections to Jowett's scheme are instructive. They would mean: an increased workload for Ministers which would be almost intolerable; administration and legislation would be delayed; very heavy work for committee members, possibly to the detriment of their work in the House itself; the risk that committee members would be divided from the rest of their party; undermining the vital doctrine of the responsibility of Ministers to Parliament as a whole.[1]

Those objections still cogently express the arguments of those who continue to be sceptical of the development of the select committee system, objections which are based on practical (work-load), political (party solidarity) and constitutional (ministerial responsibility) grounds. More significantly, Morrison's second, fourth and fifth arguments state the reasons why governments (and opposition front benches) remain sceptical, if not hostile, to developments which would enhance the power of committees. So for proponents of reform, his objections represented the case which they had to meet to overcome the opposition of those who effectively control procedural developments in the House of Commons—the business managers of the two front benches. The evolution of the Commons select committee system in the last thirty years has been the story of attempts to do just that.

Before considering the last thirty years, it is worth noting two examples of the debate about committees in the 1950s: first, the case of the select committee on nationalised industries and then, more briefly, a proposal for a committee on colonial affairs.

The Select Committee on Nationalised Industries

The socialisation programme of the post-war Labour government brought within ministerial and parliamentary purview a great range of industrial and commercial enterprises, principally public utilities. With nationalisation at the centre of the political struggle between Government and Opposition, it was inevitable that parliamentary scrutiny of the work of the public corporations established to run them should be a matter of concern. Initially, controversy focussed upon the extent to which ministers could be asked Questions about the running of the enterprises, given the statutory allocation of powers between boards and ministers. Members, particularly on the Conservative benches, were frustrated at their refusal to be drawn into answering for management issues. A select committee set up in the 1951/52 session recommended a certain amount of flexibility without altering the fundamental rule that ministers could not answer Questions on matters for which they were not responsible. However, these concessions did not satisfy Conservative Members who wanted to subject the industries to deeper scrutiny.

The following session, a further select committee reported in favour of a permanent committee to investigate the nationalised industries. The Labour Opposition saw this as an attempt to undermine the industries and argued that, as well as not interfering with day-to-day administration which was the responsibility of the boards, such a committee should not deal with policy matters which were the responsibility of ministers and for which they should account to the House as a whole. The government sought to meet Labour's concerns by excluding from the committee's remit both matters decided by or clearly the responsibility of ministers and matters of day-to-day administration. However, when such a committee was set up in 1955 it proved still-born because its members felt its terms of reference so restrictive that there was no point in its undertaking an investigation of a nationalised industry! In response, the government decided to trust to the good sense and goodwill of the committee rather than trying to embody restrictions in the terms of reference. In November 1956, even though the opposition divided the House against it, a Select Committee on Nationalised Industries was finally set up, with broad terms of reference to examine the industries' reports and accounts.

Notwithstanding that somewhat unhappy start, within ten years the committee had established itself as a successful experiment. In spite of the controversial circumstances of its birth, there was no difficulty maintaining continuity of membership or good chairmanship. Heeding Morrison's warnings about the nature of public corporations, the committee respected the statutory independence and commercial nature of the boards, avoided conducting efficiency or financial audits, but still succeeded in making a substantial contribution to the public accountability of the nationalised industries by providing a detailed survey of the work of each industry's management.

Although the committee did not draw a conceptual distinction between matters of day-to-day administration and matters of general policy, it did draw a functional distinction between what would be intolerable for the boards and what would be acceptable to them. It took evidence from civil servants rather than ministers, criticised ministerial action and recommended changes in policy. Yet these developments did not give rise to complaint that those ministers who were concerned with nationalised industries were less responsible or less answerable as a result of the committee's work. Thus the general lesson to be learned from its experience was that select committees of the House of Commons 'can and do deal with government departments on questions of policy' without impairing the fundamental features of the British Constitution.[2]

A Committee on Colonial Affairs?

In spite of the apparent success of the Committee on Nationalised Industries, the case for specialist committees made little general advance within the House in the 1950s. The 1958–59 Procedure Committee considered the issues in the context of a suggested committee on colonial affairs. This was proposed as a debating forum, without powers to call for evidence but able to receive information and advice from ministers from the department who would be ex officio members, not permitted to take decisions or make general reports to the House but able to pass resolutions drawing its attention to matters requiring closer scrutiny. The Procedure Committee firmly rejected this proposal on the grounds that it would represent a radical constitutional innovation: 'there is little doubt that the activities of such a committee would ultimately be aimed at controlling rather than criticising the policy and actions of the department concerned. In so doing it would be usurping a function which the House itself has never attempted to exercise. Although the House has always maintained the right to criticise the executive and in the last resort withdraw its confidence, it has always been careful not to arrogate to itself any of the executive power. The establishment of a colonial committee would not only invade this principle, but would also lead to the establishment of other similar committees.'

The place for discussing colonial affairs, in the Procedure Committee's view, was the floor of the House: discussion in committee would mean that many Members would be prevented from expressing their opinions. This was an unmistakable reassertion of the traditional view of the House's role, reflecting what may well be come to be seen as the high point of Executive dominance. Such a view left little room for any expansion of the work of select committees, notwithstanding the success of the Committee on Nationalised Industries.

The Estimates Committee

In the first half of the 1960s the attention of those wishing to develop the committee system focussed first on the Estimates Committee. When re-established in 1945, it retained its 1921 order of reference which required it to focus on the identification of what, if any, economies consistent with the policy implied in the Estimates might be affected. Nevertheless, whereas its predecessors had sought to scrutinise the detail of the estimates, the post-war committee decided to split up into small sub-committees taking selected estimates as the starting-point for enquiries into the efficiency of the administrative organisations responsible for particular items of expenditure.[3]

During 1960 renewed agitation amongst MPs about methods of controlling public expenditure prompted the government to announce some changes to the Estimates Committee. Its order of reference was revised and embodied in a Standing Order which made the committee a sessional committee with the same status as the Public Accounts Committee, increased its size from 36 to 43, brought supplementary estimates within its remit, and empowered it to examine variations in estimates between current and preceding years. More significantly, the revised terms of reference allowed it to take evidence on questions of policy in order to discern more economic ways of carrying it out, which reflected the post-war style of working. Thus, although still debarred from challenging ministerial policies, the committee was enabled to subject them to critical examination in the course of discovering whether they could be implemented more efficiently—an early recognition of the fact that in the dynamic processes of government policy and administration are inextricably intertwined.

By 1966 the committee had established itself as one of wide-ranging administrative scrutiny with value for money and the pursuit of efficiency as its main concerns. As far as its impact on departments is concerned, one observer wrote that because of the complex pattern of forces at work in decision-making in contemporary government 'We cannot expect much in the shape of visible effects from the work of a scrutiny committee of Parliament such as the Estimates Committee. It is one factor amongst many which influences the course of public action. But equally there is no reason to dismiss it as ineffective just because we cannot measure what it achieves.'[4] This judgement was to be repeated later by other observers of other scrutiny committees.

The assessment of the committee's impact upon Parliament could be more positive: 'The most prolific and in some respects the most influential of the instruments at the disposal of the House of Commons for finding out how the departments of State are organised, how they operate and how successful they are in achieving some of their policy objectives'[5]—a crucial informative function. However, this did not mean that the House gave much attention to the Committee's reports. Between 1945 and 1960 Estimates Committee reports were formally considered on only seven occasions by the House. The position improved after 1960 but even those debates which did occur were modest parliamentary occasions. Attendances were small, and usually a high percentage of those taking part were members of the committee who had been concerned with the report in question—again a finding to be repeated later with other scrutiny committees. Moreover, disappointingly for some advocates of reform, there was little to show that Members of Parliament made much use of the reports and evidence on occasions other than the Supply Days set aside for debate. Relatively few Parliamentary Questions were inspired by reports of the Estimates Committee.[6]

The relatively successful work of the Estimates Committee led the Procedure Committee in 1965, after the change of government, to recommend a significant extension of its powers and functions, proposing that it be empowered to examine how the departments of State carry out their responsibilities and to consider their Estimates of Expenditure and Reports. Although this proposal was rejected by the government on the ground that detailed government expenditure and administration would be bound to give place to policy discussion, it was an interesting sign of things to come.

The Crossman experiments

In the debate on the Queen's Speech in April 1966 the Prime Minister himself suggested an experiment to extend the committee system over a wider field. Mr Wilson envisaged one or two new committees to throw light on future legislation and day-to-day administration, suggesting education and housing and local government as possibilities. Ministers as well as senior officials would be available for questions. By December 1966 the Leader of the House, Richard Crossman, had developed this suggestion into the setting up of two 'specialised' committees, one on agriculture and one on science and technology.

In spite of early difficulties over staffing, overlap with the Estimates Committee, the use of expert advisers and travel abroad, Crossman was able to argue in December 1967 that the two committees should be extended for a further year and a third one—on education—added. But not all was sweetness and light. Both committees complained of being pressed for time by the need to report within one session and were irked by the long delay in debating their reports. The Agriculture Committee deliberately chose the provocative subject of the effect of entry into the EEC and experienced considerable difficulty with the Foreign Office over access to papers about the department's internal administration. Both committees encountered problems with overseas travel and complained about inadequate staffing.

In November 1968 an additional 'subject' committee was set up to consider the operation of the Race Relations Act and the admission of immigrants into the United Kingdom. In the following year the Agriculture and Education Committees were wound up and replaced by Committees on Overseas Aid and Scottish Affairs, on the grounds (according to the government) that the original intention had always been to cover more departments. Thus in all six specialist committees were appointed: three 'subject' committees (Science and Technology; Race Relations and Immigration, and Scottish Affairs; and three 'departmental' committees (Agriculture, Education and Science, and Overseas Aid). At the end of the 1966–70 Parliament these specialist committees varied in size between 13 and 18 members, drawn from both sides of the House. Their combined membership of ninety-five compared with a total membership of all standing committees and select committees of 530 (though many MPs served on more than one committee). The increasing demands made upon Members by the growth in committee activity through this period can be seen by the progressive increase in the number of sittings of committees and sub-committees—a growth of 260% in five years. What that growth had produced by the end of the decade was not a comprehensive system of select committees but a patchwork with varied origins and erratic support.

The 1969 changes focussed attention on two issues—coverage and continuity. Some reformers (and 40% of MPs responding to a Study of Parliament Group survey agreed with them[7]) wanted to see committees covering every government department. Others (supported by between a quarter and a third of respondents to the same survey) wanted committees to be more narrowly focussed and expressed concerns about manning. Certainly, the experimental committees had experienced difficulties in getting and keeping a quorum, reflecting the sharp increase in committee sittings. As regards continuity, committee members complained of the time wasted at the beginning of the session whilst the committees were being set up and the difficulty of planning a sensible programme of work when constrained by the need to report by the end of that same session.

The case for scrutiny committees of this kind had been argued before the Procedure Committee by some academic members of the Study of Parliament Group in the 1964/65 session. It was a case based very much on the benefits of a flow of information to the House. But the experience of the Crossman committees was not at first sight very encouraging to this line of argument. Attendance in the House was low when committee reports were debated—in May 1968, for example, only 17 MPs were present for a debate on a report from the Science and Technology Committee, including eleven members of the committee and two ministers. A similar lack of attention afflicted the Estimates Committee and the PAC.[8]

Reflecting on the experience of the 1960s, Crick gave a positive evaluation of the Crossman experiment. The new committees represented a 'foot in the door'. There was in his view a general acceptance of their benefits, even if scepticism continued about their extent.[9] Johnson, however, concluded more pessimistically that it could not seriously be claimed that the control or checking of the Executive by the House of Commons had been significantly strengthened. He doubted the 'exaggerated faith in the operative effects of disseminating more information both on those who produce it and on those to whom its lessons are directed. It was simply naive to assume that the House of Commons could be strengthened vis-à-vis the Executive just by improving its possibility for scrutinising the activity of government and for making information available'. If the position of the House was to be strengthened, it would be necessary to pay attention to the formal powers of committees, linking them with the work of the House as a whole, and party behaviour. 'The right to enquire and to enlighten confers no formal right to share in decisions nor does it constitute an increment of political power'.[10]

Johnson also noted that the growth of committees had not at this point significantly altered the average pattern of backbench activity. Although it had become steadily more difficult to man all types of committee adequately, there had been no cut-back in the plenary sittings of the House, no decline in Questions or the other means of holding ministers to account on the floor, and no sign that MPs believed their role was changing from that constituency grievance-man to committee specialist.[11]

The period since 1964 had been one in which reformers had had high hopes. The Prime Minster's announcement in April 1966 and the Crossman experiments had seemed to give encouragements to those hopes. But by the end of the decade, though a great deal more committee activity was taking place, its coverage was patchy and its overall effectiveness uncertain.

The Expenditure Committee

In the 1968–69 session the Procedure Committee undertook an enquiry into the methods of examination and control by the House of public expenditure. Its report recommended that the Estimates Committee should be changed to a Select Committee on Expenditure, which would work through nine sub-committees, one of sixteen members covering general issues and the other eight each covering a 'functional' field of administration. The functional sub-committees, which would comprise nine members, would consider three topics: first, expenditure projections for the relevant department(s), compared with those of previous years, and the progress made towards clarifying general objectives and priorities; second, the implications in terms of public expenditure of the policy objectives chosen by ministers and the success of departments in attaining them; and, third, departmental administration, including the effectiveness of management. Whilst the Procedure Committee specifically recommended that the Public Accounts Committee and its Select Committee on Nationalised Industries should be retained with their existing remits, they left open the future of the specialised committees to be decided by the House in the light of reactions to their Report.

The new Conservative government's October 1970 Green Paper in response to the Procedure Committee's proposals considered it beyond dispute that the specialist committees had acquired a growing body of expertise and had brought together in their reports, for the benefit of the House and the public generally, a valuable body of fact and opinion on some important issues. They had opened up new channels of communication between Parliament and interested bodies and individuals throughout the country. However, on the subject of their influence on government itself and the formation of new policies the government was more guarded, describing it as 'more subtle ... in many case it will not be visible for some time to come'.[12]

The government's main concern was that the proposed Expenditure

Committee (which it estimated would require some 80 members), if added to the existing committees, would create much too heavy a demand on MPs' time. 'There is a danger that this will have an adverse effect on the proceedings in the Chamber itself, which must remain the centre of Parliament'.[13] Indeed, in the government's view it was necessary to reduce the burden of committee work and accordingly it proposed a significantly slimmer Expenditure Committee of about 45 members to operate alongside the Nationalised Industries Committee but that only the 'subject' specialist committees should be retained.

After a debate in November which was remarkable for the absence of any expressed opposition to select committees, the Expenditure Committee was set up in February 1971 with 49 members. From the start, it was organised into six sub-committees, one general and five covering broad areas of expenditure (Defence and External Affairs, Environment, Trade and Industry, Education, Arts and the Home Office, Social Services and Employment).

Initially, the committee encountered predictable difficulties: members were appointed each session, which both delayed setting up inquiries and inhibited the development of continuity; inadequate time was allowed for debate on committee reports; departmental responses were often very slow (average response time was between six months and a year, and in 1976 there were two reports for which departmental observations had not been produced after two years. In spite of the Procedure Committee's hopes, early plans for coordination were dashed when it became apparent that the sub-committee chairmen wished to move in their own chosen directions. In consequence, there were few enquiries into specific decisions of government spending. Instead, Members took up matters which interested them or were receiving particular public attention, which resulted in some 'spectacular political investigations ... which were light years away from the committee's original remit'[14]—topics such as private medicine in the NHS or the practices of British firms in South Africa. In 1974, after many representations, the government conceded that committee members should be appointed for a whole Parliament, which brought a significant improvement to its work. Nevertheless, it continued to lack cohesion and, apart from the general sub-committee, largely ignored actual expenditure.

Although the committee produced many reports, and published many volumes of evidence, it is difficult to assess how effective all this activity was. It was not intended to be able to ensure that its recommendations were acted upon and the government was not obliged to take notice of them. In practice, in its responses some recommendations were accepted, some rejected, and in many cases general remarks were made which did not commit the government to any positive action. And when committee reports were debated on the floor of the House, the old problem encountered by other committees remained: few, except members of the committee, bothered to attend. One summing up of the

committee's work down to 1976 commented that while it had provided
a better public platform for debates than those 'charades on the floor of
the House', their effect was, unfortunately just about the same. 'It is
probably true to say that the work of the Expenditure Committee to
date has not resulted in one penny of state spending being allocated
differently, or budgetary policy being modified in any way.'[15]

Although the Expenditure Committee dominated the scene in the
1970s, that decade was also an era of proliferation of ad hoc select
committees. In the 1970–74 Parliament there were committees on such
diverse topics as the civil list, corporation tax and tax credits, as well as
the establishment of the Select Committee on European Secondary
Legislation following British entry into the European Community. And
the 1974–75 session there were ad hoc committees on Cyprus, violence
in marriage and a wealth tax. Thus, in spite of the desire for some
rationalisation after the patchwork developments of the late 1960s, the
following decade saw a continuation of the uncoordinated pattern of
growth of select committee activity.

The 1978 Procedure Committee Report

'Piecemeal development', 'patchy coverage' and 'unsystematic character'
featured in the descriptions of the committee system given by the
Procedure Committee in its report of July 1978 which was to prove so
influential. The committee had to strike a delicate balance. The overwhelming weight of evidence put to it favoured the development and
rationalisation of the committee system but the advantages of such a
development had to be weighed against two factors: 'the need to retain
the Chamber as the focus of the political and legislative work of
Parliament and to protect, and if possible enhance, the opportunities of
the individual Member to influence the decisions of the House.' Given
the need to balance such factors, it is not surprising that it concluded
that what was needed were changes of practice of an evolutionary
rather than revolutionary kind.[16]

The Procedure Committee proposed the abolition of most of the
existing committees and their replacement by twelve committees
appointed under a single, permanent Standing Order with permissive
rather than mandatory orders of reference. The twelve committees,
whose members would be nominated for the duration of a Parliament,
would be based on the subject areas of the main government departments and would be able to examine all aspects of their expenditure,
administration and policy, as well as their associated nationalised
industries and quangos.

The Procedure Committee also made a number of recommendations
designed to deal with the problems which select committees had
encountered since the early 1960s (if not before). Eight Mondays per
session should be devoted to debates on select committee reports;
government departments should respond to reports within two months;

more permanent and specialist staff should be provided with specialist advisers allowed to be appointed as the committees wished. The committees should be nominated on a motion tabled by the Committee of Selection rather than the whips, although the House should retain the ultimate right of decision, and the informal liaison committee of chairmen should be formalised.

The debate on the Procedure Committee's report in February 1979 showed the extent to which select committees had become an accepted feature of parliamentary life. The overwhelming majority of speakers were in favour of its recommendations, and even the Leader of the House, Michael Foot, after speaking strongly against any extension of the committee system at the start of the debate, had to acknowledge when winding up, that he was swimming against the tide and promised inter-party consultations.[17]

In the event, the fall of the Callaghan government meant a general election before government proposals could be brought to the House. The incoming Conservative Government's election manifesto had included a commitment to implement the Procedure Committee's report, and in June 1979 the new Leader of the House, Norman St John Stevas tabled a motion (which was agreed to) for a new Standing Order to achieve that. Although Mr St John Stevas spoke in extravagant terms of the most important parliamentary reforms of the century, it is significant that the government did not accept all the Procedure Committee's recommendations. The general structure for the new committees was accepted—but they were delegated no greater powers than the old ones. There was no provision for the eight days per session for debates nor powers to enforce the attendance of ministers as witnesses or the production of papers by government departments. These matters were covered by ministerial assurances during the debate but, as experience was to show, that is not quite the same thing. Nevertheless, after some delay while the Committee of Selection did its work, fourteen new departmental select committees were duly nominated in November 1979 and effectively began work at the start of 1980.

The New Select Committees

The departmentally-related select committees have now been in operation for four Parliaments. That fact underlines their most significant achievement: they have become a permanent part of the House of Commons arrangements. As noted in 1988, 'it is virtually inconceivable now that either the government or any substantial body of opinion in the House would seriously consider major inteference with the select committee structure, still less its abolition.'[18] This was confirmed when the Procedure Committee reviewed the select committee system in 1989–1990. In his evidence, the then Leader of the House wrote that the government started from the position that the committees had become 'an indispensable part of the work of the House of Commons

... They have established themselves as important contributors to the parliamentary functions of scrutiny, investigation and influence over the work of the executive ... The government sees the requirement for the future being one of refinement and detailed improvement, not wholesale change.'[19] This was the main burden of most of the evidence received by the committee and its own judgement was in accordance with it. As Terence Higgins, former chairman of the Treasury and Civil Service and Liaison Committees, wrote in October 1992, 'the general view is that the experiment has proved a success and the reformed system has become a permanent and important feature of parliamentary life.'[20]

What then has this reformed system achieved? Primarily three things: an extension to the range of parliamentary scrutiny; a deepening of parliamentary accountability; and a widening of the public policy debate. First, extending the range of scrutiny: all major government departments are covered by a scrutiny committee—though because of disagreement between the political parties about the allocation of places, no Scottish Affairs Committee was set up during the 1987–92 Parliament. Until March 1994, when a committee to cover Northern Ireland was established, the Northern Ireland Office has been covered separately rather than haphazardly through the other 'functional' committees. Because the committees are permanent, they are accepted as regular interlocutors, part of the process of discussion, debate and exchange of information through which the whole range of government decisions are implemented.

The second major achievement of the new system has been to deepen parliamentary accountability of the executive by adding a new dimension to the traditional procedures. Given the permanence of the committees, the work of departments (and their associated public bodies) is always a possible target for examination; action, or inaction, may have to be explained and defended, publicly and on the record. And the explanation will need to be more than a two or three line answer to a Parliamentary Question or intervention in debate. It will form part of an extended period of questioning, to which the committee may return if not satisfied. Moreover, after all the agonising in the 1950s and 1960s about distinguishing policy from administration, and the constitutional difficulties of having ministers answer to committees, the new committees have investigated policy matters as well as administration and expenditure, have interrogated Cabinet ministers as well as senior officials, without destroying the fabric of the constitution or the cohesion of parliamentary parties.

The widening of the public policy debate has been achieved because the committees have given new opportunities to those outside the House of Commons to contribute formally to it, to take part, as it were, in the grand inquest of the nation. Reviewing the effectiveness of the new system in January 1990, Terence Higgins put it like this: 'The committees have increasingly provided a forum where pressure groups and other bodies outside government have been able to bring their problems, requests and views before Parliament and to have them analysed. Much of the evidence given to committees comes from such bodies. It is valuable in enabling the committees to hear all points of view and to put often conflicting points to ministers and civil servants for comment. Additionally, the process of publication of evidence from such sources means that it can in its turn be tested or challenged; pressure groups' arguments are now subject to closer scrutiny.'[21]

Whilst there has been no significant widening of the policy community as a result of the committees' calls for evidence, what has happened is that more of the debate within that community has taken place on the public and parliamentary record. The light of publicity is thrown not only on the government's acts, omissions and intentions, but also upon the responses to and comments upon those acts, omissions and intentions.

Those achievements have taken place with, on the whole, the active cooperation of the government, notwithstanding occasional exceptions like the Westland Affair. Indeed, the committees have secured a significant improvement in time taken by departments to respond to reports—the accepted convention is now a maximum of two months— and even a limited amount of committed time in the parliamentary timetable for debates on committee reports—though such debates are still sparsely attended and cover only a small minority of the reports which are actually produced. In the first ten years of operation, only thirteen reports were the subject of either substantive motions or adjournment debates, though a further 103 were 'tagged' as being of relevance to debates on other topics.[22]

An indication of extent of the committees' scrutiny activity can be seen from the scale of evidence-taking and the number and size of reports produced in the most recent session for which figures are available (1992–93: although this was a longer session than normal, the committees were not set up until July 1992 and so for these purposes it is not untypical). In that session there were 57 appearances by Cabinet ministers before the committees and 55 by other ministers. 427 civil servants gave evidence as did 215 officials from 'associated public bodies'. The committees issued 129 reports (including evidence only reports) totalling 16,456 pages. Those reports were the product of 663 meetings. To form an idea of the total scrutiny activity of the House, which involved 300 members, one has also to add the work of the Public Accounts Committee (63 reports, 4,436 pages), the Science and Technology Committee (1 report, 305 pages), the Select Committee on the Parliamentary Commissioner for Administration (4 reports, 214 pages) and the Select Committee on European Legislation (41 reports, 1,232 pages).

As instruments of scrutiny rather than power, the committees have not radically altered the balance between government and Parliament nor have they shifted the predominant mode of behaviour of backbench MPs. They continue to operate in a broadly consensual way: in the 1992–93 session a total of 86 divisions were called: the Health and Treasury Committees were responsible between them for 53 of these; six of the committees (Agriculture, Defence, Education, National Heritage, Scottish Affairs, Social Security) had no divisions; 12 of the 86 divisions concerned the election of a chairman.

This consensual mode has not been bought at the price of avoiding controversial issues, as the reports over the years clearly demonstrate. The Defence Committee, for example, has reported on strategic nuclear weapons policy, Trident (four times), the Falklands War (twice) and the size of the Royal Navy's Surface Fleet, not to mention Westland PLC. The Treasury Committee has maintained a running commentary upon the government's economic and monetary policies, including hearings on the Budget and Public Expenditure statements. The Trade and Industry Committee held hearings on the Iraqi Gun Affair (which it will be interesting to compare with the report of the Scott Inquiry) and was the chosen vehicle to cover the government's retreat from parliamentary pressure on the coal mine closure programme in 1992.

In all this activity, two major criticisms can be made. First, taken as a whole the work of the committees has been unsystematic and its coverage of the work of government patchy, not to say idiosyncratic. In spite of the existence of the Liaison Committee with a coordinating brief, each committee is a law unto itself in the choice of topics for investigation. And the same political dynamic is often evident in the pattern of questioning, which does not always follow a coherent strategy. Members are first and foremost political animals and generalists. They will pursue those topics and lines of inquiry which fit with their perception of the political needs of the moment, which may not immediately relate to the requirements of rational or systematic analysis of policy issues, expenditure priorities or administrative systems, nor to the brief which has been put before them by the Clerk.

Second, and really a particular instance of the first criticism, notwithstanding the terms of reference of the committees, repeated encouragement from the Liaison Committee, and even draft model questions from the Treasury Committee, expenditure has been largely neglected. Some committees have held hearings on their department's annual report and the Defence Committee, as already noted, has done considerable work on the procurement of some weapons systems, but the committees as a whole have not provided the systematic and comprehensive review of public expenditure which some had hoped to see. To a large degree, this simply reflects the fact that relatively few MPs are interested in this at the level of detail which is required for such investigations and, like departmental administration, it comes low in their priorities when compared with major items of policy.

Whilst the establishment of the departmentally-related select committees was the major development of the 1980s, it was not the only important one. Concern over the control of public expenditure led to an increase in the powers of the Public Accounts Committee, the House's most venerable select committee, in the National Audit Act, 1983 — passed in spite of strong government opposition to its central features. The Act converted the old Exchequer and Audit Department to a new and independent National Audit Office (NAO) and extended its remit to cover 'value for money' investigations and the activities of any body (other than local authorities or nationalised industries) which receives more than half of its income from public funds. The enhanced independence and wider remit for the Comptroller and Auditor General and the NAO has given the PAC a renewed vigour, which it has most recently demonstrated with its report on The Conduct of Public Business.[22] Although policy matters remain formally outside its remit, the value-for-money investigations in particular have taken the PAC into the heart of controversial areas of government activity, such as housing benefits, control of local authority spending, NHS costs and defence procurement.

A further significant development in the 1980s has been the arrangements for scrutiny of European legislation. Mention has already been made of the committee established in 1974, since supplemented by the European Standing Committees, to consider the legislation. These committees deal with a major and growing aspect of government which is not the direct responsibility of British ministers, a situation which the House of Commons has not found easy to deal with. It is, however, too large a subject to be fully dealt with in a survey of this kind.

Plus ça change ...

'The evolution of select committees has proceeded in a manner which maintains the continuity of institutional forms in the House of Commons. It has been a work of cautious adaptation, sensitive to the susceptibilities of those in government but bringing renewed vitality to the traditional critical functions of Parliament'.[24] That assessment in 1988 remains true today. Caution, continuity and adaptation have been the hall-marks of the development of the select committee system in the last fifty years. There have been some apparently false starts, as with the Crossman experiments, and perhaps some detours, as with the Estimates and Expenditure Committees, but through the post-war decades the Commons has gradually shrugged off some of the more restrictive implications of Morrison's critique of Jowett but without effecting the radical change to the parliamentary system which Morrison and those like him so greatly feared. Indeed, the principal features of that system remain untouched: the Chamber of the House of Commons remains the primary forum for debate and decision; the mode of behaviour and discourse in the House is still that of cohesive, adversarial parties; single party majority government remains the norm; the Executive is still dominant. 'Plus la même chose'. Whilst select committees have grown and become more prominent, they do not provide an alternative career structure to ministerial office, even if they do provide a useful staging-post in the career of some ambitious younger MPs as well as for some of those whose ministerial days are over. On the other hand, they do provide an outlet for the increased professionalisation which has been so marked in British parliamentary politics in the last thirty years.

Although the fundamentals remain the same, change there has certainly been. Select committees have grown in number and significance, particularly if one takes the quantity of activity and published output as an indicator. Scrutiny has been extended, accountability deepened and policy debate widened. A substantial and continuous process of explanatory dialogue between ministers and their officials on the one side and backbench MPs on the other is taking place across the whole range of government, absorbing a significant and growing amount of the energies and time of all concerned.

How might the select committee system develop? If, as seems most likely whilst the present party and electoral systems remain intact, they continue as scrutiny rather than decision-making committees, the obvious developments are those which would build upon the existing system. A further extension of the range of scrutiny, including, for example, the security services, is desirable. Deeper scrutiny of administration and expenditure would be possible with more staff resources and, in particular, if the services of the National Audit Office could be made more widely available, and perhaps extended in coverage. The increased (but still relative) openness of government which will result from the 1993 White Paper *Open Government* should provide plenty of material for committee members (and their advisers and assistants) to explore.

A more radical development would be for the committees to engage with the passage of parliamentary business, such as legislation or expenditure. One of the reasons for governments' relatively benign attitude to select committees has been that, if necessary, they can afford to ignore them, at least as far as the dispatch of government business is concerned. Whilst it is helpful for governments to have the support of select committees (on which, of course, their nominal supporters are normally in a majority), it is not necessary. Adverse or critical reports from scrutiny committees are an irritant or an embarrassment, but no more. However, should the committees become engaged with the legislative or expenditure process, the government—and hence the whips—would be bound to take a much closer interest in their work, and especially in their votes. This would undoubtedly lead to a very significant shift away from the consensual mode of select committee work towards the adversarial. The dispatch of business would become the priority. Such a development seems unlikely in present political circumstances: governments, particularly governments with small majorities, are not likely to add to the number of hurdles they have to clear in getting their programme through Parliament.

Two factors may, nevertheless, generate pressure for change. The first is the growing perception that the House of Commons is over-loaded. The difficulties encountered in setting up the European legislation committees and the responses to the Jopling Report both indicate that Members see themselves as over-burdened and are pressing for significant rationalisation. The growth of select committee activity has, of course, contributed to the pressure of business, but there is little sign so far that many Members are willing to countenance reducing select committee work as a way of cutting the burden. (Standing committees would be a more popular choice for a reduced role.) But as the pressure for rationalisation becomes stronger, then the case for a more coordinated and systematic select committee structure—looking for example, at whether departmentally-related committees should deal with European business, PCA and even NAO reports—will also grow, however much individual committees protest that they should be free to determine their own priorities. Such an outcome is unlikely, but there is no doubt that the signs of overload are there, for the House as well as the government.

The second factor is the clear need for reform of the legislative process. Few, apart from government business managers, find the present arrangements satisfactory, particularly in standing committees. The need for extensive government amendments to legislation in the course of its passage, and increasingly after it has passed, has demonstrated the inadequacy of present scrutiny. This ground has been well worked over by the Rippon Commission's *Making the Law* (Hansard Society, February 1993). Legislative reform should be a priority for the House of Commons and it would not be surprising if select committees featured when it is considered—indeed, it would be astonishing if they did not. The case for using the committees for some form of pre-legislative hearings, the use of special standing committees and similar devices will all have their backers, no doubt. Reformers will need to beware how easily involving select committees in the passage of business could destroy their present raison d'etre as instruments of scrutiny.

In November 1958, the then Leader of the House, R. A. Butler, dismissed the idea of specialist committees as a wrong idea, not only difficult constitutionally, but . . . difficult from the point of view of administration. 'Any government would regard it as a muddle which is not one that fits in with normal parliamentary procedure.'[25] Nevertheless, cautious, evolutionary development over thirty years has shown that, through experiment and adaptation, British parliamentary procedure can contain, and British governments can (at least) tolerate, scrutiny and criticism of ministers and their officials by small groups of members dedicated to that task in particular areas of policy and administration. These may not be what Morrison and Butler called 'specialist committees'. But, as Shakespeare has Juliet say, what's in a name?

1   H. Morrison, *Government and Parliament: A Survey from the Inside* (Oxford University Press, 1954), pp. 154–5, 158–9.
2   See D. Coombes, *The Member of Parliament and the Administration: the Case of the Select Committee on Nationalised Industries* (Allen & Unwin, 1966), pp. 204, 205, 211.
3   See N. Johnson, *Parliament and the Administration: the Estimates Committee, 1945–65* (Allen & Unwin, 1966).
4   Ibid, p. 137.
5   Ibid, p. 131.
6   Ibid, pp. 143–44.
7   H. V. Wiseman, 'The New Specialised Committees' in A. H. Hanson and B. Crick (eds), *The Commons in Transition* (Fontana/Collins, 1970), pp. 218–19.
8   Ibid, p. 216.
9   B. Crick, 'Whither Parliamentary Reform?' in Hanson and Crick, op. cit., p. 261.
10 N. Johnson, 'Select Committees as Tools of Parliamentary Reform' in Hanson and Crick, op. cit., pp. 243 and 247.
11 Ibid, pp. 240–1.
12 *Select Committees of the House of Commons*, Cmnd. 4507, October 1970, p. 6.
13 Ibid, p. 7.
14 S. A. Walkland, 'Whither the Commons?' in S. A. Walkland and M. Ryle (eds), *The Commons in the Seventies* (Martin Robertson and Fontana, 1977), p. 247.
15 Ibid, p. 249.
16 Select Committee on Procedure, *First Report*, HC 588, 1978.
17 P. Baines, 'History and Rationale of the 1979 Reform' in G. Drewry (ed), *The New Select Committees: A Study of the 1979 Reforms* Clarendon Press, 2e 1985), p. 29.
18 N. Johnson, 'Departmental Select Committees' in M. Ryle and P. Richards (eds), *The Commons Under Scrutiny* (Routledge), p. 166.
19 Select Committee on Procedure, *Second Report: the Working of the Select Committee System*, HC 19, 1989–90, p. 18.
20 T. Higgins, 'Select Committees — A Quiet Revolution', *The House Magazine*, 26 October 1992.
21 Select Committee on Procedure, *Second Report*, HC 19, 1989–90, p. 43.
22 Select Committee on Procedure, *Second Report*, HC 19, 1989–90, p. 267.
23 Public Accounts Committee, *Eighth Report: The Proper conduct of Public Business*, HC 154, 1993–94.
24 N. Johnson, 'Departmental Select Committees' in M. Ryle and P. Richards (eds), *The Commons Under Scrutiny* (Routledge), 1988.
25 Select Committee on Procedure, *Report*, HC 92, 1958–59, Q.1159.

Backbench Influence: A Personal View

BY AUSTIN MITCHELL MP

WORKING harder to wield less power, feeling more influential but in minor matters, a more satisfying life but ultimately frustrated: such are the changes in the role and influence of backbenchers. Like all generalisations impossible to quantify, the claim is impressionistic and subject to qualification. Yet it adequately sums fifty years of growing activity for the species and increasing analysis from the academics.

Too much work falls on MPs in a system with fewer legislators per capita than other nations, yet paradoxically there are too many MPs to do the job without tripping over each other. MPs do not have one job but several: constituency ombudsman, area advocate, party activist, legislator, specialist, controller of the executive, minor media figure, propagandist with a mini bully pulpit and trainee minister all rolled into one, called 'MP' and paid £31,687. They can do as much or as little as they want; to attempt all is impossible. Some are a full-time career in their own right. With neither performance audit nor real sanction, MPs are free to attempt or evade all or any of the roles, immerse themselves in one to the exclusion of others, do little or find solace for failure in casual adultery, alcohol or the all-consuming parliamentary activity of running round in small circles thinking they are big wheels. Yet the choice and the role is a lonely one and all are on a treadmill moving ever faster. The variety of the job is its satisfaction and its curse.

What has changed is the pace and the balance between roles. The rise of the specialist committees balances the decline of the legislative role. Career politics makes Members more effective but more amenable. The politics of economic decline harnesses them tighter to the governmental chariot, forcing on them the lies, double-talk and humiliation economic failure produces, but they also strain party unity and reduce MPs to levels of unpopularity unplumbed by predecessors. There are no generalisations, just 415 ways of doing an untidy job with no clear role model.

The environment

The institution, its inhabitants and the work have all changed over fifty years. The workplace has changed least. Rebuilt in the 1940s with Portakabin ghettos slipped in everywhere the public eye cannot see, it is well calculated to deck out the politics of an 'ordinary' middle ranking power in the trappings of imperial majesty. Six thousand people now work in a building designed for fifteen hundred gentlemen. We run a

legislative factory in premises design for a gentleman's club. So convenience and efficiency are ruled out. Governments have, grudgingly and
belatedly, improved matters by taking over premises round about: the
two Norman Shaw Buildings, Abbey Yard, One Parliament Street (most
lavish of all) and 7 Millbank, reminiscent of grown-up legislatures
where they believe MPs should be given the facilities to do the job.
Once all had lockers. Now everyone who wants one has an office or a
desk and a few have suites worthy of the directors of a dodgy company.
Most are also able to accommodate secretaries nearby.

It is becoming possible to do the job with a degree of professionalism
and back-up almost enough to allow MPs to fulfil their responsibilities
and serve their constituents, though too much time and effort is still
wasted in fire-brigade activity. For too little can be rationally planned.
The institution is still run to exclude rather than facilitate, and the
Serjeant at Arms' bureaucracy remains more concerned to enforce rules
than make life or work easy for Members. The preoccupation is with
dignity and procedure not management, effective resource allocation or
accessibility. So the institution is still run as a protective device to keep
the people out and protect MPs from the world.

In other parliaments, pressures have been met by common facilities:
computer systems, research, parliamentary and secretarial staffs, better
entertainment facilities, with grants for satellite constituency offices.
Except for the Library's overstretched research facilities, Britain has
coped by paying an expense allowance to Members, currently £40,380,
a mite better than the £500 when the Secretarial Allowance began in
1969. MPs are then expected to provide for themselves, but it finances
only one office, either in the constituency or in Parliament, when both
are needed. The allowance is too much for the indolent and inactive,
several of whom keep the money in the family by employing wives (the
internal directory lists 48 MPs, 18 Labour, 27 Tory, with employees of
the same name on their staff). Yet it is too small for the conscientious
who would need a staff of, say, six where the allowance covers two,
perhaps two and a half, secretarial staff. It misses the opportunities of
bulk buying and standard systems. It allows insecurity, so we have no
pool of qualified staff with a career structure. Small wonder that the
fifty or so 'interns' provided free for three to nine months by British and
American universities are always snapped up. The allowance can only
be viewed as a start down the road, giving MPs some but not all of the
backing they need to do their job. Coupled with the electronic office
revolution, it has gone a long way to provide those MPs prepared to
work at it with mini staffs, mini communication centres sending out
faxes and press releases, and mini advice systems to cope with the
constituency. What is now needs is teams who can speak, act and think
for the MP.

Thanks to the growth in media facilities and interest, backbenchers
now have an ability to reach the people they never had before. Radio

covereage began it, though it has never lived up to its potential to provide cheap continuous coverage on a dedicated channel. Television was finally accepted in 1988 and, in an age when most people get most of their news from the television, strengthens the Commons as well as increasing interest in its business. Commonsense coverage rules and advanced remote control cameras linked to quick 'touch screen' response systems make this a real British success, but it too has not yet lived up to its potential. Only Prime Minister's Question Time is broadcast regularly: a bad joke made worse (and put under more pressure) when projected as if it were the highlight of the week rather than its nadir. Other coverage has been small-scale and partial: regional coverage of regional MPs, Summaries, Week in Parliament and longer daily coverage on satellite. The real strength of Parliament, debating serious issues seriously, is hardly ever brought home by broadcasting a full debate, and the closed-circuit potential to keep MPs in touch with what is going on the Chamber while they tackle the workload in their offices has never been tapped. Nor have we cut out the middleman. Coverage remains at the mercy of the broadcating organisations. We have no C Span and the start-to-finish coverage now available to the small Cable audience will take years to build up to the level where interested groups, educational institutions and the political class will plug in continuously.

The postwar rebuilding of the Commons doubled the number of press based in the gallery ghetto. It is grossly overcrowded, though 300 press and media compare badly with the 3,500 clustered round Congress. The media explosion of multiple television channels, local radios, now satellite and cable, strained the facilities to the maximum. Limiting entry and requiring journalists to work by club rules means they become hand-fed, allowing ministers to dole out small doses of information at profit to themselves. So news management becomes an industry and the overstretched press facilities a bottle-neck, protecting poor ministers and incompetent backbenchers. The constraint has recently been eased by moving electronic coverage to the media centre at 4 Millbank, home to eighty BBC staff, serving networks, regions and radio, local and national, to IRN, to the parliamentary units and programmes of ITN and to Sky, with studios and facilities for the regional ITV companies as well as Irish, Australian and New Zealand television, all in one building, replacing the previous cramped facilities. Too much wind-swept coverage still comes from College Green when major events happen, but there is now the basis for professional coverage almost as good as the media facilities provided for the American Congress and the Canadian House of Commons.

All a considerable improvement on what went before, strengthening backbenchers' growing media role, giving them the opportunity to reach constituents, push causes and air their egos. We have a love–hate relationship with the media, but they need MPs to break and authenticate stories, to use privilege and name names, even just to give balance. We need the media to reach the people. We are junior partners now, politics is a media game not a Commons monopoly, bit-part players in someone else's circus, not kings of the jungle. Yet we still have a role and a platform. How depressing, then, to find that the people like us less the more they get.

The Members and their work

If changes to the institution are minimal, its inhabitants have changed beyond recognition. The dark suit remains traditional apart from a few exhibitionists, but within it a new political creature, the professional politician, has been bred. From the 1930s to the 1970s the dominant two-party system meant that MPs came in after establishing themselves in a career and winning on a party ticket. The success, or failure, of that party did more to determine prospects and success than anything they could do by way of constituency service or an independent track record.

Today MPs come in somewhat younger; 52% of 1983's intake were under 40, 41% of 1987's (though this does not show up in mean ages: 49 years in 1964, the same in 1987 and 1992, because once in, MPs stay longer). Before, those from privileged backgrounds came in young to devote themselves to the struggle for the glittering prizes. Now, most do having done little of significance before in jobs with no real career prospects to keep body and soul together while pursuing the central ambition: election. The archetypal backbencher is a professional politician pursuing a career in politics by following leaders rather than party. MPs have established a degree of independence from the party which is small but sufficient to break the subordination of yore.

Professionals court and climb rather than crusade or criticise. Power is their goal, not crowning a satisfying career by a stint in the House. Career politicians compete more and climb faster. They do so by following the court formed round the Leader and hitching rides on bandwagons. Professionals view Parliament as the managerial bear-pit it is, exploit its publicity potential but eschew its drudgery to concentrate on developing their own satisfactions. Careers can crawl as well as soar but are less likely to take the path of dissent. Where once MPs struggled for possession of a party's soul or rose by dissent—the path to power of Macmillan, Churchill, Bevan, Strachey or Cripps—that road now leads only to Waikato.

Party remains dominant, just less obsessive, less effective and with less to offer. The constituency has become more important and makes much heavier demands, but there are now few party agents to ease them and less active parties have to be carried. More MPs are compelled or persuaded to live in their constituency, where they once visited. More problems come up in the politics of decline. The struggle for shares of the cake makes the MP a development officer (unskilled). The MP is the constituency's figurehead, focus and leader in its demands for grants and that constant process of lobbying ministers and Brussels which development is now about.

Constituency service, the hard grind of overpaid social work, once the exception, is the norm. Some MPs even devote themselves to it. With the work, the communications revolution and the publicity and self-promotion, comes an incumbency factor, not on the scale of the American (for theirs is a measure of money as well as service) but bigger than the five hundred or so votes once confidently estimated as the limit of the 'personal vote'. Political scientists talk of a one or two per cent bonus, particularly at the first election after winning. Thus MPs can boost, or cushion, a swing to or from the party, and the important thing is not the actual figures (which are impossible to quantify) but that personal votes are growing. Most MPs serve their constituents out of duty, yet none feel that the activity is its own reward or that the effort is without effect.

The workload has increased, is increasing and can not be diminished. MPs find themselves in the hardest worked legislature in the world. They put in the longest hours (180 days per session from 1974–6, 240 in 1992–3), pass the most legislation (an average of a thousand pages per session in the 1950s, over two thousand larger A4 pages in the 1990s) and ask the most questions. Mail and the people's demands through constituency surgeries are growing faster, compounded by economic recession, a growing desire to be heard and have the same influence as citizens as they have as consumers, added to which is the growth of pressure group activity. Analyses and MPs' own impressions both indicate that the workload is growing. In addition to constituents' concerns, there is the material generated by specialised interests and current issues. The activities of women Members speaking out on women's issues, or the God Squad on moral issues, boost the deluge. Yet more is generated by the media, either through Members appearing or through campaigns of the type which have produced panic legislation on gun laws and pit bull terriers.

Tory MPs with middle-class or commuter seats claim that much of their mail is issue orientated. Labour's relates more to problems and cases. Together, these transform the MPs' role of redressing grievances and auditing the executive by focusing on the interface between public and the machine. MPs become mediators between their constituencies and Westminster–Whitehall, making MPs social workers, issue explainers and early warning systems to indicate when things are going wrong, as they did on the poll tax or the Child Support Agency. Problems, complaints, grievances and worries pour into the MP as the local face of the system and as the residuary legatee of power. MPs encourage the process, turning themselves into Citizens Advice Bureaux, Ombudsmen and the political arm of the growing 'problem industry'.

As such, we are well qualified to audit the machine and tackle the problems it throws up. This is largely a post-box role, sending the complaints on to proper authorities, but it still allows opportunities for pressure, legal talent, effort and skilled exposition. Our main strength is the ability to take complaints to the top. There, decisions made by harassed staff are rechecked and, where necessary, put right. This happens in a sizeable minority of cases, so constituents feel the MP has used power on their behalf, an impression we make no attempt to dispel, however untrue. Even where the verdict is unchanged, all get an explanation which may satisfy. Government itself benefits, because an increasingly complicated system interacts with the people across an ever wider range of issues. Complaints via MPs signal where things are going wrong and provides a safety valve more effective than all the Citizens' Charters.

This new role has grown only to be curtailed. Few MPs now follow Enoch Powell's approach of sending back local government problems, but influence on housing allocations has largely been eliminated by shortage of housing stock, while tighter rules and meaner benefits curtail the ability to win special needs allocations. Government has handed whole areas to agencies from whose decisions there is no appeal. MPs plead and their complaints are given priority. Yet in the last analysis the only way to win is to 'go nuclear' by naming officials or embarrassing the agency in Parliament. Some Members do that, but most have too little time. Handing over powers to non-accountable quangos run by businessmen also undermines the role of the MP, for health trusts and opted-out schools do not always welcome interventions, while TECs have been known to threaten training organisations which appeal to MPs: customer care and Charter power is their ethos, much of it PR, all of it ultimately unresponsive.

Once the MP was a generalist telling government what the constituency would not stand for. That role is now dead. In a fast-moving world MPs find it difficult to keep up. Able to deal with things retrospectively, they are less able to analyse quickly, as distinct from commenting as situations develop. They have been replaced by the media, self-appointed voice of the nation and sponsors of the polls by which government measures public opinion more accurately than MPs ever could. We are now grist to a media mill not powers in our own right. So we have to specialise since as society becomes more complex, government listens only to specialised opinion: in the universities, the interest groups, the media, the think-tanks, in business and trade associations. We can be influential by plugging into this, a process facilitated by the proliferation of All-Party parliamentary groups, currently 233 in number, many serviced by outside organisations, all allowing MPs to follow their interests.

Select committees are a better training ground. Their real role is to test the intellectual basis of government policies, making governmemt better at justifying and opposition better informed. So competition for membership has become more intense, with whips on both sides more inclined to use the power of selection as patronage and more ready to assert greater influence. Membership confers access to information and the ability to develop knowledge, skill and contacts, all vital training grounds not previously available, so they are doled out carefully to reward friends and advance careers. The committees have not fulfilled their earlier promise, however, but are stuck in a rut. They have become more partisan, with the party majority more dominant. Where cross-party alliances once produced decisions embarrassing to the government, this is now rare. So reports are either diluted or they split, as in the abortive report on party finances from the Home Affairs Committee. The work is still valuable, though more the evidence than the analyses, yet the real potential for dramatic public hearings calling ministers and civil servants to account or high-powered reports setting out a new agenda have been deliberately frustrated.

The committees have undermined themselves by taking up big subjects without the intellectual or research strength to cope, or by pursuing fashions without the strength to lead them. Royal Commissions are out of fashion. Yet instead of trying to replace them, the select committees have allowed themselves to be used as cheap-jack substitutes, making ephemeral reports, less soundly based than they should be. Members have not been prepared to do the work. Though they have imposed heavier burdens on MPs and developed their specialist expertise, the benefits have accrued to individual MPs not the wider public. As an effective check on government, they have been useless, while their role as a critique on government thinking has declined. Fortunately specialisation has grown outside the committees' nucleus. Members not brought into government seek solace — and income — as consultants, but few in that species of internal exile which is the lot of dissenters have become in effect D.I.Y. departments: Bill Cash is the Department of Anti-European Affairs, Chris Mullins his own Minister of Justice, Ken Livingstone an Economics Department, Frank Field Mr Pensions, I am interested in Accountancy and Audit. All are happy in their work but largely ignored by a front bench which does not relish competition.

Extra work, more specialised expertise, the growing constituency role, the incumbency vote, all lead to increasing independence. As party creatures, MPs were totally dependent. Today, party is less rewarding and effective, and MPs have a small degree of distance. Labour brought its MPs few benefits in its time of trouble. John Major has created an atmosphere of 'sauve qui peut'. MPs attempting to decouple their fate are less impelled to prostrate themselves, even though they now establish their dissent more quietly than the faction fighting of old. There is life after and outside the party, not much yet but some and growing, and independence grows with it.

The parties, particularly Labour, are even becoming dependent on MPs. Once Tories were expected to contribute to their local party, so selection became an auction. Today, Labour's weakness, the decline in numbers and the increasing expense of modern campaigning, have introduced that principle to the people's party. MPs are required to contribute 1% of income to the party nationally, a similar sum goes to the regional party and many give whatever they can afford (or the party can extract) locally. This Danegeld is supplemented by Office Allowances through the use or provision of equipment such as faxes, telephones and copiers, even party use of secretaries, paid by the House of Commons. Labour is collapsing in on its MPs. The Tories are not, but they have fewer agents and can provide less backing to their MPs.

The same collapse goes on in the Commons. A management consultants' report on Labour says of its backbenchers: 'They are by far the largest resource available to the party. Yet backbenchers are not organised into any formal policy and campaigning structure as such in which they can help the party ... In effect the formal structure of the party ignores more than half the resources which are at its disposal to help it achieve its goals. This problem can only be solved if the talent of the backbenchers is harnessed and managed effectively.'

This is the latest symptom of a long process of using backbenchers to help local parties in Tory seats. The abortive proposal of the PLP review group, that shadow spokesmen and spokeswomen should not have teams of mini-shadows to increase patronage but work with backbench groups, was ignored because of the clamour for jobs; and any proposal which ignores the individualistic competitive nature of MPs will face a similar fate. Front-benchers do not want anyone, particularly competing backbenchers, interfering in their policy reserves. Backbenchers do not want to pull triumphal chariots. Yet the proposals underline a developing trend. MPs on both sides are already unpaid canvassing teams in by-elections, local and Euro elections, perambulating party workers in the recess, unpaid media trainers and compulsory attenders at fund-raising functions. As the parties get weaker, they will have to work harder to merit the backing it is failing to give them.

The changing role of parties

Bagehot portrayed MPs as men of dignity and status influencing government by debate. Some believe that picture still prevails, indeed Speaker Weatherall discerned nineteen occasions in which government had changed or modified policy as a result of debate. In fact, Bagehot's picture became irrelevant as it was written. The rise of party put the executive in charge of the legislature. Government will only listen if it can be thrown out. Only the electorate can do that, so the MP is no longer there to exercise independent judgement but as a member of a party elected on a party ticket to support or oppose what government proposes. The party majority means that the executive drives a legislative streamroller. Opposition MPs can heckle, ask parliamentary questions and argue with the government until they are red (or hopefully some day blue) in the face; they can neither stop nor detour it. Mrs

Thatcher drove the steamroller in one way, John Major in another, but both flatten an opposition which can only make noise, delay measures and appeal to an opinion outside which is not very interested most of the time.

Party is less popular, less relevant, less respected but still dominant. The Labour government of the 1970s had first a small, then no majority, but that constrained troops prepared to oppose the government on matters below 'confidence' level and such as the 40% requirement on the Scottish and Welsh devolution referenda or Rooker/Wise amendment indexing tax allowances. They nevertheles remained loyal on central issues, rebelling only to the left in ways the Tories could not support rather than endangering their government. Margaret Thatcher changed the nature of her party but Tory MPs went along with it, just as they have under her less determined successor. Grumbling is not revolt, the Duke of York style works: the troops march up and down again though the dissent is louder, the laggards more numerous.

Both parties have become more like each other. The Tories have become more ideological and factional, Labour's left–right conflict has given way to a court versus country division. The anti-leadership ethos has gone and Labour has become leadership-driven as the Tories always were, though Labour's leader is more powerful because internal management structures built for debate can be steered as debate dies away. As a party built for government, the Conservatives have the most effective system of internal management to relay the opinions of the troops up and the orders of leaders down. Management means consultation. Leaders need to know the parameters of manoeuvre to lead effectively. So the whips office, party committees and the 1922 Committee itself are all effective instruments of a two-way process to which Labour has no counterpart. Disused battlefields do not make good sounding boards.

So Labour, in theory built on democracy, in fact gives its backbenchers less influence than a Tory party with a leadership ethos. Once Labour MPs elected their leaders. Their choices were usually the inevitable ones: Gaitskell, Wilson and Callaghan, though their last choice, Michael Foot, was so disastrous that they lost the power to choose to an electoral college of Parliamentary Labour Party, unions and constituencies. There, the parliamentary vote accounts for only a third of the total. Subsequent choices of both leader and deputy have been ratifications of the inevitable and the new system is weighted towards inertia. Leadership contenders rise by attracting attention in the House, then get on TV and in to the Shadow Cabinet (a list of who is up and who is down in the parliamentary stakes) and use that as a platform to get on the National Executive rather than battling their way up through the outside organisations. As a result, the number of MPs on Labour's NEC has been fairly steady: 17 in 1960, 12 in 1985, 13 in 1993, but the number of Shadow Cabinet members there in a custodial role has risen to over half, currently 7 out of the 13. The leadership is well in control of the whole party and a leader once installed is impossible to remove.

The Tories have moved the other way. Originally, the choice was made by the 'magic circle' sounded out mysteriously to produce the leaders. In the 1960s, it was changed to election by MPs alone, a system which produced Mrs Thatcher but also got rid of her when she became a liability and threatens the same for John Major. MPs have tasted power. It is negative, for they can destroy rather than create, but with politics more focused on electoral survival that is what MPs really want—which makes the media increasingly powerful in the same negative way.

Because of the emphasis on management, the Tory whips' office is more important and more sophisticated than Labour's. Tory whips assiduously attend every meeting, plug into every grouping, talk to their flocks, while Labour's are less energetic, less listened to by MPs and less respected by the leadership. Labour's committees, former battle-grounds, are now trying to find a role as education classes and backing groups for front-benchers. In the Tory party they are more flexible, for meetings can be held quickly as trouble arises, allowing explanations and bringing ministers into contact with the range of parliamentary opinion. Labour's are more routine and shadow ministers are less at their beck and call. The contrast is brought out by John Horam, the only MP who has had experience of both systems in government: 'When Labour was in power in the 1970s the party meetings and committees were always much more interesting and lively. I remember a series of clashes and confrontations with left-wingers like Dennis Skinner dressing down ministers and even the Prime Minister: "We know what you're about Jim. We're wise to what you're doing." It was a real discussion about real issues and it mattered. Things are different in the Conservative Party. It's never as directly expressed but their fmachinery of consultation is more effective because of that. It's also much more flexible because meetings of subject groups are set up quickly as soon as a crisis blows up and we're talking directly and quickly to the minister who has to explain himself and justify what he's doing.'

Conservative party structures have never been the forum for a long running debate between entrenched blocks of the type which dominated Labour's committees and PLP meetings up to the mid-1980s. In power, ministers like Denis Healey routinely swatted off attacks from the right and from the left. The subject groups were no real check; and though the PLP debated serious issues and critical resolutions, it was easily brought back into line in its rare votes by the arrival of the pay-roll vote, dark-suited, serious and always late. They came in 12.30pm onwards to vote down the unacceptable without having heard what it was. On the Conservative side, real issues are broached in the more polite, less confrontational voice that the party uses and the 1922

Committee is a sounding board not a power, though ministers appear before it to explain and be criticised. Except on Europe, ministers deal with real problems directly rather than defending themselves against attacks from different ideological standpoints, magnified and filtered through blocks which uses the structures to carry on their long-standing arguments.

Both parties changed in the 1980s. Labour more. Loss of office produced a nervous breakdown and a left–right conflict (mainly between the PLP and the outside party) and its internal repercussions as bitterly contested committee elections and policy discussions produced travelling caucuses, moving from one group to another to vote for their policies in a way which had not happened before. Or since. Messy, argumentative, divisive, it was ultimately disastrous, resulting in Labour's defeat. Yet it was also lively, interesting and exciting, grappling with real issues and discussing real policy problems in a way which has not happened since. Discussion has been deliberately damped down as divisive; the party no longer wants to argue.

In the late 1980s the party over-compensated for these follies by submission to the leadership. Richard Rose described Labour as a party of factions, the Tories as one of tendencies. Labour's factions died or splintered just as Tory tendencies came out into the open and the groups began to attack each other as if they were in the Labour Party. Labour's Campaign Group is what Tribune was but smaller and less influential; Tribune has become a leadership rally, Manifesto had packed up. In party elections there is now little block voting, no faction fighting, just courtiers with degrees of enthusiasm, loyalists who are more or less energetic. Thus the PLP is now a forum for complaints and grumbles rather than confrontation. The subject groups are echo chambers for the front-bench spokesmen, their officers loyalists picked, even elected, by the front-benchers, their role to provide speaking teams and backing groups rather than sustaining a critique or playing a part in the development of policy.

Even the party Conference, Labour's parliament, has become its leadership rally, tamed because there is a deep instinct for loyalty in the Labour Party and a desire to over-compensate for the failures of the early 1980s. Yet rather than relying on it, the party leaders have deliberately reduced the role of the Conference and the outside party, taking control of the NEC, formulating policy from the top down, rather than letting it bubble up or be thrashed out by the old dialectic. The way to do this was developed in the Policy Review. Its committees worked like Royal Commissions drawing up policy drafts which were then put before Conference to accept or reject. The process worked so well it paved the way for the policy structure Labour now has: front-bench spokesmen put drafts before the Policy Forum which ratifies rather than debates because it is offered no coherent alternatives, and its decisions in turn pre-empt Conference's acceptance. Thus Labour has become what the Tory party once was, accepting rather than arguing, grumbling about the process but accepting it because it so desperately wants to win. The process makes better, if duller, and certainly safer policy but also dims enthusiasm. Membership has fallen as manageriability has grown.

Backbench influence

The Conservative Party has grown more fractious. Those instinctive loyalists, the military men and the country gentlemen, have been replaced by what Julian Critchley describes as the careerists and arrivistes. A party dedicated to resisting change has become radical and interventionist. As it did, so new arguments emerged, a process begun by Ted Heath, weak in the arts of leadership, never conciliatory and frugal with the knighthoods Tory backbenchers like (for their wives' sake of course). Margaret Thatcher's restless radicalism imposed even more strain, but she was more successful at winning elections and handled the party better: listening, flattering, arranging personal contracts and handing out honours. Both leaders put the party under strain, leading to greater dissent and far more split votes though none seriously inconvenienced the government. Under Ted Heath (1970–4) Tories defeated their own government six times, half of them on three-line whips, and in opposition (1974–9) dissented on 204 votes, nearly a fifth of the total. By the time Mrs Thatcher came to power, the dissident votes had got larger: from 1979–83 ten or more Tories voted against their party on 16 occasions, over 40 on four of these; in later Parliaments dissent continued but its effect was less because of the large majority, although it did result in the spectacular defeat of the Shops Bill in 1986. No action could be taken against rebels. Government's bluff had been called and independence became addictive.

Economic policy, crucial to success or failure, was almost wholly immune from backbench influence. Mrs Thatcher got away with a massive, and unnecessary, deflation from 1979–82. It brought the economy to its knees but the party marched on loyally in the main. Opposition was easily beaten off. The same happened in the second great deflation, and it was George Soros, not the backbenchers or disgruntled ministers, who sprang the party from the ERM trap. In legislative matters government was more inclined to back down rather than risk a vote, as the Thatcher government did on eye test and hospital bed charges, student grant proposals, BBC World Service and the initial sale of Leyland. Where it was attached to a policy, however, it could get its way as it did on the poll tax, even though that was the main cause of Mrs Thatcher's later downfall. Initially, it went through with ease: four Tory MPs against it before the 1987 election, 18 afterwards. John Major is open to pressure and changes his mind, yet the party still follows. Even on the emotional issue of pit closures, fleetingly hailed as a backbench triumph, a number of backbenchers delayed the closures but failed to stop them. Conservative backbenchers dissent and are beginning to taste power, but it is a blocking role, not effective invigilation.

Except on Europe, for the EC cuts right across traditional loyalties. Labour critics concentrate on economic integration which makes it more difficult to run a national economy for growth and jobs. On the Tory side, sovereignty and the nation's ability to control its own destinies are the issues. Both parties are split and leaders walk a tightrope. Issues of principle were left by both Callaghan and Thatcher governments to ritual late-night battles between Europhorics and Euro-sceptics, a fun feature which amused both sides and accomplished nothing. John Major inherited the whirlwind with the Maastricht Treaty. Twenty five Eurosceptics voted consistently against it, though the government's authority was deeply involved. Labour's rebels from that party's supportive line fluctuated between 66 and 80. The Treaty was passed by a tacit conspiracy between front-benchers. Labour thundering about a Social Chapter so vague as to be meaningless, and the government defeated only on a symbolic issue and the comparatively unimportant Committee of the Regions. Had Labour opposed the Treaty root and branch, it might have killed it, though government sceptics could well have found the usual excuses for not pursuing their scepticism to the point of defeating their own government. In the final vote they did, indeed, come back into line gritting their teeth. The legacy of this episode was mistrust on both sides, however.

On European issues backbenchers have had real—but negative—influence. Macro-policy generally is still dominated by the executive, but in micro-policies, not of central importance to government, back-bench influence has increased, as has the propensity to rebel. The Tory government precipitated intermittent rebellions on such issues as dog licensing, rail privatisation and the Financial Services Bill of 1986 when committee revolts by two backbenchers allowed Labour to strengthen the legislation. Yet the law of distance applies: the further an issue is from the central preoccupations of government, the greater the pos-sibility of dissent: backbench influence increases in such cases as more were prepared to abstain or cross party lines.

'Moral' and conscience issues have been the area of greatest growth in backbench influence. Traditionally, these are free votes. In the 1980s and 1990s they have become both more important and more numerous, partly because divided and embarrassed parties preferred to leave such matters to individual Members. Capital punishment was decided early. Although Margaret Thatcher attempted to make it a Tory issue to complement 'law and order', liberals frustrated her. Sunday trading came up in 1986 and 1993–4, the first time as government policy, with the government supporting total deregulation, but was then unable to carry it because 72 Tories, mostly sabattareans, joined with Labour (only 3 abstentions) to stop it. There was also a series of free votes on abortion, embryo and foetus research, homosexual age of consent and women priests in the Church of England. Embarrassed leaderships handed decisions to MPs, who were then bombarded with information and pleas, mostly highly organised.

Some backbenchers resented the pressure, craving the safety of a party line to relieve them of deciding for themselves and protect them generally. Most relished the feeling of power and importance which come from being courted. So turn-out was much higher than usual on Fridays when the House is usually left to play-way politics. Two decades earlier, homosexual law reform and the legalisation of prostitution had lured only half the House to vote, the rest presumably hiding from the issue. As a whole, today's MPs are ready, even eager, to stand up and be counted in the widening areas nervous parties have given up, which will make it more difficult to prevent the spread of that independence into other areas. The only way to rebuild party cohesion would be for parties either to control MPs more effectively or offer more to them. In fact, they can do neither and the backbench taste for power must grow as party is seen to have so few clothes.

Early Day Motions (EDMs) illustrate the new pluralism. Getting backbenchers to put their views on this Commons' graffiti board has changed from a casual statement of opinion to an industry. Interest and concern groups press MPs to sign, MPs pursue each other, and backbenchers' willingness to state their views has become a clamour. Less than two hundred EDMs per session in the 1950s, so few that academics could study them, became over a thousand in the 1980s and since then two thousand in the 1990s.

In the two full weeks the Commons sat in April 1994, 76 and 45 were tabled. Never have the opinions of so few been pursued by so many. To so little effect, except to make the Members signing feel important. EDMs are a part of the parliamentary PR role which is so vital to backbenchers, the pretence that airing an issue is equivalent to doing something about it. That deception embraces Questions, Adjournment Motions, Ten Minute Rule Bills and interventions to raise matters of urgent important. For many constituents, possibly most MPs, this is enough.

For those MPs who want something more positive, the most satisfying form of backbench influence, decided like so much else in political life by a lottery, is legislation. Passing a Private Members' Bill is a career high and a unique experience because the responsible MP has to be legislator, shaping the bill; minister, running a department and taking soundings of the interested groups; whip, mobilising the troops; media manipulator, organising opinion and focusing it on the Commons; and he or she may also become a popular hero, pushing good and important causes. All this work is beyond the resources of Members, which is why most take a 'hand me down' bill from a pressure group prepared to do much of the work.

Like everything else, activity has increased: from around 50 bills per session in the 1950s to 80 or more in the 1970s and over a hundred more recently. Yer the successes have diminished proportionately from nearly half to around a tenth. The odds are long. Only twelve or thirteen Fridays are set aside for Private Members' Bills and ten for Motions, so the only bills with a prospect of success are the first twenty, and really only the first ten, in the sessional ballot which confers priority. Many are called, few are chosen. The number of bills passed is less than a score, usually just over a dozen, three-quarters of them from the preferred ballot track and usually none of the flood of Ten Minute Rule Bills which have been reduced to a joke.

Deciding what bill to introduce is a nice choice. MPs can take a bill from the government pigeon holes of useful measures for which there has been no time, pass it easily and get their name on the statute book where it is instantly forgotten. At the other extreme, they can make a gesture more appropriate to a Ten Minute Rule Bill by raising an issue too controversial to pass, as Nick Budgen did with his bill to make the Bank of England independent. Most such controversial bills are wasted opportunities—which does not stop a number of MPs making the gesture. Between the two extremes come important measures which stand a chance because they divide or wrong-foot the government and could pass with a fair wind. My own House Buyer's Bill won its second reading because it put the government in an embarrassing situation and this forced it to implement the principle. Kevin Barron's Ban on Tobacco Advertising and Alf Morris' Disabled Rights Bill (taken up again in 1994 by Roger Berry) were also backed by Tories, the latter having posed a real threat to the government. Yet neither passed, for the groups which mobilise anger and give the appearance of threatening opposing MPs where it hurts, in the ballot box, are really impotent to deliver, while Private Members' Bills are very vulnerable because the time limits allows them to be talked out easily or done down under the guise of helping, improving by amendment.

Risk adds to the excitement and the challenge. The backbencher can end up a hero, as Alf Morris and Kevin Barron did without passing their bills. Even better, backbenchers can change things, as did the abolition of the solicitors' monopoly of conveyancing which unleashed competition on the house purchase market. Few parliamentary roles are more satisfying. Yet the satisfaction is temporary, the opportunity comes to few and some MPs never even come up in the ballot.

Conclusion

The backbench workforce is shrinking as front-benchers multiply. The remaining 440 or so (with perhaps 20 incapacitated at any one time) must work hard and become more professional. Their workload is heavier, their task more complicated, their influence greater, but still not substantial. To increase their influence, they must still rise in the party. The most dramatic change is in the workload, more minutiae imposing a head-down role of frenzied activity. So Bagehot's Commons, 'a big meeting of more or less idle people' giving leisured consideration to public policy, becomes accidental groupings of impossibly busy people. Some roles, such as legislator—to which the House still devotes over two-fifths of its time—have declined in interest and value. Others, such as party man or woman, impose more work to bring less satisfaction. Those of specialist and constituency servant grow exponentially, and with them both interest and workload. Those who can keep their heads above the rising tide have influence and a prospect for the top, but the backbenches have become an outward-bound course not a leisurely preparation for power.

What was a part-time job, paid as such, is becoming a full-time profession, almost paid as such. What was amateur is becoming professional. What was done out of duty is driven by competition. A dignified role for gentlemen has become a pressured, harried and over-worked course for hacks. Instead of checking the power of the executive, a job MPs have pretended to do without ever succeeding, we have become intermediaries between the executive (with its machine) and the people, creating a new role focusing attention on myriad minor matters rather than the big issues. We are the defender, salesperson, promoter, leader and figurehead of the constituencies. As for debating, that has transferred to a broader arena of which the Commons is only a part.

When the job was dignified, many came in to enjoy a ring-side seat on history, feeling they were doing a useful, if nebulous, job of public service. Today, the job is more hectic and difficult but regarded as a transition to something else, preferably—but not essentially—power. In neither case was the job particularly satisfying in itself, once because not fully absorbing, now all the roles collected together under the rubric do not constitute a job to absorb ambitious professionals once they know the ropes. The apprenticeship period is getting longer. The job is more demanding, though much of the routine can be put on to the shoulders of staff. Some love it and are satisfied; movers, shakers and 'ministrables' crave something more, have mastered it and use the backbenches as a platform to reach for power.

The latter came into the job to advance themselves as well as the cause of their party. Their aim is to be professional ministers not professional backbenchers and given the scale of the modern executive, most can. If their party wins office, their chances are two to one; half the Tory incomers of 1979 have held office of some kind. Yet they may not make it for all sorts of reasons, and their party may not ever reach power: Labour's long exile has taken several careers beyond their sell-by dates. So, just as the archetypal Member uses the job as a stepping stone to power, those who do not make it a platform from which to fulfil themselves develop a new career or become politico-business-media-legislative-entrepreneurs; and as the job develops, so do all these alternative fulfilments.

Most now come in younger, often before they know the world, its opportunities and corruptions. Some find consolation and a career in the constituency, though to be a good constituency MP is still discounted and somehow downgraded by the ambitious. Others become media figures, a few so bitten by the bug that they go out to do it full time: no crime, that, for it is good for people to choose a destiny which fulfils, however late. Some past their peak, hang in and coast along to the honours' queue. Some become consultants and jobbing businessmen, particularly in the politico-business field which is growing in importance. Others compensate by status, trips, writing books, becoming 'personalities' or casual adultery, in different ways all roles offering interest, excitement or income but built on the basic backbench job.

Backbenchers have become more influential but in narrower areas. To grasp real power, they must move out of the backbenches and climb not now a slippery pole but a career pyramid. The bottom steps of this now involve proving themselves effective as backbenchers, an art form rising stars were previously able to neglect. More are anxious to climb higher. For those who do not make the top, the multiplying distractions of the backbenches are also opportunities, a full but hectic life, a platform from which to do interesting things in Parliament or outside, an automatic entry to most places, a status which is unique. While some regard backbench work as the consolation prize for failure, many find it a career.

Nevertheless, as the worker bees of a busier system, backbenchers work too hard to appreciate what they are doing, are pushed too hard to do the job satisfactorily, and find it more difficult to keep up with the pace. Whatever the MP's dedication to it, no constituency can ever be served properly, and demands increase in ratio to commitment. It is equally impossible to do the parliamentary job fully. We live, therefore, with a permanent feeling of never quite being up to or with the job.

Parliamentary reform would make more influence and satisfactions available but its pace has slackened—not because the institution is perfect but because MPs have lost appetite and are finding new burdens impossible to shoulder. The Procedure Committee suggested timetabling of bills, the Jopling Report looked at civilised hours, the Hansard Commission reported on the legislative process and made important suggestions, such as the introduction of committee hearings for outside representations. All would have been considerable improvements but all demanded extra work. So nothing was done, MPs do not want more work.

There is no obvious way out of this trap. The treadmill will move faster, more minutiae will distract us from fundamentals. A reform of the whole system, taking power and functions from both Commons and executive to spread it round, would make backbenchers more effective by substituting a limited but specific role for a slim chance of total power. An effective second chamber, devolution to regional assemblies, a Bill of Rights, weakening the grip of the constituency by the German form of proportional representation, weakening the parties, though not their grip on individuals, by list PR, would all help but constitute a constitutional revolution of a type as desirable as it is unlikely in this conservative nation. So things will go on much as they are. Ministers will burn out quicker. Backbenchers may even burn out before they make that grade. The rest will run faster to stand still.

Short of remodelling either the British or the human constitution, disposable MPs are another answer; but as the job becomes more interesting, more are inclined to stay. Older MPs do find it more difficult to keep up the pace, but there is little chance that it will push them out so long as there is no performance audit and nothing to deter them from coasting to semi-retirement in situ. To make all MPs as effective as some requires a stick as well as an even bigger carrot. If those who have not performed effectively in ten years go, perhaps to some political band of alderman, the rest could be a well prepared pool. So a forecast for the backbench future based on the trends of the past must be more of the same. However, the myth of parties as the only road to a better world is disintegrating, along with their cohesion and authority. In the ruins of government by party, backbenchers shamble and mill, half uncomprehendingly, to a new, better and more exhausting role in the pluralistic and confusing system that emerges. But the transition is slow — and messy.

The Growth of the Constituency Role of the MP

SINCE the 1880s, the single-member constituency has been the norm in British politics. Some two-member seats (two MPs being elected by the same electors) and a number of University seats (the electors being graduates and not residents of a particular area) survived until 1950. Since 1950, the single-member constituency, with the MP returned to Parliament by citizens residing in a geographically-defined and exclusive area, has been universal.

The relationship between MPs and their constituencies is subject to no formal rules. There is no official job description. What constituents appear to expect of their Member of Parliament and what the Member has done over the years in response to the demands, or perceived needs, of the constituency have varied. Though a number of generic names are sometimes given to the MP's role in relation to the constituency — most commonly and recently that of 'social welfare officer' — the tasks undertaken are several and separable. Those tasks have undergone some notable changes, both qualitatively as well as quantitatively, over the past forty years. The purpose of this article is to identify the several constituency roles of the Member of Parliament, the extent to which they have changed, the reasons why those changes have taken place, and the implications of those changes for MPs in future years.

Constituency roles

Constituents appear to ascribe several roles to their local Member of Parliament. Those roles can variously be gleaned from the requests made, frequently in writing, to the MP. The requests may come from one or more individuals or from particular organised interests within the constituency. A study of the correspondence received by Tony Benn, then MP for Bristol South-East, in 1972–73 suggested three principal roles: as an agent of information exchange, providing information and advice to constituents who wanted to pass on their views or receive an explanation about a particular issue of concern; as a powerful 'friend', intervening in a dispute with a public official; and as an official constituency representative, lending his or her name to a particular cause or organisation.[1] This constitutes a useful but limited taxonomy. A study of the requests made of MPs in earlier decades of this century, as well as more recently, permits a more substantial categorisation. Indeed, from such a study, it is possible to identify seven constituency roles of the Member of Parliament: (1) safety valve, (2) information provider, (3) local dignitary, (4) advocate, (5) benefactor, (6) powerful friend, and (7) promoter of constituency interests. The first three roles are primarily, but not exclusively, internal to the constituency. The rest normally involve the MP taking some action beyond the borders of the constituency, usually but not always in relation to some public body. The first six are essentially roles pursued on the basis of approaches made to the MP. The seventh is frequently pursued by the MP on the basis of such requests but may also be undertaken by the MP without specific prompting. Some MPs may undertake other tasks without prompting, but the generalisation holds.

(1) Safety valve. For citizens with a point of view they wish to express about some aspect of public policy, the local MP serves as a visible political figure to whom that point of view can be expressed. Writing to the MP can serve as a safety valve, allowing citizens to express themselves in a way that might not otherwise be possible. The act of writing may be sufficient in itself. The MP may acknowledge the letter, even comment on it, but the role of the MP is largely passive and may extend to no more than reading the letter. With an efficient or trusted office staff, it may not even extend to that. If the MP decides to pass the letter on and seek and authoritative response, or decides to respond with a substantive personal reply, the nature of the role changes, the MP then acting as an information provider.

(2) Information provider. Some constituents will approach the local MP seeking advice or information. A constituent may want advice on who to approach with a particular problem. A sixth-former or undergraduate may write seeking data about the MP's role, activities or political views. A worried constituent may seek information about government or party policy on a particular issue. The information may be provided directly by the Member without recourse to any other body or may be supplied from material obtained from local authorities, government departments, or other agencies.

The two categories of safety valve and information provider are separable but are subsumed within the 'information exchange' role identified earlier. Benn received information from constituents or constituency organisations—such as reports of meetings and motions passed—that was acknowledged (safety valve) and requests for information that he provided, either directly or on the basis of information supplied by other bodies (information provider).

(3) Local dignitary. Election to Parliament confers status. The Member of Parliament constitutes a local dignitary. It is common for the local MP to be invited, with the mayor and other civic dignitaries, to official functions and other events within the constituency. Sometimes the event involves a non-speaking role but will often entail speaking—for example, opening a local fête or when presenting awards at a school

prize-giving. It is common for the MP's spouse to be invited in place of the MP, especially among Conservatives, and in mid-week when the MP is is Westminster, but the invitation derives from the status of the MP.

(4) Advocate. This role is not dissimilar to that identified in the analysis of Tony Benn's constituency as the official constituency representative, but it goes somewhat broader than that term implies. It involves the MP giving his or her name in support of a particular cause. It is listed at this point because it derives from the MP's status as a dignitary, but it goes — or rather can go — beyond the symbolic role of the local dignitary. The MP may serve as a passive advocate, allowing the name to be added to the headed notepaper, but equally may be an active advocate, marching in demonstrations or making speeches on a public platform. Such action may not be aimed at an official body but at a wider public and may seek to confer some authority on the cause being promoted. The nature of the cause and the activity may involve the MP going beyond the borders of the constituency in order to pursue advocacy of the cause.

Also under this heading comes in large part the local party role of the MP. The MP is returned under a party label and will seek to promote the cause of the party not just at Westminster but also in the constituency. The MP may do this willingly and without prompting, but the local party may be expected to encourage this activity. The MP may speak at local party meetings, take part in local debates, and write an occasional column for a local newspaper. Such activity may be seen as partisan rather than undertaken on behalf of constituents as a whole, but it has equally to be noted that much of the activity undertaken by MPs on behalf of constituency interests is in pursuit of the demands of particular individuals or groupings within the constituency and not some recognisable constituency-wide interest.

(5) Benefactor. This involves the MP serving as the provider of benefits to particular individuals, usually those who are needy or greedy. The role differs from that of powerful friend in that the latter involves intervening in a dispute in order to achieve a redress of grievance. The role of benefactor involves the MP providing some help, including sometimes financial help, without reference to any other body or seeking to obtain some preference — such as an honour — for a constituent without any dispute being involved. The role is one that has been historically significant but has declined in significance in recent history.

(6) Powerful friend. Constituents may ask the MP to intervene in a dispute with a public body, or even a private body, in order to achieve a redress of grievance, either by achieving a changed decision or by obtaining an authoritative explanation of or apology for some action taken or not taken. Members of Parliament are able to utilise procedures

that a constituent cannot—such as tabling a parliamentary question, raising an issue in debate in the House of Commons, or referring a case to the Parliamentary Commissioner for Administration (the Ombudsman)—and they enjoy priority over members of the public in having letters considered within government departments. To constituents, the MP may thus appear a useful ally in seeking to achieve a desired outcome. The MP may not be able to deliver what the constituent wants, but to constituents who know little of the ways of government, the knowledge that the MP is taking action on their behalf serves as something of a reassurance that avenues that might otherwise be neglected are being pursued.

(7) Promoter of constituency interests. The interests of a constituency and the interests of particular constituents are not necesssarily synonymous. Individuals, or indeed groups, may ask the local MP to take some action on their behalf. The sum of their demands does not necessarily represent the interests of the whole. Indeed, given the heterogeneous nature of most constituencies, it may be difficult to identify a common interest. Nonetheless, in a number of cases, there are some general interests. Most MPs would regard it as in the interests of their constituency not to lose the biggest employer in the area and usually (though not necessarily in all cases) to attract new industry and jobs. A local firm under threat of closure may approach the local MP to act as a powerful friend in order to achieve some support from public agencies. However, the MP may also adopt a more proactive role, seeking to promote—without prompting—the interests of the constituency through calling attention to its value and what it has to offer, be it to consumers or to employers. Indeed, some MPs have achieved reputations for promoting local interests in this way, such as some Scottish MPs promoting the Scotch whisky industry.

The constituency 'role' of the MP thus encompasses a number of tasks. Those tasks are notable not only for their number but also for the extent to which they have changed in recent decades—some becoming more prominent than others—with the workload they impose on MPs becoming notably demanding. MPs are finding it increasingly difficult to cope.

The changing role: the early decades

In the first few decades of the century, the MP was not necessarily inundated with requests from constituents. He (not until after 1919 could one write she) was nonetheless not free of such demands. In the demands made of them, Members resembled their predecessors of the nineteenth century. MPs were dignitaries and often men of wealth and considerable influence. They were invited to civic functions and they were important targets for job seekers and those wanting some public honour or recognition. As prominent and powerful figures, they were often seen also as potential benefactors of the local community. In the Conservative Party especially, they were also generally seen as benefactors of the local party. Members frequently made donations to the local party and the promise of a sizable donation was often what determined their initial selection as candidates.

The extent to which the local MP was in demand in the roles of both local dignitary and benefactor is shown in the experience of the MP returned for Ashton-under-Lyne in 1910, the young Canadian millionaire Max Aitken: 'A flood of requests poured in: to join local societies, attend and open bazaars, become patrons of pageants, judge dog shows, grace annual dinners and balls, present prizes, watch football matches . . . Nearly always, a donation or subscription was involved . . . There was also a stream of begging letters from individuals. All were looked in to; Aitken was prepared to be generous, but hated being taken for granted . . . Often he would ask his agents to give a needy family food or clothes rather than cash.'[2]

Such beneficence appears to have declined in succeeding decades. Labour MPs did not have the resources to provide such support and Conservative MPs, especially after the second world war, did not have the resources either. On the Conservative side, the Maxwell-Fyfe reforms ensured that Conservative MPs in the 1950s no longer made significant contributions to their local parties. The House became more middle class. The benefactor role thus appears to have declined, leaving essentially the role of local dignitary as the principal constituency role of the MP.

Even the role of local dignitary does not appear to have been one that MPs necessarily embraced with enthusiasm. MPs in the first half of the century were often powerful figures whose focus was Westminster or their business affairs. Despite his financial generosity, the young Max Aitken disliked the demands made on his time by the constituency. His constituency was five hours by train from London. He made it clear that he was not prepared to sacrifice his business interests and within ten weeks of his election was talking of giving up parliamentary life. Many MPs were not even prepared to give the amount of time to their constituencies that Aitken did to his. Most did not live in or near their constituencies and some paid what amounted to annual or twice-yearly visits to the constituency.

This relative neglect was still apparent in post-war years. Austin Mitchell cites the example of the new MP in 1945 being met by the local station master and asked if he would be paying his annual visit at that time of year. 'A. V. Alexander hardly ever visited his Sheffield constituency during or after the war, producing such disgruntlement that his successor George Darling was selected on the radical promise of quarterly visits.'[3] Similar examples could be found well into the 1950s and 1960s. Tom Driberg, Labour MP for Barking from 1959 to 1974, was loathe even to fulfil the role of local dignitary. He rarely attended social functions and when he did would announce after half-an-hour that he had had enough and demand to be driven back to London. He had an agreement with the MP for a neighbouring seat that when the two of them were invited to an official function locally, they would 'both go or neither go—and on the whole go to as few as possible'. His approach to the other tasks was similar. Constituency surgeries—meetings at which constituents could come and raise problems in person—were regarded as a chore. 'He often gave the impression that every moment spent in the constituency was an excruciating ordeal for him.'[4] He was more concerned with politics at the national than the parochial level.

The extent to which such MPs were typical rather than exceptional is difficult to ascertain. There is a good deal of anecdotal evidence suggesting that such cases were far from isolated. What is known is that most MPs in the 1950s and 1960s did not live in their constituencies and that they received few letters from their constituents. In the 1959–64 Parliament, less than one third-third of MPs listed addresses that were within their constituencies.[5] It has been estimated that the typical MP in the 1950s received between twelve and twenty letters a week,[6] a volume that could be handled without difficulty by Members. Though most MPs did hold regular surgeries, more than a third did not,[7] and those that were held took place with a frequency that varied enormously.

The MP thus found that the tasks he or she was called upon to fulfil were not too numerous nor too demanding. That of local dignitary continued to be the most obvious, along with that of advocate, with the MP supporting local worthy causes. Some MPs also served as promoters of local interests, notably Labour MPs who spoke in support of what they saw as the needs of their constituencies. (These needs were seen in general—and political—terms, such as the need to maintain full employment and, in mining areas, to support the coal industry.) For MPs who wished to devote their energies to interests other than their constituencies—be it business, leisure, or the floor of the House of Commons—then they were no significant impediments to pursuing those interests.

The demands made of the modern MP

The era of the MP able to ignore the various roles of the constituency Member soon passed. There were already some underlying signs of growing demands made of MPs by constituents in the 1950s. As we have seen, most MPs held surgeries. There is little evidence that they were as numerous or held as frequently in earlier decades as they were in this. The number of letters received from constituents were not numerous, but they were apparently more numerous than in earlier years.[8] However, the most significant increase in the demands on MPs came in the 1960s and, on an even greater scale, in succeeding decades.

The 1960s saw a notable growth of the MP's postbag. Of MPs surveyed in 1967, most estimated that they received between 25 and 75 letters a week from constituency sources. Approximately one in five Members claimed to received 75 or more letters a week. The same survey found a somewhat higher proportion of MPs holding surgeries than had been shown by the survey of 1963, with a greater proportion being held more frequently.[9]

Succeeding decades have seen a notable increase in the number of letters written to MPs. A survey by the Letter Writing Bureau in 1986 found that the typical MP received a postbag of between twenty and fifty letters a day, with more than half coming from constituents.[10] In other words, the MP was receiving in one day more letters from constituents than he or she used to receive in one week in the 1950s. The increase in the number of letters also generated an increase in the number of letters written by MPs to ministers on behalf of constituents. By the early 1980s, approximately ten thousand letters a month were being written to ministers, mostly in pursuit of constituency casework. By the end of the decade, the figure had increased to fifteen thousand.[11] The experience of Edwina Currie, junior minister in the Department of Health and Social Security — the largest single recipient of MPs' letters — in the late 1980s provides a useful illustration of what it entailed for one minister: 'If you wanted a reply signed by me, you had to write to your own MP. Lots did, In a typical week, when Parliament was sitting, when I'd made a speech, when the Department of Health was in the news, I would expect to sign over 300 such letters . . . In a normal year I must have signed 10,000.'[12]

A survey carried out by the Cabinet Office Efficiency Unit in 1990 found that ministers answered 250,000 letters a year, most of them from MPs.[13] Even allowing for a sizable proportion of letters written to non-parliamentarians, this suggests a continuing increase in the volume of parliamentary correspondence.

The greater activity of MPs on behalf of constituents is not confined to Westminster. Members now spend more time in their constituencies than before. In part, this reflects the fact that far more MPs now live in their constituencies than was previously the case. An analysis of MPs' addresses in the 1987–92 Parliament found that MPs returned at the 1983 and the 1987 general elections were more likely than pre-1983 returnees to list addresses in or near their constituencies. A majority of the MPs returned for the first time in 1987 listed a constituency address.[14] A survey of Members carried out by the Commons all-party reform group in 1984 found that a majority of MPs who responded spent at least eight days a month in the constituency. One in five said that they spent thirteen or more days of every month in the constituency. Though we have no comparable figures for earlier years, the evidence so far presented — and the findings of the Review Body of Top Salaries that the amount of time spent by the average MP on constituency work increased from eleven hours a week in 1971 to sixteen hours in 1984[15] — would suggest that this constitutes a greater commitment than was made by MPs in previous decades.

The activity of MPs devoted to constituency work has thus increased substantially. The greatest demands made of MPs appears to be as powerful friends. Of the requests received by Tony Benn in 1972–73, two-thirds sought his intervention in a dispute with a public official. Of the constituency casework of seven MPs, covering a three-month period at the turn of 1986, 90% of the cases were invoked by individuals — rather than groups — and were concerned overwhelmingly with the particular needs of the individual. The MP was being asked to intercede with the administration rather than to take political action.[16] Council housing and benefits provoked the largest number of letters. This was in line with the experience of Tony Benn and, according to a 1993 MORI survey of MPs, these topics remain among those most frequently raised in MPs' postbags.[17]

The amount of time spent by MPs in their constituencies also suggests that the role of local dignitary has assumed an even greater prominence than before. There are some data to suggest a greater prominence than before as a safety valve and advocate. About 16% of Tony Benn's correspondence took the form of information or views offered by constituents. (About 8% sought information.) The volume of mail now received by MPs that does not take the form of personal letters by constituents (e.g. form letters, postcards, and brochures from firms and lobbying organisations) points to more material flowing in to MPs as safety valves and as advocates. Mail generated by groups rather than individuals did not figure as a separate item in the analysis of Tony Benn's correspondence. An analysis of a new MPs' mailbag in 1991 found that not only was it a significant item, but that it accounted for the majority of the items received in the mail by the MP.[18] The 1993 MORI poll of MPs also found an issue of policy — animal welfare — among those generating the most mail.

The increase in mail providing MPs with information and trying to get them to serve as advocates for particular causes is notable, though can not be encompassed solely within the rubric of constituency demands. Much of this mail comes from outside the constituency, the product of mass mailing by particular groups or the result of an MP's known interest in the subject. Nonetheless, it is known that much lobbying is channelled through constituents. In 1985, for example, the Education Secretary withdrew plans for an interest in the parental contribution to student grants under intense pressure from Conservative MPs. The MPs themselves had been put under pressure by parents, who had written to them or turned up at their surgeries. In 1986, the campaign against the Shops Bill — to deregulate Sunday trading — was organised at the constituency level, opponents being encouraged to write to their local MP and make their views known.[19] In 1994, supporters of a lowering of the age of consent for homosexual conduct to sixteen organised an intense campaign based on constituency-level pressure, a tactic that came close to achieving a largely unexpected success.

Promoting constituency interests is not a new role for MPs. Members, as we have noted, have variously helped promote industries heavily concentrated in their constituencies. In 1936, for example, Aneurin Bevan—Labour MP for Ebbw Vale—played some part in getting the local steel works reopened. We have no data that allows us to demonstrate a clear increase in such promotional work undertaken by MPs. What is known is that such work—lobbying ministers on behalf of local firms or industries, leading delegations to see ministers—now constitutes an important part of constituency activity by some, though not all, Members of Parliament. It can be inferred from the evidence presented that such activity has increased over the past decades.

Of the remaining two roles, that of information provider remains a role that MPs are variously called on to fulfil. As we have noted already, a small proportion of Benn's correspondence fell into that category. Anecdotal evidence from MPs suggests that, if anything, requests for information are more numerous now than in previous years. Among those making demands on MPs' time for information are researchers, who either seek interviews or ask Members to complete questionnaires. Such has been the increase in the number of these requests that some MPs decline all that do not emanate from the constituency and another will only fill in a questionnaire if the sender donates some money to b favourite charity. As with lobbying mail, though, such requests can be encompassed solely within the rubric of constituency mail. S may be, as from local students, but most probably can not.

The role of benefactor has declined considerably, though not point where it can be said to have disappeared. The MP—if a ment supporter—may lobby government to achieve a knigh other honour for some local worthy (often a local party wor aspects of the role have largely gone, though not quite cr least one Conservative MP, for example, is known to pensioner's poll tax for her (without her knowledge); ar ing complaints from a constituent about draughty wind went round one morning and put up some draught-r at her windows. Such examples are rare and hardl munificence provided by wealthy MPs earlier ir though, the only one of the several constituency r that has declined in significance in post-war v increased in significance, notably so in the ca ful friend and as an advocate. The importa why?

Not all MPs are notably constituency a as we have seen, can be variously sub-divi shown, the constituency role itself is but one of several roles pursued by MPs.[20] Some MPs prefer to pursue the role of policy advocate or ministerial aspirant rather than that of constituency member. That reflects the particular preferences of Members. However, regardless of personal preferences, Members of Parliament are now under greater pressure that before to devote time and energy to their constituencies and, to a greater or lesser extent, Members generally adopt a responsive mode in dealing with these pressures. That is, they act in order to meet the demands made of them, instead of ignoring or dismissing them. Some adopt a minimalist approach, doing as little as possible. Some MPs not only have other things to occupy their attention, but a few are plain lazy. Nonetheless, the generalisation holds. Why, then, the increase in the demands made of MPs by those within their constituencies? And why have MPs adopted a responsive mode?

Reasons for change: increased demands

There is no single reason why the demands made of MPs has increased so notably over the past forty years, but four variables can be identified as causal factors.

Growth of the electorate. One simple explanation is to be found in the increase in the number of electors. The greater the number of citizens, the greater the number of demands likely to be made of MPs. In 1900, the electorate numbered less than seven million. By 1992, it exceeded 43 million. However, the increase in the number of electors is not by itself sufficient to explain the substantial increase in constituency demands in recent decades. The proportional increase in the volume of constituency correspondence since the 1950s (our figures suggest it has more than quadrupled) has far exceeded the increase in the size of the elecorate over that period.

Growth of the public sector. Post-war years have seen a significant growth of the public sector. The welfare state came to fruition with the creation of the National Health Service in 1948 and with the passage of the 1945 Family Allowance Act, the 1946 National Insurance Act and the 1948 National Assistance Act. There was also a massive expansion in the provision of public housing. The result has been that contact between the citizen and public bodies is far greater than ever before. The greater the degree of public provision, and the greater the degree of contact between citizen and public agency, the greater the potential for problems to arise in that relationship and for the citizen to harbour a grievance.

Greater knowledge. An increase in citizen grievances may not in itself translated into an increase in the demands made of Members of Parliament. Constituents have to know about the availability of their and how to go about making contact. Post-war years have seen an expansion in secondary education, producing a more educated population. The growth of the mass media has also raised awareness of the political process and of political issues. What has been termed cognitive mobilisation has resulted in more people joining groups and attempting to influence the political process. Increased group activity would explain the greater demands made of MPs to act as advocates for particular causes. However, a greater awareness may also have facilitated contact between individuals and MPs.

The importance of citizen awareness of the MP's availability is also borne out by the findings of social attitudes surveys in the 1980s. When asked in 1984 what action they would take to influence the passage of legislation they deemed unjust, a majority of respondents said they would contact the MP: this was the most popular form of personal action. A similar response was achieved two years later when respondents were asked what they would do to influence government.[21] The questions did not focus directly on personal grievances, but the responses indicate a high level of awareness of the availability of the MP as a recipient of representations from citizens. The data themselves are not sufficient to demonstrate a link between a more educated electorate and a greater willingness to make demands of the local MP, as there is no comparable survey data for earlier decades this century. The link can only be made by inference, but it is a reasonable inference to draw.

Success breeding success. Where MPs have responded to demands from constituents, and achieved some response, the knowledge of their action has often not been confined to the constituent making the demand. There has been a ripple effect—family and friends getting to know of the MP's action. There may be a wider audience if the measures taken by the MP are covered in the local media. This adds to the awareness of the availability of the Member of Parliament. What adds to the attractiveness of making contact is the perception that the MP is effective in achieving the desired response. In many cases, constituents are satisfied with an authoritative explanation of why some action was taken—and, in most cases, that is what MPs get for constituents, rather than a changed decision. The perception of constituents is what is important. A 1978 survey found that, of those who contacted their MP, 75% reported a 'good' or 'very good' response. An earlier Granada survey found that the closer the contact, the greater the belief that the MP was doing a good job. The British Social Attitudes Survey found that respondents not only 'would' contact the MP in order to influence unjust legislation but that more respondents deemed it the 'most effective' action than any other.

The more MPs do on behalf of their constituencies, the more their action is known about within the constituency. Given that such action is deemed to have some effect—and is what constituents expect their

MP to be doing—then the greater the encouragement to other constituents to follow suit.

Reasons for change: MPs' responsiveness

To identify reasons for an increase in the demands made of MPs by sources within their constituencies is not to identify the reasons why MPs devote so much time to constituency work. Why do MPs choose to respond to the demands and to do so in the way that they do, devoting a substantial proportion of their time to carrying out the various constituency roles we have identified?

One motivation is essentially the moral one: that it is 'part of the job' and constituents expect the MP to carry it out. That moral imperative is longstanding. Arguably, there is no other reason why MPs should have devoted time to constituency work in post-war Parliaments. Most MPs sat for—and continue to sit for—safe seats. They know they are likely to be re-elected, regardless of whether they do much or no constituency work. Yet is that moral imperative sufficient to explain their efforts on behalf of constituents in recent decades, giving more time and attention to constituency work? There are three significant changes that could be said to have contributed to the willingness of the typical MP to spend more time than before on constituency work: (1) a change in electoral politics; (2) a change in local party politics; and (3) a change in the nature of MPs themselves.

Change in electoral politics. The waning of the class-party nexus since the 1960s has resulted in a more volatile electorate. This is reflected in massive swings in voting intentions and in seats changing hands in by-elections. The success of the Conservative Party in winning four consecutive general elections from 1979 onwards has masked an underlying volatility: in March 1990 and again in March 1994, the Conservatives trailed Labour in the opinion polls by more than twenty points. In the five years after winning the 1989 Richmond by-election, the Conservatives failed to hold a single seat in a by-election. By-elections do not, of course, threaten sitting MPs, but they often threaten the governing party and, occasionally, the main opposition party, raising the spectre of defeat for the MP at the next general election.

Such volatility gives MPs—even if sitting for ostensibly safe seats—cause to doubt their own parliamentary immortality. They therefore appear keen to bolster their own support within the constituency. Being constituency active may not be sufficient to influence many voters, but it appears that it may have some effect at the margins.[22] Constituency work does not sway normally hostile voters to switch their votes. Where it may be important is serving as a magnet for existing supporters. For an MP seeking re-election, the support of those who voted for him or her last time is vital. A supporter who is thinking of defecting to another candidate may be less likely to do so if the incumbent has a good reputation as a constituency Member. If the supporter is dissatisfied with the party's performance *and* with the performance of the local MP (assuming the same party), then it would be plausible to conclude that the combination increases the likelihood of the supporter switching sides. For the MP, therefore, the moral imperative is complemented by a political imperative: the need to achieve re-election.

Change in local party politics. Local parties have historically maintained certain expectations about the involvement of 'their' MP (where their candidate was the winning one) in constituency activities. However, that expectation for much of this century—as we have seen—appears not to have been excessive. Neglect of the constituency occasionally resulted in some grumbling among local activists. On occasion, the MP was denied readoption as a candidate (as in the case of Ebbw Vale in 1929), but such occasions were very rare. Recent years have seen the expectations increase. Maintaining a high constituency profile is deemed good for party morale. Party activists are more likely to give of their time if the MP appears to be working hard as well in the constituency.

However, there are two further incentives. The change in the Labour Party rules in 1981, requiring all Labour MPs to go through full-scale reselection procedures in every Parliament, put pressure on Labour MPs in dispute with their local parties. The reputation of being a 'good constituency Member' was an effective shield against attempts at deselection. Though several Labour MPs were denied reselection in the 1980s, in only one instance does a Member with a reputation as a good constituency MP appear to have been involved. Others under threat staved off the challenge.

The reputation of being a good constituency Member can carry weight not only with the MP's existing local party but also with other local party associations. This is significant given the frequency of boundary changes. An MP may be elected with a large majority. That majority—as we have seen—cannot always be taken for granted. But neither can the existence of the seat. Members may thus lose their seat by being voted out or by the seat disappearing in boundary changes. Not only are there numerous MPs presently in the House who have sat for another seat, there are actually three MPs who have each sat for three geographically-distinct seats. To have a reputation for good constituency service is useful in seeking another seat. To have a reputation as an appalling constituency Member is not likely to increase the chances of finding a candidature elsewhere.

Change in the nature of MPs. Recent decades have seen the emergence of a more career-oriented MP. The 'traditional' MP, especially on the Conservative side, was one who may have harboured ministerial ambitions, but who nonetheless had other interests and recognised other pursuits as being equally or more important than politics. Service in Parliament may come at the end of a career or may be a form of public service prior to taking up some other career, or a form of service combined with another career. The careerist MP is one who makes politics a full-time — and life-long — career. The growth of the careerist MP has significant implications for parliamentary activity.

Constituency activity for the careerist has a dual importance. Given that politics is essentially the be all and end all of life, then re-election is a necessary but not sufficient condition for achieving one's political ambitions. However much one might be a ministerial aspirant, some attention has to be given to the constituency in order to ensure re-election (and, indeed, readoption), not least given the changes in electoral and party politics that we have identified. Furthermore, the greater the number of careerist MPs, the greater the competition between them to get noticed. Pursuing issues on behalf of constituents — and constituency causes — is one way of achieving attention, either directly or indirectly. Tabling parliamentary questions or achieving an adjournment debate on constituency issues helps get the MP noticed in the chamber. The traditional MP would usually table a question infrequently. Careerist MPs often attempt to table questions up to their allowed maximum, scurrying around for appropriate subjects on which to base the questions. One recent survey of Members found that nine out of every ten who responded said that, among the reasons for tabling questions, was to make ministers aware of points of concern to constituents. More than 80% said they sent answers to their questions to the local press.[23]

These changes, then, in combination have generated a body of MPs willing — as we have said, to a greater or lesser extent — to respond to the growth in the demands of constituents. For some, the moral and political imperatives are so strong now that they adopt a proactive, rather than a reactive, stance, actually seeking out constituency griev-ances rather than waiting for constituents to bring issues to them. (One study puts the figure at 27% of Members.[34]) The contrast with the stance taken by the traditional MP in the immediate post-war decades could not be starker. The change in the constituency role of the MP has clearly been a qualitative as well as a quantitative one.

Consequences

There are 651 MPs and 651 ways of handling the different constituency roles of the MP. There are some variations between Conservative and Labour Members. These have not been drawn out because they are not on a scale to affect the picture presented. Depite the variations, a number of generalisations are possible about the consequences of the growth in the constituency role of the Member of Parliament.

The growth in constituency activity, and what MPs have done in response, has arguably been beneficial for the political system. In contact between constituents and MPs, 'familiarity breeds content'. In most cases, MPs deliver something that constituents are satisfied with, usually information. There is also the benefit to those individuals or groups who get the help they sought, be it an explanation or a changed decision. Even if constituents do not make use of the services of the local MP, knowledge that the MP is there is itself of importance.

There is a cost to Members. Carrying out the various constituency roles provides many MPs with job satisfaction and also offers some means of gaining knowledge about the problems faced by individuals. Against that must be set the fact that the roles are time-consuming and call on Members to carry out tasks for which, in many cases, they are not well-equipped. Most MPs are not trained counsellors nor lawyers specialising in the sphere of individual rights. The more time that is consumed by constituency casework and projects, the less time there is to devote to other important work. MPs have to establish priorities and those at the bottom of the list then lose out. MPs have tended to compartmentalise their work—distinguishing between their Westminster and their constituency roles—but the demands of constituency work threaten that distinction. If constituency work starts to crowd out Westminster work, producing a more parochial orientation, then the capacity of the House of Commons to subject government actions and public legislation to sustained scrutiny is diminished.

To cope, MPs have to achieve a reduction in the constituency burden and/or increase their own resources to handle that burden. If the hypothesis concerning the effect of the enlargement of the public sector is valid, then one would expect a diminution in the size of the public sector to result in less constituency casework. However, the other variables we have identified remain. Though ministerial responsibility may have less scope than before, citizen complaints concerning privatized public utilities and 'Next Steps' Agencies may well be channelled through MPs. The moral and political imperatives will ensure that many Members will pursue such cases on behalf of their constituents.

To cope, MPs need greater resources, especially at the constituency level. More and more MPs have constituency-based secretaries, and fax or computer links with their constituency offices, but the improvement in resources has not kept pace with the demands made on them. Unless a significant enhancement of resources takes place over the next few years, MPs—already burdened with increased pressures from other sources as well—are in danger of being overloaded with work. That is neither healthy for MPs nor for the political system.

1   F. Morrell, *From the Electors of Bristol* (Spokesman, 1977), pp. 22–36.
2   A. Chisholm and M. Davie, *Beaverbrook: A Life* (Pimlico, 1993), p. 85.
3   A. Mitchell, *Westminster Man* (Thames Methuen, 1982), p. 183.
4   F. Wheen, *Tom Driberg: His Life and Indiscretions* (Chatto & Windus, 1990), p. 335.
5   P. Norton and D. Wood, *Back from Westminster: British Members of Parliament and their Constituents* (University Press of Kentucky, 1993), p. 40.
6   P. G. Richards, *Honourable Members* (Faber and Faber, 1959).
7   R. E. Dowse, 'The MP and his Surgery', *Political Studies*, 1963.

8   N. Chester and N. Bowring, *Questions in Parliament* (Clarendon Press, 1962), pp. 103–5.

9   A. Barker and M. Rush, *The Member of Parliament and His Information* (Allen & Unwin, 1970), p. 174.

10 J. A. G. Griffith and M. Ryle, *Parliament: Functions, Practice and Procedure* (Sweet & Maxwell, 1989), p. 72.

11 P. Norton, *Does Parliament Matter?* (Harvester Wheatsheaf, 1993), p. 150.

12 E. Currie, *Lifelines* (Sidgwick & Jackson, 1989), pp. 231–2.

13 T. Elms and T. Terry, *Scrutiny of Ministerial Correspondence* (Cabinet Office Efficiency Unit, 1990).

14 Norton and Wood, *Back from Westminster*, p. 35.

15 P. Norton and D. Wood, 'Constituency Service by Members of Parliament: Does it Contribute to a Personal Vote?' *Parliamentary Affairs*, 1990, p. 199.

16 R. Rawlings, 'The MP's Complaints Service (I)', *The Modern Law Review*, 1990, p. 30.

17 MORI 'Summer 1993 Survey of MPs', *British Public Opinion*, 16 (10), 1993, p. 5.

18 Norton, *Does Parliament Matter?* p. 176, n. 2.

19 See F. A. C. S. Bown, 'The Defeat of the Shops Bill, 1986', in M. Rush (ed.), *Parliament and Pressure Politics* (Clarendon Press, 1990), pp. 218, 221.

20 D. Searing, *Westminster's World* (Harvard University Press, 1994).

21 R. Jowell and S. Witherspoon, *British Social Attitudes: The 1985 Report* (Gower, 1985), and R. Jowell, S. Witherspoon, and L. Brook, *British Social Attitudes: The 1987 Survey* (Gower, 1987).

22 Norton and Wood, *Back from Westminster*.

23 M. Franklin and P. Norton, 'Questions and Members', in M. Franklin and P. Norton (eds), *Parliamentary Questions* (Clarendon Press, 1993), pp. 109–110. See also R. Rawlings, 'The MP's Complaints Service (II),' *Modern Law Review*, 53 (2), 1990, pp. 161–2.

24 See B. Cain, J. Ferejohn, and M. Fiorina, *The Personal Vote* (Harvard University Press, 1987).

The House of Lords: Time for a Change?

BY DONALD SHELL

THE handful of peers who have sat in the House of Lords throughout the last fifty years have witnessed many changes in their part of Parliament. Their House has been leavened with life peers, graced by women and invaded by television cameras. The Chamber itself is much better attended than it was in their youth, and the House as a whole works far harder than it did then. Many folk, not least peers themselves, would argue that the Lords appears to have become more important in the whole business of government than it was a half century ago.

Yet, more remarkable than any (or all) of the changes that have taken place have been the continuities that have characterised the House. And it is therefore appropriate to begin this article by drawing attention to the fundamentally unreformed nature of the House. Above all, it remains a predominantly hereditary body. Over 60% of its members are there because they inherited this right. Of the remainder, not a single one is elected; all owe their position to the recommendation of successive Prime Ministers. The House of Lords remains an institution unscathed by democracy.

The unreformed House

Imagine the task of conducting around Westminster a delegation of officials from Eastern Europe here in the UK to learn the ways of democracy. Explaining the House of Lords must present something of a challenge. That most of those entitled to sit, to speak, and to vote in the second chamber do so simply because they inherited this right seems extraordinary. That Britain, a country thought to have pioneered the development of democracy, should retain as part of its Parliament a second chamber still dominated by the aristocracy, seems paradoxical. That towards the close of the twentieth century, far from feeling embarrassed about this state of affairs, many seem to take pride in the continued existence of the House of Lords as a sort of tribute to English genius, or the triumph of English pragmatism, must surely bemuse overseas observers.

Having perhaps parried some difficult questions from those seeking know-how about democracy on the place of hereditary legislators, it would then have to be explained that the remaining members of the House are not elected, either directly or even indirectly, that they are not appointed by the House of Commons, or by local Councils, or even by a committee of any kind. Rather, every single one of them has become a member of the second chamber because the Prime Minister of the day had decided to recommend them for a peerage. Yes, the former Prime Minister, Baroness Thatcher had roundly declared at the opening of her maiden speech in the House of Lords (2 July 1992) that according to her own calculations she was responsible for the elevation of no fewer than 214 of those entitled to sit and listen to her. Mr Wilson could claim professional paternity for a slightly larger number.

Inquirers about the party breakdown in the House must be told that whatever the complexion of the government of the day, the Conservative Party always enjoys control in the House of Lords. At the end of the most recent session, of those eligible to turn up any time and speak or vote in the House, 453 were Conservative, 111 Labour, 56 Liberal Democrat, 256 cross-bench, with 55 in other categories. Conservative spokesmen may emphasise that their party does not have an overall majority, but with over 48% of the House taking the Conservative whip, and around 30% sitting on the cross-benches, Conservative preponderance is assured. When Prime Minster, Mrs Thatcher took care to recommend almost twice as many Conservatives as Labour Party supporters for elevation to the House. Far from evening up the party balance in the House, she seemed determined to ensure an increased Conservative majority. That she was allowed to do this is surely curious; that no outcry greeted such behaviour is remarkable.

Hopefully, our East European guests would not have been visiting the House when it recently debated Lord Diamond's bill which sought to give women a greater chance of inheriting peerages (7 March 1994). To listen to their lordships reasons for decisively rejecting this modest proposal, designed to reduce the 45 to one male/female imbalance among the 760 or so hereditary peers, would surely have induced amazement and embarrassment. Anxieties about the possibilities of bad feeling within families if the expectations of male heirs were to be removed, or indeed if so-called courtesy titles had to be withdrawn, were prominent. Perhaps, it was suggested, a Royal Commission could examine the possibility of extending female rights to inherit, but only where otherwise a peerage would, tragically it was thought, become extinct. The whole debate was characterised by expressions of proprietal sentiments towards seats in Parliament, very similar to those which must have been expressed during debate about the abolition of rotten boroughs at the time of the 1832 Great Reform Bill. This debate showed the House at its introspective worst, blatantly defending the rights and privileges of present members and flagrantly out of touch with surrounding society.

It is possible that our East European guests would have been present for another recent debate, that on the constitutional role of the contemporary House (13 April 1994). If so, far from hearing disquiet voiced about the House or calls for its reform, they would have heard peers expressing enormous confidence in themselves and their part of

The House of Lords   225

Parliament. Indeed, they would have listened to peers revelling in self-congratulation on the array of talent and experience they could collectively display. The anomalies of the present House were freely admitted and it was acknowledged that no one would ever think of inventing such a chamber today. But the House bequeathed by history did actually work, or so it was claimed; it performed a useful role, and furthermore it did this without causing difficulties elsewhere, or even imposing much cost on the public purse! If any change at all were needed, this should only be marginal adjustments to improve the present laudable contribution made by the House. Most of the active peers plainly enjoy their membership of the Lords. They take pleasure in the self-perceived wisdom of their own counsels, even when no one else, including those in government, appear to have noticed what they have said. Naturally enough, such complacency need not trouble the government. The minister replying to this debate was happy enough to express satisfaction with the present powers and composition of the House.

To say that such a House is deeply offensive to democratic values is surely a truism. But what is as remarkable as the continued existence of the House is the fact that so much satisfaction is expressed with it and that so little public debate surrounds the survival of this feudal relic. The preamble to the 1911 Parliament Act spoke quite specifically of the intention to 'substitute for the House as it at present exists a Second Chamber constituted on a popular rather than a hereditary basis'. Consistent with that intention, the Bryce Conference was appointed in 1917, and this made recommendations for fundamental reform of the second chamber. These and many other proposals were debated with some persistence for another decade or so. But then the debate fizzled out; and though it has spluttered to life now and again since, what is striking about recent years is the absence of the sort of vigorous and far-reaching debate that characterised the earlier part of this century.

Fifty years is of course a relatively short time in the history of an institution that reaches back over six centuries. Significant reforms tend to be discussed for decades before anything is accomplished. From the passing of the Great Reform Act in 1832, schemes to reduce the power of the House had been considered continuously, until in 1911 such a change was made. From the mid-nineteenth century onwards, proposals to introduce life peers were regularly advanced. Eventually, this simple reform was achieved in the mid-twentieth century. Likewise, the desirability of allowing peers by succession to escape from the House, and in particular to remain eligible for the House of Commons, had long been acknowledged before this change was introduced in 1963. The exclusion of women from the House had been recognised as anomalous once women had attained membership of the House of Commons, but attempts to rectify this anomaly were rebutted until this too was altered during the Macmillan years. Proposals for further reforms have been made over the last half century, especially for removing or limiting the rights of hereditary peers. Eventually, no doubt, such a change will occur. But not yet. The House remains in the 1990s a decidedly ancient institution, still displaying with some pride its unmodernised form.

But even though fundamental reform has been absent, and wide ranging debate about the House spasmodic, some changes have taken place, and to these we now turn.

The Parliament Act 1949

The only measure to make any change in the formal powers of the House during the last fifty years has been the Parliament Act of 1949. The background to this lay in the concerns felt within the Labour government that the Lords might make some determined use of the two-year delaying power accorded to it under the 1911 Parliament Act, especially towards the end of the 1945 Parliament. It was, after all, only just over thirty years (well within the living memory of many senior politicians) since the House of Lords had felt unabashed at using its powers in a quite decisive way. In a sense, the 1911 Parliament Act had strengthened the legitimacy of the House in exercising power because it had replaced an absolute veto—a drastic power which had been recognised as generally unusable—with a statutory suspensory veto. So was the House not fully within its rights to use such a power? The 1911 Act appeared to have been based on the assumption that the delaying power was part and parcel of a healthy democracy. It had been argued that delay allowed public opinion to express itself, and in deference to such opinion minds within government might be changed, or else the expression of such opinion—in an election—might change the government.

The fact that since the first world war the power to delay legislation had not been used seemed more a consequence of prolonged periods of Conservative dominated government rather than of an attitude change on the part of their Lordships. The arrival of a Labour government, with for the first time a clear overall Commons majority, unleashed once more concern that the House would at some stage make vigorous use of the powers it still retained. In 1945 such fears had been assuaged to some extent by the Conservative leader in the Lords, the fifth Marquess of Salisbury, annunciating what came to be known as the 'Salisbury doctrine', a sensible and necessary rule to guide the House at a time when the Commons had an overwhelming Labour majority and the Lords an overwhelming Conservative majority. Under this the House, or at least the Conservative Party in the Lords, accepted that it would be wrong for it to vote down at second reading any bill which had been clearly foreshadowed in the governing party's previous election manifesto. The House showed little sign of departing from this principle in the early years of the Attlee government. But in some quarters it was feared that such restraint might evaporate as the excitements of a general election drew closer. The reluctance of some members of the Labour Cabinet to agree to the postponement of steel nationalisation in the summer of 1947 was partly assuaged by the government's commitment to proceed with a bill curtailing further the power of the Lords, so that any legislation introduced in the penultimate session of a Parliament could be assured of passage to the statute book notwithstanding determined opposition from the Lords.

Many Conservatives thought this a good moment to seek a more extensive reform of the House. So, following the second reading of the Bill, official all-party talks were announced. At these, agreement in principle was reached on several issues, such as the admission of women, the entitlement of peers to stand for and vote in elections to the Commons, and the removal of the right to take part in the work of the House based solely on inheritance. On power, however, the two parties could not agree. But it is worth noting how close they came to a compromise. Labour argued that there were greater dangers in modern conditions in the machinery of government acting 'too slowly rather than too quickly', and insisted twelve months delay from Commons second reading, or nine months from Commons third reading, was all that should be allowed to the upper House. But the Conservatives were 'unable to agree to what they regarded as the virtual elimination of the suspensory period', though they were prepared to consider a period of twelve months from Commons third reading.[1] So the talks and the prospect of an agreed reform of the House broke down on a difference of three months in the delaying power of the House.

Labour pressed ahead with the 1949 Parliament Act, and the Conservatives used their power in the Lords to impose delay on its enactment. This measure cut the period during which the House could delay legislation from two years spread over three parliamentary sessions to one year spread over two sessions, with the twelve months being measured from the date of a disputed bill's second reading in the Commons in the first session. In practice, this would ensure that the actual period of delay for a disagreed bill would in all likelihood be no more than around six months. It did not cover statutory instruments, on which the House of Lords veto power remained, nor did it appear to cover any bills which went first to the House of Lords rather than the Commons. The subsequent use made by the House of this power is discussed further below.

The Life Peerages Act 1958

Having failed to achieve a comprehensive reform of the Lords when in office, Labour's policy back in opposition seemed to be to leave the place well alone, anticipating its demise either as a prelude to a new second chamber or to a unicameral parliament. A leading member of the party in 1953, Patrick Gordon-Walker, argued that the House was best left anomalous and that it should not be changed at all, because 'if one admitted women or permitted life peers . . . one would be tempted to go further and create a more rational body'.[2] The House of Lords reached its lowest ebb in the post war period in the mid 1950s. The task of sustaining the Opposition front-bench fell to a handful of elderly and increasingly infirm Labour peers. Apart from a travel allowance, their toils were unrecompensed. Attendance of peers was low; in 1957 Peter Bromhead observed that the number present at debates tended 'to dwindle after 5.30pm', though until then there were 'generally at least 30 present'.[3] If the number normally present was scarcely sufficient to sustain the work of the House, occasionally much larger attendances were a cause of embarrassment. The highest attendance of the decade occurred in 1956 when the House voted by 238 votes to 95 to retain the death penalty, thus overturning an abolitionist private member's bill that had passed the Commons. The many rare attenders who on this occasion came to vote for the death penalty revived debate about 'backwoodsmen'.

The Macmillan government decided, in traditional Tory style, that in order to conserve, reform was necessary. Hence without the support of the Labour Party it introduced the Life Peerages Bill, a simple measure which provided for the creation of peerages for the lifetime of the holder only. Because there was no reason why this new category of member should exclude women, provision was at last made for women to enter the House. Labour voted against the bill because the party did not wish to see any enhancement in the legitimacy of an undemocratic chamber. This gave rise to the odd spectacle of the party of the left voting to keep the House entirely composed of hereditary peers, a few bishops and judges excepted, and incidentally an entirely male preserve. It is one of the ironies of the House of Lords that subsequently many who expressed opposition to reforming the House, including Gordon-Walker, found their way there as life peers. Initially, the idea was that life peers would be 'working' peers, and for a few years lists of life peers were announced separately from the regular honours lists still containing hereditary awards. But when Labour came to power in 1964 the Prime Minister announced that he would not be recommending any hereditary honours. For almost twenty years thereafter no new hereditary peerages were awarded.

Looking back the 1958 Life Peerages Act can be seen as a turning point in the fortunes of the House. Recruitment to the House not only broadened, so as to include more party loyalists and a wider cross section of the meritocracy than hitherto, but the rate at which new peers arrived in the House approximately doubled. Between 1964 and 1970 Mr Wilson as Prime Minister recommended 141 life peers, including 78 Labour Party supporters. Many of these became active members of the House, a fact which undoubtedly helped it begin its journey back from the brink of collapse into becoming once more a significant part of Parliament. The growth in attendance was no doubt further facilitated by the introduction of a financial allowance enabling peers to claim out-of-pocket expenses incurred in attending the House; this was initially set at three guineas a day, but thereafter steadily rose until in the early 1990s, for peers claiming overnight accommodation, the daily allowance was over £120, payable in addition to travel expenses. A further minor change was the introduction of a standing order allowing peers who did not anticipate attending the House to apply for leave of absence. It was hoped that this provision would diminish the likelihood of further unwelcome publicity surrounding the sudden appearance of large numbers of 'backwoods-men', but it was in effect no more than a rather poor cosmetic. No requirement to take leave was introduced, even for rare or non-attenders, and a peer who took leave could cancel this at a month's notice.

The Peerage Act 1963

Though life peers had been introduced to the House, peers by succession who wished to disencumber themselves of their peerage, which was also a disqualification from membership of the House of Commons, could not do so. Among others, Quintin Hogg had gone reluctantly from the Commons to the Lords in 1950; he had appealed to Attlee, the Labour Prime Minster, to introduce legislation to allow those who inherited peerages to disclaim them and thereby remain in the Commons, but Attlee was not disposed to intervene. When in 1960 a young and ambitious Labour MP, Tony Benn, inherited a peerage he adopted a different strategy. When a by-election was called because of his acces-sion to a peerage, he stood and was convincingly re-elected to the House of Commons from which he was disqualified. Minds were suddenly and sharply focused on the need for change. After some huffing and puffing the Peerage Act was passed, and this enabled Tony Benn, Quintin Hogg and the new Conservative Prime Minister, Lord Home, among others to renounce their peerages. The passage of this change was assured because a sufficient number of leading figures in both parties wanted it. At the same time, some further tidying up took place, allowing the few women who had inherited peerages in their own right to be admitted to the House, along with all the Scottish peers who hitherto had elected sixteen of their number to the Lords.

Thus by the mid-1960s a number of adjustments had been made to the membership of the House. There seemed the real possibility of the modernising trend encapsulated in the 1958 Life Peerages Act and the 1963 Peerages Act being continued. If all new peerages were for life only, and if disclaiming caught on among hereditary peers, then after a few years removing peers by succession would have seemed more like a natural development. With Labour returned to power in 1964, and enjoying a 100-seat majority after 1966, the time seemed ripe for building further on these changes.

The Parliament (No. 2) Bill and since

In 1967 the Labour Cabinet initiated all-party talks about possible change, and these led to the 1968 Parliament (No. 2) Bill, which expressed agreement reached by both front-benches.[4] If enacted, this would have resulted eventually in the exclusion of all peers by succession; as such peers died, their heirs would inherit their peerage but not the right to a seat in the House. In time, therefore, the House would become a House entirely composed of the nominees of successive Prime Ministers. But only those who attended over one-third of the sittings, and who were below a set retirement age, would have had the right to vote. Others, including existing holders of hereditary peerages, could attend and speak but not vote. Peers themselves supported these proposals with near alacrity (251 to 56 in the division lobby), presumably conjecturing that if enacted they would offer a more secure basis to their House than it could otherwise expect. In the Commons the bill was approved at second reading but it then ran aground in committee as backbench opponents on both right and left conspired to destroy the measure. To both Enoch Powell and Michael Foot the anomalies of the existing House were preferable to any reformed version. Many other members of both parties were concerned at the extension of prime-ministerial patronage inherent in the proposals.

What is remarkable, looking back, is the extent of common ground between the two main parties, both of whose front-benches supported these proposals—if without enthusiasm. Within a few years Labour policy had reverted to outright abolition and a unicameral parliament, while under Mrs Thatcher the Conservatives lost interest altogether in reform of the House. In the first twenty-five years of the post-war period, three Acts of Parliament had brought changes to the House of Lords, in 1949, 1958 and 1963, and a further bill seeking to make major changes to the House had been introduced in 1968. The twenty-five years since then have seen no further attempts to reform the House. During the 1970s a polarisation between the parties took place. When Labour was in office after 1974 the difficulties it faced with the House of Lords were much greater than in either earlier post-war Labour administration. In 1976 the Labour Party conference overwhelmingly endorsed a policy of abolition, but the party's 1979 manifesto more modestly proposed the removal of the remaining powers of the House to veto or delay legislation. The commitment to abolition of the House and acceptance of a unicameral parliament was included in the 1983 manifesto, but by 1992 the party was proposing to replace the House with an entirely elected chamber without any power to delay normal legislation, and without any ministerial presence. This presupposed that some folk would want to be elected to such a eunuch-like body.

As Conservative leader, Mrs Thatcher had responded to Labour's abolitionist commitment by establishing a committee under Lord Home. If Labour were even half-serious about abolition, it was only prudent for the Conservatives to have an alternative ready staked out, and one that looked a plausible basis for conserving a second chamber. The Home Committee recommended the removal of hereditary peers and a one-third appointed and two-thirds elected House.[5] But once safely installed in office, Mrs Thatcher turned the energies of her party in other directions. About the constitution she preferred to have a blind spot. Though some of her colleagues continued to press for reform, Mrs Thatcher found that prevailing arrangements suited her well. As the House of Lords became more of an irritant to her in the mid-1980s, she preferred to bully it into submission, and she took care not to allow her party's numerical superiority to be eroded. As the decade progressed, the Conservative Party ceased to think about the constitution at all. It had no need for such concern. It benefited too much from the status quo. No doubt when back in opposition again troublesome thoughts about 'elective dictatorship' will once more return.

The direction of change until the 1970s had been gradual reform. This might easily have been consolidated in various ways. For example, when the Peerages Bill was being debated, expectations, and in some quarters concern, had been expressed that this might result in large numbers of peers leaving the House, perhaps even a wholesale exit. But in the event, only eight individuals renounced their peerages within twelve months of the passage of the Act, and only seven more did so in the next thirteen years, and none at all since 1977. The tide of opinion seemed to turn, so much so that in the 1980s three heirs of disclaimers who had died took up these renounced peerages and became active in the House. In 1992 John Major even revived use of the 'writ of acceleration' procedure to speed the arrival in the House of the heir to a peerage (Robert, courtesy title Viscount, Cranborne) before the current holder of that peerage (the sixth Marquess of Salisbury) had died. And after almost twenty years without a single new hereditary peerage being created, Mrs Thatcher reintroduced such peerages from 1983 onwards. These may seem detailed points, but they indicated how the direction of opinion had changed. From shifting towards reform, the House was drawing back to its traditional position. Perhaps this reflected a wider change of mood in society, an unwillingness to continue the slow advance towards democracy that had characterised the earlier part of the century.

A more active House

Reform resulting from legislation may have been relatively slight throughout the post-war period, and non-existent since the 1960s, but the House has nevertheless continued to change, both by adapting its own procedures and through the altered behaviour of peers themselves. In particular, the activity of the House has grown. More peers attend, more vote and speak, and do so more often, than in the early post-war years. Numbers attending the House have expanded, from a daily average of less than one hundred in the early 1950s, to over two hundred by 1968–69, then over three hundred by 1983–84, and to almost four hundred a decade later. The average sitting day was under four hours through most of the 1950s, with the House usually sitting some 400 hours all-told in a normal length session. By the mid-1960s the House sat on average over five hours per day, and by the late 1980s the average had risen to around seven hours, with the House sitting about a thousand hours a session. Monday sittings had become normal and Friday sittings unexceptional. In the three sessions 1951–54, 318 peers were recorded as having spoken in the House, but only 58 did so frequently (more than eight or nine times a year). By 1989–90 as many as 521 peers spoke in a single session, with over three times as many speaking frequently as had done so in the earlier period. In the early 1950s the number of divisions was about 15 per session, but by the late 1980s it was closer to 200 per session; furthermore the average number of peers voting in divisions had doubled in the same period. For many years the division in 1956 on the death penalty question in which 333 peers had voted was cited as the largest in the post-war period. But that number was surpassed in the 1970s, and in 1993 no fewer than 622 peers were recorded as voting in a division on the European Communities (Amendment) Bill, (on a proposal to require a referendum before implementing the Treaty of Maastricht).

Such figures reflect growing professionalism within the House. More peers view their membership as a job and give it a significant proportion of their working time. One consequence of this has been increased pressure on those procedures of the House that provide for scrutiny and criticism of government. From a customary one or two starred questions per day in the 1950s, the maximum number of four per day were almost invariably asked by the 1980s. Until the 1969–70 session the number of written questions averaged out at less than one per sitting day; by 1992–93 the average was thirteen per sitting day. Though the House remained remarkably free of procedural restrictions on the rights of peers to speak and to table questions or motions, rationing devices had had to be adopted. Among these had been the introduction of time-limited debates in the early 1970s, and the subsequent growing use of such debates. But away from the floor of the House peers had also become very much more active through select committee work, especially the European Communities Committee, first established in 1974, and the Science and Technology Committee, established in 1980.

But the pressure of parliamentary business has also increased because of the rise in the quantity of legislation. In the 1940s fewer than a thousand pages of primary legislation per year were enacted; by the late 1980s the quantity was two to three times as great. The amount of secondary legislation had grown even more. These figures on their own do not, of course, tell us very much about the actual work of the House of Lords. But certainly during the 1960s and onwards the activity of the Lords in revising legislation has steadily grown. From spending some two to three hundred hours a year in the 1950s dealing with bills, the House was spending around seven hundred hours a year by the late

1980s. This reflected the legislative fecundity of governments as well as the growing assiduity of peers. That the House has become much busier is not in doubt. However, the effectiveness of what it does also deserves some comment, as does the possibility that procedural or other reforms could enable the House to function better than it does at present. To these questions we now turn.

The legislative work of the House

Revising legislation brought from the Commons has always been a very high priority for the House of Lords. Reading Peter Bromhead's study of the work of the House in the 1940s, one is struck by the similarity between the contribution made by the House then and since. Having accepted that it would be wrong for the House to vote down the principle of manifesto bills, peers applied themselves to the task of discussing the detail of the great socialist reforms of the Attlee period. Large numbers of amendments were made, many consequent on undertakings given in the Commons, others enabling discussion to take place on sections of bills guillotined in the lower House. Thus 'to the government itself the committee stages in the Lords were often of great value'. In the 1946–47 session the Lords passed 1,222 amendments, of which only 57 were rejected by the Commons. In 1947, when the Transport Bill emerged from the Commons, *The Times* commented: 'If a revising chamber did not exist it would have to be invented.'[6]

With the return of the Conservatives to power in the 1950s, the pattern of activity was different; some bills upon which MPs had spent much time went through the Lords very quickly because Labour peers hardly considered it worthwhile making what they saw as mere token protests. A few bills excited considerable controversy among Conservative backbenchers, most notably the legislation to introduce commercial television, against which Lord Hailsham led a vigorous assault without, however, deflecting the government from its intentions. In the early 1960s a somewhat reinvigorated Labour Opposition put up more resistance to government bills than hitherto, with the bill to alter local government in London in the 1962–63 session in particular meeting prolonged opposition.

With Labour back in office from 1964 to 1970, both the usefulness and obstructiveness of the House of Lords was again demonstrated. Its usefulness was evident in the number of amendments government ministers regularly introduced to their own bills, but its obstructiveness was seen in its opposition to some government measures. In 1969 the Lords refused to give way to the Commons on amendments to the House of Commons (Redistribution of Seats) Bill, but the Labour government found a way of securing its objective—of delaying redistribution until beyond the next general election—without the need for this bill at all. The previous year the House had rejected by 193 votes to 184 an order concerned with sanctions against Rhodesia. This was a somewhat curious episode; because the legislation concerned was a statutory instrument, the Lords still had a veto power, but having rejected it, Conservative peers let it be known that if the order was relaid their opposition would not be sustained.

Their action did, however, result in the Labour government breaking off talks with the Conservatives about the reform of the House. Perhaps this was what some Tory backbenchers wanted. When Richard Crossman introduced the Lords reform proposals to the Commons, he referred to the fact that if a second chamber did not exist, two extra legislative stages would be needed in the Commons. He also spoke of the value of the House in the field of 'unconventional legislation', by which he meant the contribution peers made to the enactment of a series of private members bills, albeit ones enjoying tacit government support, often spoken of as the permissive society legislation. The arrival of life peers had been associated with the development of a much more liberal attitude within the House. Whereas in 1948 and again in 1956 peers had voted down Commons' proposals for the abolition of the death penalty, in 1965 peers were ready decisively to accept abolition. Subsequent to this, the upper House did a good deal to push public opinion along in the direction of liberalising the law on abortion and homosexuality and other matters.

When the Conservatives came back to power in 1970, they found the Labour Opposition in the Lords much stronger than any they had previously experienced. In particular, some Labour peers exploited the relative freedom from procedural constraints in the House to mount a sustained campaign against the Industrial Relations Bill. Though this made little difference to the bill, on other measures the Heath government did give ground to the Lords, especially following defeats involving cross-bench and Conservative back-bench peers. Much more serious difficulties arose, however, under the Labour government of 1974 to 1979. Labour had no clear Commons majority. Yet unlike 1950–51 and 1964–66, when Labour had had a very low majority, the government did bring forward some highly contentious legislation. Though peers kept to the Salisbury doctrine, this did not prevent them passing some bills back to the Commons with significant amendments inserted against the government's wishes, often described as 'wrecking' amendments. The process of reversing these in the Commons was fraught — and could fail if the government lost the support of even a single Labour MP.

On two bills, Parliament Act procedures were invoked because at the end of the session in which they had been introduced agreement between the two Houses had not been reached. The precise points at issue concerned the application of the 'closed shop' principle to journalists under a trade union reform bill of 1975, and the inclusion of ship-repairing in the bill nationalising shipbuilding in 1976. The fact that compromise was reached between peers and government ministers on both these bills before Parliament Act procedures had run their course did little to diminish Labour anger with the House. It was against this background that the party adopted a unicameralist policy, proposing to do away with the Lords altogether.

To the Thatcher governments of the 1980s the House was frequently an irritant but never a serious obstacle. Tensions within the Conservative Party between Thatcherites and traditionalists not infrequently surfaced in the House of Lords. In particular, legislation relating to local government and its various responsibilities, notably education and housing, was frequently amended against the will of the government. Ministers regularly gave ground to the Lords, with the House even being described as the real opposition during the 1983 Parliament when the Labour opposition in the Commons was at its lowest ebb. But in the late 1980s there appeared to be a hardening of ministerial attitudes to the Lords, with the government endeavouring wherever possible to overturn any defeat it suffered there. This culminated in the use of the Parliament Act procedures to pass the War Crimes Act of 1991, a bill which the government chose to persist with notwithstanding strong opposition in the Lords, not least from the judicial peers, as well as much opposition from within Conservative Party ranks. It was certainly not a manifesto bill, and not at all the kind of legislation envisaged as appropriate for Parliament Act procedures when these had first been formulated. The subsequent failure, at least to the time of writing, to bring any prosecutions of alleged second world war criminals living in Britain was seen by many peers as a vindication of their collective wisdom in opposing the measure.

If the revision of legislation has generally been regarded as the most important aspect of the work of the House, it is not so much the excitements caused when the Lords disagrees with the Commons, but the usual day in and day out business of amending bills which is in view. If the productivity of the House were to be measured in terms of the numbers of amendments passed, then its record is impressive. By the late 1980s some 2000 amendments per sesssion were being made to government bills. But such figures probably have more to do with the ill-thought out nature of much legislation when first introduced than with any particular skill or diligence by peers. Some commentators saw a decline in consultation between government and organised groups during the Thatcher years as correlated with a decline in the quality of legislation as first introduced to parliament.[7] This it was argued had led to the development of a legislate-as-you-go mentality, which in turn imposed increased burdens on the House as a revising chamber. Certainly, the House became during the 1980s the object of much greater attention from interest groups. From a practical point of view, many groups found that for securing detailed adjustments to bills, the Lords was at least as useful as the Commons.[8]

The deliberative work of the House

It has always been difficult to assess the value of non-legislative debate in the House of Lords. There is no doubt that the House does contain an array of expertise on many subjects. As such, this can make for very well informed debate, and certainly over the years peers themselves have continued to emphasise the high quality of debate within their chamber and been reluctant to see time spent on non-legislative debate eroded. Such debate may at times influence some sections of public opinion and may also receive some attention from within some part of government. The arrival of television cameras in 1985 helped to publicise the activities of the House, which has often been perceived as more courteous and responsible in its style than the Commons. But many of the debates held in the Lords can only be seen as occasions on which peers talk to each other. Most pass entirely unnoticed even in the 'quality' newspapers, and there is little evidence to show they have any impact elsewhere either.

But the House has made increased use of select committees since the early 1970s. One of the first to be established examined a private member's bill on sex discrimination in the 1972–73 session. It is ironic that despite peers' unwillingess to address this issue in respect of the hereditary membership of their own House in the 1990s, they did much to advance the anti-discrimination cause in the early 1970s. Subsequent ad hoc select committees dealt with a miscellany of topics with mixed results. A report on overseas trade in 1985 represented a powerful and much quoted indictment of government policies. Inquiries into laboratory experimentation on animals and into charity law cleared the way to legislation in these areas. Other select committee reports, such as one recommending the abolition of the mandatory life sentence for murder, met with less success.

The most important initiative in respect of select committee work came in 1974 with the establishment of a committee on the European Communities. Up to a hundred peers became involved in up to seven sub-committees providing an in depth examination of selected items of draft Community legislation as well as related matters. To oversee this, a full-time salaried post was created for the chairman of this Committee, which has certainly made a useful contribution to the examination of draft European legislation and its potential impact on Britain. Alongside the European Communities Committee, the House in 1979 decided to establish a Select Committee on Science and Technology. The immediate precipitant for this was the reorganisation of select committee activity in the Commons which included the aboliton of a select committee of MPs bearing the same title. Between the European Communities Commitee and the Science and Technology Committee, and their various sub-committees, as well as a steady stream of ad hoc committees, the House has over the last twenty years mobilised a considerable proportion of its membership into providing a critical scrutiny of areas of public policy. It has done this in a form complementary to the Commons, rather than as rivals to the lower House. Like all committee work, the quality and the effectiveness has varied considerably.

In 1993 the activities of the European Communities Committee were cut back slightly. The ostensible reason for this was a feeling that too many of the resources available to the House had become invested in it. In particular, peers wanted more freedom to establish ad hoc select committees, and they also wanted to set up a committee to examine on an on-going basis the provisions contained in bills to delegate legislative power. This was a subject which had received increasing attention in the House, largely because of the activities of a small group of peers. Perhaps because the House of Lords itself felt inhibited from using its power in respect of delegated legislation, this was a subject to which peers increasingly gave attention when debating bills. Lord Rippon, who had chaired the Hansard Society inquiry into the legislative process, became the first chairman of this new committee on the scrutiny of delegated powers. Again, this could be seen as the House endeavouring to do what the House of Commons lacked the time or the inclination to do.

Useful — but still in need of change

Any examination of the functions of the House can point without too much difficulty to useful work performed by peers. It would be odd if this were not the case. The House of Commons is far from being a perfect legislature. There is plenty of work for a second chamber to do. And the House of Lords does contain within its ranks a great many highly experienced politicians as well as many others who have achieved distinction in various walks of life. Other much less distinguished folk often represent a family tradition of public service. So one would expect some good to come from the Lords. The details of draft legislation are often debated in an unsatisfactory way in the Commons; the use of the guillotine is frequent, and the imperatives of party conflict take precedence over the need for careful and methodical scrutiny of legislation. Governments of all persuasions have found the House of Lords a necessary adjunct to the legislative process. Peers themselves have sought to enhance the effectiveness of their House by developing select committee work.

But whatever usefulness the present House possesses should not be taken as an excuse for avoiding the question of reform. Reform is necessary because retaining the present House symbolises Britain's half-hearted commitment to democracy. Governments that urge upon other institutions the need for modernisation while ignoring the House of Lords lose credibility. To talk of developing a classless society while leaving the present House of Lords in place is a nonsense. Furthermore, the present composition of the House, including as it does a ridiculous imbalance in party strengths, ensures that governments need not take the House very seriously.

The House lacks the legitimacy to resist government effectively. It would now be foolish to rely on the House to provide satisfactory protection for the fundamentals of the constitution. The House is too ready to settle for being mildly awkward to government when it ought to be persistently difficult. If the government choose to reverse Lords' amendments to bills, then peers prefer to give way rather than to use their powers to hold up legislation. The only recent exception to this was the War Crimes Bill, which peers felt able to resist precisely because it was not a bill upon which the government could apply a whip in the Commons. On delegated legislation peers have in effect accepted a convention forbidding them from voting against statutory instruments, lest they accidentally use the veto power they still possess in this area.

But if reform is to take place, of what should this consist? It seems unlikely that the deliberations of the 'good and the great', or for that matter all party conferences, will ever produce a generally agreed scheme of reform. Such efforts in the past have always failed. But one or other party might decide to push through an alteration when it is calculated that this will suit its interest. The Life Peerages Act suited the Conservatives because it bolstered an otherwise dying House. Labour might in the future carry an equally simple piece of legislation excluding all peers by succession, notwithstanding Conservative hostility. This at least could be achieved without any great expenditure of legislative time, and it would please the overwhelming majority of Labour supporters. Nor is such a change likely to meet with sustained opposition from the modern Conservative party. Such a step would clear the ground for further reform, most obviously the introduction of an elected element into the House.

If any form of election is dismissed on the grounds that the House of Commons would not tolerate any element of rivalry from a upper House even partially elected, then this is tantamount in modern conditions to calling for unicameralism. There is a sense in which the House of Commons badly needs a rival. At least the first concern of any parliamentary reform should be to strengthen Parliament vis à vis government. It is the weakness of the present House of Commons that leaves the House of Lords looking moderately satisfactory to many folk.

1   Cmnd 7380, 1948.
2   P. Gordon-Walker, 'Delaying Power' in S. Bailey (ed.), *The Future of the House of Lords* (Hansard Society, 1954), p. 128.
3   P. A. Bromhead, *The House of Lords and Contemporary Politics* (Routledge & Kegan Paul, 1958), pp. 32–33.
4   See *House of Lords Reform*, cmnd 3799, 1968.
5   *Report of the Review Committee on the Second Chamber*, Conservative Political Centre, 1978.
6   See Bromhead, *op. cit.* pp. 158, 167.

7   See *Making the Law: Report of the Hansard Society Commission on the Legislature Process*, chairman Lord Rippon (Hansard Society 1993).

8   See N. Baldwin, 'The House of Lords' in M. Rush (ed.), *Parliament and Pressure Politics* (Clarendon Press, 1990).

INDEX